Now Concerning Spiritual Things

Now Concerning Spiritual Things

Authentic Spirituality in Pluralistic Contexts

Fitzroy John Willis

WIPF & STOCK · Eugene, Oregon

NOW CONCERNING SPIRITUAL THINGS
Authentic Spirituality in Pluralistic Contexts

Copyright © 2019 Fitzroy John Willis. All rights reserved. Except for brief quotations in critical publications or reviews, no part of this book may be reproduced in any manner without prior written permission from the publisher. Write: Permissions, Wipf and Stock Publishers, 199 W. 8th Ave., Suite 3, Eugene, OR 97401.

Wipf & Stock
An Imprint of Wipf and Stock Publishers
199 W. 8th Ave., Suite 3
Eugene, OR 97401

www.wipfandstock.com

PAPERBACK ISBN: 978-1-5326-8044-1
HARDCOVER ISBN: 978-1-5326-8045-8
EBOOK ISBN: 978-1-5326-8046-5

All biblical quotations, unless otherwise noted, are taken from the New Revised Standard Version Bible, copyright © 1989, Division of Christian Education of the National Council of the Churches of Christ in the United States of America. Used by permission. All rights reserved.

Manufactured in the U.S.A.   10/24/19

To my wife, Bonnie, and our kids, Abigail, John, Stephen, Anna, and Sarah—living testaments that every good and perfect gift comes from our faithful God!

Contents

Acknowledgments | ix
Introduction | xi

Part I: Authentic Spirituality in the Old Testament

Chapter 1: Authentic Spirituality in the Old Testament:
An Emphasis on Prophecy | 3

Part II: Authentic Spirituality in the New Testament

Chapter 2: The Context of 1 Corinthians | 29

Chapter 3: Spiritual Things | 42

Chapter 4: The Criterion of the Manifestation of the Spirit
(1 Cor 12:1–31) | 53

Chapter 5: The Criterion of Love (1 Cor 13:1–13) | 75

Chapter 6: The Criterion of Edification (1 Cor 14:1–40) | 89

Part III: Contemporary Implications of Authentic Spirituality in Pluralistic Contexts

Chapter 7: The Basis, Acceptability, and the Appropriation
of Paul's Criterion for Authentic Spirituality | 109

Chapter 8: Implications of Authentic Spirituality for
the Contemporary Church | 122

Chapter 9: Implications of Authentic Spirituality for
the Contemporary Worship Service | 133

Part IV: Conclusion

Chapter 10: Authentic Spirituality in Pluralistic Contexts | 171

Bibliography | 177
Name Index | 189
Subject Index | 193
Scripture Index | 197

Acknowledgments

I am thankful to God for the grace that has allowed me to complete this book. This grace of God has been evident through several people.

Dr. Petrus Gräbe, you have been the most excellent mentor in every way. Your kind and ever-encouraging voice helped me to stay the course and complete this work. Thanks for your willingness to support me every time I needed it. Words can hardly express my gratitude for all the time you have spent guiding me towards the completion of this thesis. Dr. Matthew Gordley, your careful and very insightful feedback helped to sharpen my thinking and improved the content of this work. Dr. Jan Van der Watt, thank you for being willing to read this work as it developed. I pray it will in some way be worthy of your involvement.

I wish to acknowledge the significant role that various Regent University professors have had on my theological and personal development. Besides those previously mentioned, I acknowledge the mentorship, support, and constructive feedback that have been given to me over the years by Dr. Graham Twelftree. I thank him for being a friend, mentor, and pastoral figure that continuously prays for my family and me. Dr. Lyle Story, I probably have taken all the classes you have taught. There probably is no greater influence on how I go about the task of studying the Bible. Thanks for allowing me to have served as your TA. I learned so much from your professionalism, exemplary teaching, and the pastoral way in which you relate to students and all whom God allows you to influence. A special mention is also due to Dr. Amos Yong, who has tremendously impacted my theological development. You inspired me to challenge my own presuppositions and always provided much needed constructive criticism. I have tried to learn and grow from the example of scholarship and professionalism you have demonstrated.

Last, but not least, I wish to acknowledge the support of my beautiful wife, Bonnie, and five kids—Abigail, John, Stephen, Anna, and Sarah. It has been a long and at times stressful journey, but I am grateful for such a loving and supportive family who allowed me to research and write—seemingly forever. Hopefully, you all will be proud of the work you have made possible. Bonnie, I especially thank you for being my partner, wise counselor, and editor. You have been tremendously patient with me throughout this process, and I truly appreciate it. I love you and the kids, in Jesus' name!

Introduction

In pluralistic contexts, there are many opinions concerning authentic revelation from God, or authentic spirituality.[1] For example, the Qur'an is the central religious text for Muslims. For Jews and Christians, the Tanakh and the Christian Bible, respectively, are the primary sources of divine revelation. But even within these various traditions, there are differences of opinion as to what constitutes authentic spirituality. The various Christian denominations, beliefs, and practices alone serve to evidence this. Indeed, some Christians believe that the manifesting of spiritual activity is criterion for a revelation of God. Pentecostals, for example, believe that the charism, or gift, of tongues is the initial evidence of being baptized in the Holy Spirit. Other Christians believe that such spiritual activities have ceased with the closing of the canon of Scripture, and any such spiritual manifestations are therefore not authentically spiritual, for only Scripture reveals God. Moreover, even within specific churches, there is a need for discernment, or criteria, in terms of understanding if, how, and when God is speaking to individuals. There is no consensus as to what should be normative relative to communication in the worship service, or for general Christian living.

It is not just people of the monotheistic faiths, however, that stand to benefit from criteria for what is authentically spiritual. This is because in the contemporary postmodern context, the criterion for truth seems to be consensus, or what any given community tolerates. But, can such varying opinions be right simultaneously? Can relativism be an effective means of evaluating truth from falsehood in a pluralistic world? To address such questions, I will focus on two major concerns.

1. Herein, the concept of "authentic spirituality" will be considered synonymous with "divine revelatory experience." The presupposition of this work is in accord with the Christian theological tradition, which considers that there is one God who has been revealed as Father, Son, and Spirit. Further, experiences can only be considered revelatory if they have as their source this same divine being. Therefore, truly divine revelatory experiences are authentic, and revelatory claims that do not arise from this God can be considered false.

The first concern is the construction of a general perspective for what is authentic spirituality. This process necessitates the filling of a void in scholarship concerning criteria for authentic revelatory experiences and the functioning of *charismata*[2] in which the role of the Trinity, in general, and the Spirit, in particular, are almost universally overlooked. My argument is that an overwhelming majority of scholars have overemphasized spiritual gifts (*charismatōn*) at the expense of other "spiritual things" (*tōn pneumatikōn*), and they have deemphasized the role of the Spirit in the study of criteria, or criteriology, for what is authentically spiritual. Consequently, a more balanced approach relative to the role of the Spirit in such studies is needed. This study seeks a more balanced, dialogical, ontological, and biblical criterion for authentic revelatory experiences—what I am calling charismatic criteriology. In other words, this work is a comprehensive study of criteria as they relate to authentic spirituality—including the functioning of the *charismata*.

Rather than continuing the historicist, polarizing, and dichotomous tendencies of modernism—which creates "objective" and "subjective" categories, and asserts, for example, that concepts such as faith and reason, spirit and matter, are antithetical—as well as the subjectivizing tendencies of postmodernism—which seems to disregard the value of traditional authoritative sources such as the Bible—this study seeks to conduct essential dialogue about authentic spirituality with the presupposition that all sources of truth about God are complimentary, rather than antithetical to each other.

To construct a perspective for what is authentic spirituality, this study also addresses the concern that scholarship relative to 1 Corinthians 12–14, which deals with criteria for the functioning of the *charismata*, has failed to fully communicate the Pauline message. In terms of scholarship on 1 Corinthians 12–14, there has been a comparatively lower emphasis on various other *pneumatikōn* or "spiritual things" (1 Cor 12:1) that Paul addresses, and an overemphasis on the role of the Spirit and the *charismata* (gifts of the Spirit). Relative to charismatic criteria, there has generally been an omission of the role of the Spirit due to an overwhelming emphasis on Christology. Such scholarship reduces the edification one can obtain from Pauline thought, since other important aspects relative to what the apostle considers truly spiritual are not being considered.

---

2. The word *charismata* is a transliteration of the Greek term χαρισματα. Unless the original Greek is being highlighted, the English transliteration will be used herein to convey the same word. The concept of χαρισματα will be discussed in detail in part II of this work. For now, however, it can be said that χαρισματα are gifts of the Spirit (1 Cor 12:4, 7–11), and "charismatic" refers to things pertaining to the χαρισματα.

This study, however, is an opportunity to engage in dialogue with Old Testament (OT) prophets, the apostle Paul, and scholars throughout church history up to the contemporary context, to gain insight on how to discern, as well as how to live and communicate, what is authentically spiritual—regardless of one's context.

I am also inquiring how to bridge the religious impasse between believers and a post-Christendom and pluralistic context where individuals may consider themselves to be "spiritual" yet are offended by the person of Jesus. Additionally, this study investigates ways in which the church could continue the mission of Christ in the world, because it seeks answers to questions like: What are the implications of charismatic criteriology on the worship service? How should the church function in the world? How should the church be structured? What role should race, gender, and socioeconomic background play in the church? And, does the church have authority in the world? If so, what is this authority and its extent?

The other concern of this study involves hermeneutical considerations associated with the communication of divine truths, especially to pluralistic contexts. Can careful interpretation of texts provide revelation as to what is authentically spiritual? And how can one discern when an authentic revelation from God is being communicated? Such questions are worthy of exploration, if for no other reason than the fact that human nature and communication is fallible. Is it not true that, on the one hand, someone known to be a false claimant to revelatory experiences, or someone who speak presumptuously for God, can at times put forth claims that are authentically spiritual? On the other hand, is it not also true that one who is generally considered to be authentically spiritual might lie or attempt to mislead others—deliberately or not? And, as already alluded to, some churches may only accept a more rational, "objective" way of communicating, as opposed to others who embrace a more supernatural and "subjective" way of communicating divine truths. How can one discern if what is being communicated is representative of God? Towards this end, and in consideration of the present global, pluralistic, and post-Christendom society, where many are offended by the gospel of Jesus Christ, this study hopes to contribute a way theology could be done to more effectively communicate divine truths to all. This approach has three main hermeneutical considerations, which will be discussed as three excursions.

First, instead of being just christocentric or pneumatocentric, this work is a more comprehensive biblical theology—a Trinitarian perspective. Unlike much Western and contemporary scholarship, the perichoretic unity of the Godhead as well as the *hypostatic* diversity of Father, Son, and Spirit will be considered before coming to conclusions about God. For, speaking of God must always mean the Father, Son, and Holy Spirit in the presence of one another, in total reciprocity, in immediacy of loving relationship, being one for another, by another, in another, and with another. No divine Person exists alone for its [their] own; they are always and eternally in relationship with one another.³

This Trinitarian perspective is more robust than a theology of the first, second, and third article,⁴ which, respectively, interprets Christianity's witness of Christ from the perspective of God the Father, God the Son, and God the Spirit. This is because it theologizes through a christocentric lens, but maintains a Trinitarian balance by remaining conscious of the perichoretic activity of God. And, unlike a Reformed theology of the second article, which also emphasizes Christ, the activity of the Spirit is not considered to have ceased in the apostolic era, or with the closing of the canon of Scripture. Rather, the continuous work of the Spirit throughout the history of the church, including in the contemporary context, is celebrated.

This robustly christocentric Trinitarianism is important for at least four reasons. First, it reflects the impetus behind the apostle Paul's writings. For Paul, "living is Christ and dying is gain" (Phil 1:21). Thus, he appeals to the Corinthians by the name of Jesus Christ (1 Cor 1:10), proclaiming the gospel (cf., 1:17, 23; 2:1–16; 3:10) based on his revelation of Jesus Christ through the Spirit (1 Cor 2:10–13; Gal 1:12–16; 2:2). Second, Christ is inseparably linked to the Spirit, who empowers him to glorify the Father. Third, unlike the subjectivity associated with the person of the Spirit and the Father—whom no one has ever seen (John 1:18; 6:46; 1 John 4:12)—Christ has been an objective presence in the world, revealing the Father (John 14:9). Finally, while a scholar such as Lyle Dabney, for example, focuses on a theology of the third article to effectively witness in a post-Christendom world, because of the subjectivity associated with the Spirit—and the three previous reasons—this work advocates the love exemplified or personified in Christ as essential for effective communicating to all people in this global, pluralistic, and post-Christendom world.

In terms of the second hermeneutical consideration, or excursion, unlike much of modern rationalistic emphasis on "objective" truth and the concomitant rejection of what is "subjective," along with the postmodern affinity for the supernatural, but disdain for what is purely rational and traditional, this study is contextual in at least two ways. On the one hand, it is conversant with various sources of knowledge about God and is

---

3. Boff, *Trinity and Society*, 133.

4. These three articles are described by Dabney in his "Starting with the Spirit."

accountable to feedback from these sources of truth. So, tacit knowledge such as that derived from faith and spiritual gifts, as well as rational or philosophical claims to truth, are considered in the epistemological process, along with Western, Eastern, and Southern modes of thinking. On the other hand, this study is "open to experience that is made possible by experience itself."[5] Stated differently, this study seeks to be sensitive to existential and ontological realities.

Finally, contrary to a postmodern tendency to reject what is traditional and authoritative, our third excursion considers, and is informed by, traditional tools of discourse such as the Bible, doctrinal formulations, personalities, and historical movements that have shaped the way society has come to understand dialogue about God. For there is no presuppositionless understanding, and the "person seeking to understand something has a bond to the subject matter that comes into language through the traditionary text, and has, or acquires, a connection with the tradition from which the text speaks."[6] Rather than hindering truth, tradition allows truth to emerge as it filters out what blurs truth and allows for the consideration of new sources of understanding. I pray the following pages will make clear how one can discern when things are truly revelatory of God.

Part I and chapter 1 of this study gives proper perspective to the entirety of the project by providing the OT context for studies relative to authenticating spirituality. It is a dialogue with key contributors about criteria for genuine OT prophecy. The chapter's focus is to gain clarity concerning questions like: Are there observable outer experiences that serve as criteria to authenticate prophecy? What is the role of divinity and humanity in determining criteria? Are there different criteria for prophets and for the people? What is the role, if any, of factors such as tradition, context, and hermeneutics in determining criteria? And, is there a model prophet from whom one can determine or establish criteria?

Part II of this study consists of chapters 2–6 and focuses on the New Testament context relative to authentic spirituality. Chapter 2 addresses the context of 1 Corinthians in terms of comparing the first-century Graeco-Roman and Corinthian context. It presents the history of the Corinthian church and epistle, as well as the 1 Corinthians epistolary context—all of which is essential for the exegetical work that follows.

Chapter 3 is preparatory to the three chapters that follow it. Therein, the various spiritual things that Paul addresses are outlined.

---

5. Gadamer, *Truth and Method*, 350.
6. Gadamer, *Truth and Method*, 295.

Chapters 4–6 are three exegetical chapters concerning, respectively, the three chapters of 1 Corinthians 12–14, which deal with Pauline criteria for authentic spirituality. The chapters are constructed from the five Pauline criteria determined by Marthinus Bezuidenhout.[7] Chapter 4 is entitled "The Criterion of the Manifestation of the Spirit (1 Cor 12:1–31)" and addresses the first three criteria: the confessional criterion (12:1–3), the criterion of common benefit (12:4–11), and the criterion of service (12:12–30). Interspersed between the first two criteria, the first of three excursions relative to how Paul communicates his message is entitled Paul's "Trinitarian" theology.

Chapter 5 concerns the criterion of love (13:1–13) and includes the second excursion, which focuses on Paul's contextual theology. Chapter 6 concerns the criterion of edification (14:1–40) and includes the final excursion, which addresses the various historical and traditional tools of rational discourse that Paul employs.

Part III of this study consists of chapters 7–9. Chapter 7 highlights some major similarities between the ancient and contemporary contexts. The basis, acceptability, and the appropriation of Paul's spiritual instructions are also discussed. The discussion serves as a validation, or a platform, from which contemporary implications of Paul's criteria for authentic spirituality can then be addressed.

Both chapters 8 and 9 address contemporary implications of the derived thesis about authentic spirituality. Chapter 8 explores implications for the contemporary church, and chapter 9 deals with the contemporary worship service—including an analysis of Reformed and contemporary interpretations of criteria for the functioning of the *charismata*.

Finally, part IV concludes this study. It consists of chapter 10 and briefly points out the problems that were addressed, and the unique contributions to those issues made with this work. Additionally, constructive comments on authenticating spirituality in pluralistic contexts are posited. May the ensuing dialog truly help us discern and apply the things characteristic of God in our lives!

---

7. Cf. Bezuidenhout, *Pauliniese kriteria ten opsigte van die beoefening van die charismata: 'n eksegetiese studie van 1 Kor. 12–14* (translated as *Pauline Criteria Concerning the Practice of Charismata: An Exegetical Study of 1 Corinthians 12–14*).

Part I

Authentic Spirituality in the Old Testament

It is fair to say that most commentators do mention the idea of criteria when discussing authentic spirituality. Bezuidenhout, for example, focuses on criteria for the functioning of *charismata*.[1] But his work only deals with Pauline criteria based on 1 Corinthians 12–14. While a major portion of this study will also address Pauline thought, part I and chapter 1 will expound the OT antecedent to such thought and assess whether there is a criterion or criteria for discerning authentic spirituality in the OT.

---

1. Bezuidenhout, *Pauliniese kriteria*. See also "Trinitarian Nature of the Pauline Criteria."

Chapter 1

Authentic Spirituality in the Old Testament: An Emphasis on Prophecy

1.1 Introduction

MY emphasis in this chapter will be on OT prophecy, not only because of the centrality of the prophets in religious history, but also because prophecy is considered among the *charismata* (1 Cor 12:10)—which is significant in consideration of authentic spirituality. And even though the OT does not use the term *charismata* to describe prophecy, since the term χαρίσματα was coined by the apostle Paul and is limited to the Pauline corpus and 1 Peter 4:10 of the Christian Bible, it is generally agreed that the charism of prophecy that the apostle Paul describes in the New Testament (NT) is in direct continuity with OT prophecy.[1] Moreover, the OT "messenger formula" of "thus says the Lord" and the ascribing of prophecy as a gift from the Spirit in the NT (1 Cor 12:4, 7–11) make it clear that such prophecy was considered to be revelatory of God and authentic spirituality. To be sure, it is to divine revelation that Paul attributed genuine prophetic activity in the OT. Despite this truth, the OT background to prophecy is usually excluded or only briefly summarized when discussing the charism of prophecy described in the NT.[2]

That being said, in an uncertain religious climate where false prophets (Balaam) at times speak a true oracle from Yahweh, speak presumptuously

---

1. For example, Aune, *Prophecy in Early Christianity*, 195, says Pauline prophecy is correctly related to OT tradition. And, "Undoubtedly, Paul's conception of the prophetic role was primarily informed by OT models" (196). John Hilber, in his article entitled "Diversity of Prophetic Phenomena and NT Prophecy," 254, says NT prophecy is in continuity with OT prophecy, and NT prophecy "was conditioned at the outset of the NT period according to the standards of the OT." Additionally, J. Baker, "Prophecy, Prophets," says, "prophecy and the prophets form the greatest line of continuity between the OT and NT."

2. Hildebrandt, *Old Testament Theology*, xvi.

in Yahweh's name (Hananiah, Zedekiah), and where true prophets might lie (old prophet in 1 Kings 13) or attempt to mislead people (Miriam, Saul, Gehazi), there is need to have tests for prophecy. Indeed, because human nature and communication is fallible, and if it is true that prophecy is always accompanied by false prophecy, then there is need for criteria to discern what is authentic,[3] on the part of both the prophet and the people.[4] This charismatic criteriology, then, is no mere academic exercise. There is practical and spiritual significance in determining prophetic criteria, especially since "OT abuses of prophecy are just as relevant to our contemporary situation as they [were] in the OT context and in the early church."[5]

This chapter seeks to clarify what was brought in the way of prophetic understanding through tradition, from the times of the OT through antiquity, to establishing a criterion for genuine prophecy within a present-day context—which should go a long way toward constructing a conclusive statement regarding criteria for authenticating prophecy that perhaps will give proper perspective to the entirety of this project.

1.1.1 Defining the term "prophet"

Before addressing this issue, however, it will be instructive to define the term "prophet" and the concept of prophecy in the pluralistic OT context. Interestingly, the root of the English word "prophet" is not found in the OT. The term "prophet" is derived from the Greek word *prophētēs*, which is a combination of the words *pro*, which means before, and *phēmi*, which means to say something, orally or in writing.[6] Thus, the word "prophet" conveys the idea of "communicating before." More specifically, a prophet communicates for God, before the people of God.[7] In the OT, three main words are used to refer to prophets. The more familiar of these Hebrew words is *nabi*. It is used in designating members of a prophetic guild, court prophets, and even false prophets. Thus, the definition given by Lasor et al. of a prophet (*nabi*) as one communicating for God, and for the people of God, is oversimplified in that it limits the term to "prophets of Yahweh"— whom this work considers to be "true prophets."

---

3. Dunn, "Prophetic I-Sayings," 19.
4. McNamara, "Discernment Criteria in Israel," 6.
5. Hildebrandt, *Old Testament Theology*, 182.
6. Bauer, *Greek-English Lexicon*, 864 and 1053. Hereafter referred to as BAGD.
7. Lasor et al., *Old Testament Survey*, 221–22.

Unlike Lasor et al., Joseph Blenkinsopp suggests "the prophet [*nāḇī*] was one who proclaims a message on behalf of another, generally a deity."[8] Blenkinsopp affirms the seemingly contradictory passive and active basis of prophecy that Alfred Guillaume suggests when he defines the *nāḇī* as "one who is in the state of announcing a message which has been given to him."[9] For Guillaume, the prophet is passive because he or she is called by a deity, and the prophet is active in that he or she announces or proclaims a message. Additionally, the prophet is an instrument to accomplish the things of God. Indeed, Jan Ridderbos seems to have been correct in positing that the word *nāḇī* has an external meaning, and concerns people who have in common external things, primarily a claim to be the mouth of God.[10] The *nāḇī*, then, is primarily a proclaimer or forth-teller, but the *nāḇī* can also be a predictor or foreteller.[11] The other two words that refer to a prophet are *rōeh* and *hōzeh*. Both can be translated as "seer," and seems to have given way to the word *nāḇī*, for 1 Samuel 9:9 says, "he who is called a prophet [*nāḇī*] now was formerly called a seer."

1.1.2 The concept of prophecy

Based on the definitions for the prophet, it is fair to say that prophecy involves the proclamation of a prophet. Certainly, the OT considers prophecy to be supernatural (cf. Amos 3:7ff.; Jer 1:5ff.) in that it has its source in God. But a modern scholar like Hermann Gunkel, for example, considers prophecy the utterance of the human soul. He asserts that there is no difference between true and false prophecy, for prophetic claims originate in the human soul and do not have their source in God.[12] An apparent disagreement like this between the OT and some scholars suggests at least two things about the nature of prophecy. In the first place, it is an essential feature of prophecy to demand criterion for its authentication, both by the prophet and by their audience. Additionally, it seems that one criterion for prophecy would include the source—human or divine—of the revelatory claim.

Regardless of what this study will eventually unfold about prophecy and its criteria, it is noteworthy that scholars have suggested that there are two stages of OT prophecy.[13] One stage—the earlier stage—consists of the

---

8. Blenkinsopp, *History of Prophecy in Israel*, 36.
9. Guillaume, *Prophecy and Divination*, 112.
10. Ridderbos, "Nature of Prophecy," 112.
11. Sawyer, *Prophecy and the Prophets*, 1.
12. Gunkel, "Secret Experiences of the Prophets," 357–59.
13. Cf. Holscher, *Propheten*, 197. Lindblom, in his *Prophecy in Ancient Israel*, 47,

books of Samuel and Kings and is often termed "nebiism." This older type of prophecy is characterized by ecstatic and observable outer experiences. The other stage—the later stage—includes the prophets of Amos to Malachi, and are called the classical, writing, or reforming prophets. These later prophets are often considered to have rejected ecstasy, but stressed the word of Yahweh.[14] These issues, as will be elaborated on below, are important in the discussion of prophetic criteria in the OT. Suffice it to say for now that regardless of the chronological appearance of the prophets, OT tradition regards true prophecy as a gift from God to his people.[15]

But the concept of prophecy was not unique to the OT and the people of Israel. The context of prophecy in the ancient Near East, for example, should be considered as the background for OT prophecy. In fact, it has even been suggested that Israelite prophecy is based on Canaanite influence in the times of the Judges.[16] Whether or not this hypothesis is true, the OT is clear. For Jeremiah 27:1–15 suggests that the nations of Edom, Moab, Ammon, Tyre, and Sidon also had prophets—who were prophesying falsely in the name of Yahweh. In addition to the witness of Jeremiah, 1 Kings 18:19 references prophets to Canaanite deities. Four hundred and fifty of these prophets were of Baal, and four hundred of Asherah. The OT witness of prophetic activity outside of Israel is confirmed, for example, because Egyptian prophets influenced the established social order;[17] and Mesopotamian prophets are mentioned in the tablets from the Mari archives (eighteenth century B.C.E.).[18] Collectively, this evidence suggests that one can be considered a prophet even if they are not communicating the revelation of Yahweh. But if Yahweh is the one and only true God—as is the presupposition of this work—authentic prophecy concerns only what Yahweh reveals. It is to the criteria for determining what is authentically revealed by Yahweh that this study will now focus.

---

agrees with Holscher.

14. Cf. Mowinckel, "'Spirit' and the 'Word.'"

15. Mcnamara, "Discernment Criteria in Israel," 6. Cf. Hos 12:13; Deut 18:15–18.

16. Haldar, *Associations of Cult Prophets*, 91–110.

17. Wilson, "Early Israelite Prophecy," 7.

18. Wilson, "Early Israelite Prophecy," 8. Cf. Craghan, "Mari and Its Prophets," 32–55.

1.2 Are There Outer Experiences that Can Be Considered Criteria of Authentic Spirituality?

To begin this inquiry regarding criteria for what is genuinely prophetic in the OT, it is perhaps appropriate to first ask what might be the most obvious question relative to this subject: are there any observable outer experiences that one can point to as criteria or a criterion for a genuine prophet or prophecy? The work of Sigmund Mowinckel addresses this very issue. In his "The Spirit and the Word in the Pre-Exilic Reforming Prophets," Mowinckel examines the notion that the older prophets of the OT (primitive nebiism) were characterized by ecstatic experiences associated with possession of the immanent Spirit of Yahweh, while the later pre-exilic reforming prophet's consciousness and prophetic message was characterized by the word of Yahweh.[19] This study by Mowinckel was important because studies concerning prophetic criteria generally neglected the role of the Spirit for the word of Yahweh. And if the Spirit was discussed, it was often done in a negative light. For example, ecstasy—which is associated with the Spirit—was considered connected to false prophecy,[20] probably because it was known in Canaanite religion such as Baalism.[21] Moreover, studies, for example, by Friedrich Giesebrecht[22] and Paul Volz[23] concluded that in most of the reforming prophets (Amos, Zephaniah, Nahum, Habakkuk, and Jeremiah), the idea of the ecstasy-producing Spirit of Yahweh is missing, rejected, and even considered undesirable. These studies also asserted that the reforming prophets never associated their prophetic vocation and possession of the word of Yahweh with their possession of Yahweh's Spirit. Seeming exceptions, such as Ezekiel (11:19; 36:26-27; 39:29) and Isaiah (42:5; 44:3), which emphasize the Spirit of God in the life of the people of Israel, are considered additions by postexilic authors, or not concerning prophecy.[24]

Mowinckel, in a qualifying way, disagrees with these findings and concludes that it must not be inferred that the reforming prophets lacked ecstatic character, for the reforming prophets' seeming disregard or disapproval of the concept of the Spirit of Yahweh is because, being theocentric, the word of Yahweh was their preferred source of prophetic revelation.[25] But

---

19. Mowinckel, "'Spirit' and the 'Word,'" 199.
20. Holscher, *Propheten*, 97.
21. Baker, "Prophecy, Prophets," 969.
22. Giesebrecht, *Berufsbegabung der Altestamentlichen Propheten*, 142.
23. Volz, *Geist Gottes und die verwandten Erscheinungen*, 62.
24. Mowinckel, "'Spirit' and the 'Word,'" 203.
25. Mowinckel, "'Spirit' and the 'Word,'" 209–10.

ecstasy—which was characteristic of primitive nebiism, as Gustav Holscher and other scholars, both prior to and subsequent to Mowinckel, have acknowledged—was also present in the reforming prophets. Indeed, Holscher considers ecstasy to be characteristic of all the prophets.[26] To Gunkel, ecstasy is "the fundamental experience of all types of prophecy."[27] Walter Jacobi says, "ecstasy is of the essence of prophecy."[28] Theodore Robinson remarks that "every prophetic oracle arose out of an ecstatic state."[29] Johannes Lindblom maintains that it is misleading to distinguish two phases of OT prophecy because ecstasy is found in all the prophets, and the difference between the prophets does not arrive from the experience of ecstasy but in the frequency and character of the ecstasy.[30] James Crenshaw adds that "one cannot deny ecstatic behavior to genuine prophecy, for there seems to be no clear-cut distinction along these lines between true and false prophet."[31] Furthermore, Robert Wilson gives four compelling arguments for the continuity between early prophets and later writing prophets and criticizes what he calls superficial distinctions based on the existence of ecstasy and participation in the cult.[32] For Wilson, first, ecstasy "appeared sporadically throughout the entire history of Israelite prophecy. Second, both the early and writing prophets were involved in the cult. Third, the OT itself does not distinguish between early and writing prophets—both are called *nābî*. Finally, form critical studies have shown that there is continuity in the speech form of the early and writing prophets." Consequently, Wilson warns that OT prophecy is a complex issue and the individuality of the prophets should be considered before generalizing about them and their ecstatic message.[33]

Considering such agreement that ecstasy is universal to prophecy, it makes sense when Mowinckel explains that the reforming prophets seeming dismissal of the outward ecstatic phenomenon is not an attack on the idea or phenomena of the ecstasy-producing Spirit of Yahweh. Rather, the reforming prophets are reacting against extreme ecstatic behavior, or the frenzy and madness of the "ecstatic" behavior some prophets claimed.[34]

---

26. Holscher, *Propheten*, 148.
27. Gunkel, "Secret Experiences of the Prophets," 358.
28. Jacobi, *Ekstase der alttestamentlichen Propheten*, 4.
29. Robinson, "Prophetischen Bucher," 4.
30. Lindblom, *Prophecy in Ancient Israel*, 47.
31. Crenshaw, *Prophetic Conflict*, 54.
32. Wilson, "Early Israelite Prophecy," 4–6.
33. Wilson, "Early Israelite Prophecy," 5–6.
34. Mowinckel, "'Spirit' and the 'Word,'" 207.

This latter conclusion by Mowinckel, along with Wilson's caution regarding the complexity of OT prophecy and the need to be careful about generalizing about it, is also relevant for this study regarding OT prophetic criteria. So, before proceeding with this discussion it will be instructive to more clearly define the concept of ecstasy and then the prophetic message commonly claimed to be the "word of Yahweh."

1.2.1 The concept of ecstasy

What is ecstasy? It is worth noting that the term "ecstasy" lacks a universally accepted definition. Thus, Holscher, as already stated, defines ecstasy by differentiating between an older and later form. For Mowinckel, the older ecstasy is marked by observable outer experiences such as dancing, music, convulsions, delirious frenzy, and "a wild stammering *glossolalia*," which the reforming prophets consider "madness, intellectual, moral and religious abnormality and worthlessness."[35]

Despite such a judgment, however, it is important to remember, as discussed above, that the reforming prophets themselves are also ecstatic. That being said, the outer experience of ecstasy—Holscher's later form—for the reforming prophet, however, was different than that of primitive nebiism, because it is manifested as an occasional tranquil vision,[36] trances, words, and impulses.[37] This ecstasy of the reforming prophets is characterized by clear publication of divine truths as well as the absence of stammering and half-intelligible speech. It is also manifested by a consciousness of being called by Yahweh (Isa 6; Jer 1) to deliver a religious and moral message characterized by sudden spiritual clarity and reasoned judgment. This consciousness of being called, for the reforming prophet, is evident "when their whole consciousness, the sum of their emotions and will, centered upon a single idea and aim, to the exclusion of all side issues and restraints,"[38] all their inhibitions are removed. The reforming prophets cannot escape the compelling force of their call. Yet, they do not ascribe the Spirit of Yahweh as criteria for their call.

Such apparent rejection of the Spirit could be because the ecstatic compulsion does not cause the prophet to lose self-control. Indeed, during ecstasy,

---

35. Mowinckel, "'Spirit' and the 'Word,'" 207–10.
36. Cf. Isa 6; Jer 1; 24; 38:21ff.; Amos 7:1ff.; Holscher, *Propheten*, 181; Hertzberg, *Prophet und Gott*, 83ff.
37. Mowinckel, "'Spirit' and the 'Word,'" 210, 214.
38. Mowinckel, "'Spirit' and the 'Word,'" 209–10.

the prophet's individuality or personality is not destroyed.[39] Instead of being a loss of control on the part of the reforming prophet, the ecstatic phenomenon evidences the coming of the word of Yahweh, and to that extent, says Mowinckel, the Spirit of Yahweh, or the "ecstatic element," is to be considered a criterion for authenticating a prophet, even if the reforming prophets do not affirm this.[40] Implicit in Mowinckel's ascribing of ecstasy as a prophetic criterion is the idea that an outer experience (ecstasy) can be a criteria for authenticating prophecy. This becomes clear when one considers that, for Mowinckel, in ecstasy the external phenomena are noticeable.[41]

Mowinckel, however, makes clear that instead of the ecstasy-producing Spirit of Yahweh, what the reforming prophets explicitly considers the criterion that authenticates their prophetic call is the word of Yahweh.[42] This word of Yahweh has been considered a separate category of revelation from ecstasy.[43] But before concluding on this assessment, it is important to learn more about the word of Yahweh.

1.2.2 The concept of the word of Yahweh

According to Mowinckel, the word of Yahweh includes what is seen and heard in visions (internal experience), as well as what is heard externally by the prophet.[44] Thus, the word of Yahweh can be both an inner and outer experience that can be observed if the prophet's auditions can also be heard by observers. Further, the word of Yahweh is active in that it integrates the feelings, thought, and will of the prophet, compelling them to obey Yahweh's commands. This compulsion aspect of the word of Yahweh is analogous to the compelling force of the ecstasy produced by the Spirit and can be clearly discerned because of the prophet's consciousness of being called and when it is fulfilled. There is also another similarity between ecstasy and the word of Yahweh. For, just as ecstasy has been considered a criterion for prophecy, the word of Yahweh, which is authenticated through an ecstatic experience, is also regarded as a criterion.[45] In light of the parallels between ecstasy and

---

39. Lindblom, *Prophecy in Ancient Israel*, 197. I. M. Lewis, *Ecstatic Religion*, 55, notes that initial experiences of ecstasy may be involuntary, but subsequent experiences can be controlled.

40. Mowinckel, "'Spirit' and the 'Word,'" 215.

41. Mowinckel, "'Spirit' and the 'Word,'" 214.

42. Mowinckel, "'Spirit' and the 'Word,'" 211.

43. Grether, *Name und Wort Gottes*, 83ff.

44. Mowinckel, "'Spirit' and the 'Word,'" 214.

45. Mowinckel, "'Spirit' and the 'Word,'" 211.

the word of God, as well as the dynamic nature of the ecstatic phenomenon, it seems too simplistic to say that true prophets emphasize the word of God and false prophets emphasize the Spirit.[46] The OT does not affirm such a distinction between the word of God and the Spirit. To the contrary, there is an apparent inseparability of ecstasy and the word of Yahweh, for both phenomena are outer experiences, are considered criterion for prophecy and each other, and are compelling occurrences to the prophet.

But if ecstasy and the word of Yahweh are inseparable, relative to prophetic criterion, why is there a seeming subordination of ecstasy to the word of Yahweh by the reforming prophets? Some possible reasons for this have already been alluded to from Mowinckel's work. For example, expressions of ecstasy are considered extreme, and the reforming prophets are theocentric. The supposed infallibility of the criterion of the word of Yahweh, however, is perhaps at least one other reason. Additionally, the criterion of the word of Yahweh must be coupled with the criterion of inner content, for there is a moral criterion to the word of Yahweh.[47] In other words, "the reforming prophets quite consciously adopt as their criterion . . . the clear purport, the moral and religious content of the word. And this moral criterion is not only a formal, but a factual mark of genuineness."[48] Further, the word of Yahweh must have "correspondence with their [reforming prophet] religious and moral consciousness and their apprehension of Yahweh as a moral God, who exacts true piety of heart."[49] Hence, the word of Yahweh must not contradict what is already known of Yahweh in Israelite tradition, for such a contradiction would evidence that one does not have Yahweh's Spirit.

1.2.3 An in-depth look at the question of observable outer experiences

Having now reasoned, with the help of Mowinckel's work, that the ecstasy produced by the Spirit of Yahweh as well as the word of Yahweh have both been considered prophetic criteria as well as inseparable and compelling outer experiences, it is now time for a more focused look into the question of whether or not there are observable outer experiences that can be considered criteria of authentic prophecy. On this issue, scholars have generally answered no. H.

---

46. This notion, for example, is implicit in the works of Giesebrecht, *Berufsbegabung der Altestamentlichen Propheten*, 42; and Volz, *Geist Gottes und die verwandten Erscheinungen*, 62, which Mowinckel is reacting to.

47. Mowinckel, "'Spirit' and the 'Word,'" 215–16, 223.

48. Mowinckel, "'Spirit' and the 'Word,'" 217.

49. Mowinckel, "'Spirit' and the 'Word,'" 225.

H. Rowley, for example, suggests that criteria for authenticating prophecy belong to the spiritual realm and not to outer experiences.[50] To Lindblom, outer experiences cannot be criteria because prophecy is an inward enlightenment effectuated by the Spirit,[51] and in the OT (cf. Jer 28:10–11; 23:31) both true and false prophets had similar outer experiences. In this latter statement, Lindblom is affirming what Gottfried Quell has already observed. Quell's study of Jeremiah 28 showed that Hannaniah—a false prophet—evidenced the same forms of speech and symbolism as Jeremiah—a true prophet. Thus, Quell concludes, outer experiences cannot be considered criteria to determine authentic prophecy, for only the inner witness of a genuine prophet can determine authenticity.[52] Martin McNamara agrees with this interpretation of Quell, and adds that outer experiences can only be considered criteria for determining false prophecy.[53]

Even Mowinckel seems to suggest that outer experiences cannot authenticate prophecy. The Norwegian scholar says that in ecstasy the prophet is conscious of being given thoughts, words, and impulses that do not emanate from themselves but "may be concentrated into visual and auditory hallucinations and illusions . . . which seem to come from without . . . in reality all their experiences are inner experiences."[54] Mowinckel is right to imply that the ecstatic experiences come from within, because despite originating from the Spirit, ecstasy issues through the spirit, or the inner consciousness of the prophet. Thus, for the prophet, the effect of the working of the Spirit (from outside the prophet, or on the prophet) is an inner experience of the Spirit that is manifested as observable outer experiences like tongues, prophecy, dance, and impulses. In this sense, then, ecstasy, like the word of God, can be considered both an inner and outer experience, for ecstasy is an extreme case of a mental condition (inner experience) where the external phenomena become conspicuous.

For Mowinckel, the external experiences of ecstasy can be considered prophecy-authenticating criteria—for the prophet.[55] But, as it is for the word of Yahweh, this ecstatic criterion must be combined with the criterion of inner content, or consistency with what is already known of Yahweh through Israelite tradition. This is because ecstasy—as is the case for the word of Yahweh—is not an infallible criterion, at least not by itself, for ecstasy is

50. Rowley, "Nature of Prophecy," 18–19.
51. Lindblom, *Prophecy in Ancient Israel*, 174–77.
52. Quell, *Wahre und falsche Propheten*, 65.
53. McNamara, "Discernment Criteria in Israel," 10.
54. Mowinckel, "'Spirit' and the 'Word,'" 214.
55. Mowinckel, "'Spirit' and the 'Word,'" 215.

characteristic of all prophecy (both true and false).⁵⁶ Additionally, ecstasy seems to be a criterion that is limited to the prophets, who themselves may entertain doubt relative to the ecstatic phenomenon. Because of such uncertainty, the role of humanity and divinity as it relates to prophetic criteria will now be investigated.

1.3 What Is the Role of Divinity and Humanity in Establishing Criteria?

In his study on the effect of prophetic conflict upon Israelite religion, James Crenshaw acknowledges that ever since Quell's interpretation of true and false prophecy there has been a denial of valid criteria for authenticating prophecy. Following Mowinckel's study, which, as has been alluded to above, asserts the prophet is able to authenticate that which is prophetic, Quell investigates whether there is a single criterion by which the populace as well as the prophet can determine who is a true prophet of Yahweh. Quell validates Mowinckel's assertion and concludes that because prophecy operates on the divine (Spirit) as well as human (prophet) realm, only the inner witness of a genuine prophet can determine authenticity, and the criteria for discernment must be pneumatic.⁵⁷ In contrast to Mowinckel, however, who suggests the Spirit and the word of Yahweh are criteria, because of the subjectivity of the pneumatic and inner witness of the prophet, Quell asserts that there can be no criteria to authenticate prophecy. Ironically, this assertion is self-contradictory, for despite the subjectivity of pneumatic experiences, the implicit notion that discernment criteria must be pneumatic is itself a criterion. What this pneumatic criterion entails, including whether it functions by itself, remains to be determined. Nevertheless, in light of these conclusions by Mowinckel and Quell, as well as that of a scholar like Ridderbos, that there are important human as well as divine factors in prophecy,⁵⁸ Crenshaw is convinced that human limitation and divine sovereignty combine to create tension as to what is authentically prophetic and seeks to clarify the role of both divine and human factors in determining prophetic criteria.⁵⁹

In order to accomplish his aim Crenshaw recognizes the seven major criteria that have been discussed in literature concerning prophetic criteria, and separates them into two categories. The first consists of what he calls

56. Baker, "Prophecy, Prophets," 969.
57. Crenshaw, *Prophetic Conflict*, 18.
58. Ridderbos, "Nature of Prophecy," 120.
59. Crenshaw, *Prophetic Conflict*, 4, 110.

"message-centered criteria," and pertains to four criteria that relate to the divine message of the prophet. Crenshaw's second category of criteria consists of three criteria relative to the human claimant to prophecy. These two categories of prophetic criteria will now be discussed in turn.

1.3.1 Crenshaw's divine message–centered criteria

The first of the divine message–centered criteria is the fulfillment or non-fulfillment of prophecy. This criterion has been debated based on OT texts such as Deuteronomy 18:21–22, which says, "you may say to yourself, 'how can we recognize a word that the Lord has not spoken?' If a prophet speaks in the name of the Lord but the thing does not take place or prove true, it is a word that the Lord has not spoken. The prophet has spoken it presumptuously; do not be frightened by it."[60] This verse seems to be an explicit criterion for determining authentic prophecy.[61] That is, if one is to be considered a prophet from Yahweh, what he or she proclaims must be fulfilled. If the prophetic claim is not fulfilled, the claimant is a false prophet and their proclamation should not be cause for fear. For Crenshaw, however, as it is for J. Hempel, who addresses the issue of unfulfilled predictions,[62] this criterion is limited and can only be used successfully in authenticating past events. It is of little value when one considers the dynamic nature of many prophetic words, including the conditional aspect of prophecy.

The conditional aspect of prophecy is evident in Jeremiah 18:7–10. For Jeremiah, the Lord says,

> At one moment I may declare concerning a nation or a kingdom, that I will pluck up and break down and destroy it, [8] but if that nation, concerning which I have spoken, turns from its evil, I will change my mind about the disaster that I intended to bring on it. [9] And at another moment I may declare concerning a nation or a kingdom that I will build and plant it, [10] but if it does evil in my sight, not listening to my voice, then I will change my mind about the good that I had intended to do to it.

---

60. All biblical quotations, except those from 1 Corinthians 12–14, are taken from the NRSV unless otherwise noted. All quotations from 1 Corinthians 12–14 are this author's own translation.

61. Other verses that express this same principle that all prophetic claims must be fulfilled to be considered authentic include 1 Kgs 22:28; Isa 30:8; Ezek 33:33; and Jer 28:9.

62. Hempel, "Vom irrenden Glauben."

Because prophecy is often conditional, or dependent on future actions relative to people and nations, the criterion of fulfillment is limited to divine good pleasure and of value only when restricted to the time of the prophet and his contemporaries, but no time limit can be set on prophecy. In addition to being conditional, prophecy is also dynamic in nature. This latter feature of prophetic words is seen, for example, in Deuteronomy 13:1, which suggests that even if prophetic claims are fulfilled, this is no sure sign of a true prophet, for prophecy should not contradict the established revelation of God—the moral criterion.

Crenshaw's second divine message-centered criteria relates to the promise of weal or woe. According to this criterion, true prophets predict woe or judgment and the false prophet proclaims weal or prosperity to Israel.[63] This presupposition is based on passages such as Jeremiah 28, where Jeremiah seems to imply that true prophets prophesy "war, famine, and pestilence against many countries and great kingdoms," and false prophets—those who have not been sent by Yahweh—generally prophesy peace (vv. 8–9).[64] Jeremiah communicates this apparent criterion after the prophet Hananiah claims he has a message from the Lord that promises within two years there will be an end to the captivity of the people of Judah at the hands of Babylon—including the return of the king as well as the vessels of the temple to Judah (vv. 2–4). Hananiah's message of weal can be contrasted with Jeremiah's message of woe. According to Jeremiah, the God of Israel says that Judah will continue in its captivity with Babylon, for the Lord has "put an iron yoke on the neck" of Judah (v. 14). Unfortunately for Hananiah, Jeremiah also had a message of woe for him. Jeremiah prophesied to his fellow prophet, "Listen, Hananiah, the Lord has not sent you, and you made this people trust in a lie. Therefore, thus says the Lord: I am going to send you off the face of the earth. Within this year you will be dead, because you have spoken rebellion against the Lord" (vv. 15–16). The subsequent fulfillment of Jeremiah's prophecy and the concomitant non-fulfillment of Hananiah's prophecy suggest that Jeremiah is the true prophet and Hananiah is the false prophet. Thus, Crenshaw declares, a criterion of weal or woe is invalid because both true and false prophets sometimes prophesy weal and woe.[65] Evidence of this is seen when Isaiah—a true prophet—prophesied words of welfare to Ahaz, the king of Judah (Isa 7:3–4), as well as future

---

63. Crenshaw, *Prophetic Conflict*, 52–53.

64. Other passages that seem to support a criterion of weal or woe include Ezek 13:1–10 and 1 Kgs 22:5–8.

65. Crenshaw, *Prophetic Conflict*, 53.

woes (7:17). Likewise, Micah 3:5 speaks of false prophets who prophesy weal and woe as it is convenient for them.

The third divine message criterion concerns the revelatory form in which the divine message is received. Two of these revelatory forms—the Spirit (ecstasy) and the word of God—have already been discussed. The third revelatory form is a dream. In terms of criterion, it has been asserted by Crenshaw that Jeremiah prophesied that only false prophets prophesy based on dreams.[66] This assertion is based on Jeremiah's prophecy that the Lord says, "I have heard what the prophets have said who prophesy lies in my name, saying, 'I have dreamed, I have dreamed!'" (Jer 23:25), and "See, I am against those who prophesy lying dreams, says the Lord, and who tell them, and who lead my people astray by their lies and their recklessness, when I did not send them or appoint them; so they do not profit this people at all, says the Lord" (23:32). But the thrice-repeated idea of lying evidences that these verses are specifically addressing those who prophesy lying dreams and it should therefore not be taken as a criterion that those who prophesy by dreams are false prophets. Obviously implicit in this observation, then, is the idea that dreams can be an authentic form of prophecy. This is affirmed in the OT, for example, with Jacob's dream at Bethel (Gen 28:10–17) regarding the promised fulfillment of the Abrahamic covenant (cf. Gen 12:1–3; 17:1–22); Joel's prophecy concerning a future outpouring of the Spirit that will be marked by prophecy, dreams, and visions (Joel 2:28); and the Lord speaking to Aaron and Miriam from a pillar of cloud, saying "hear my words: when there are prophets among you, I the Lord make myself known to them in visions; I speak to them in dreams" (Num 12:6). The internal and subjective nature of the revelation through dreams, however, would rule them out as criterion to authenticate prophecy.

The final divine message–centered criterion concerns allegiance to Yahweh or Baal. Based on Deuteronomy 13:1–3, and in light of there being prophets who prophesy to and by Baal (cf. Jer 2:8; 23:13), it has been supposed that a criterion for authentic prophecy is faithfulness to Yahweh rather than Baal.[67] The author of Deuteronomy records that even if there is a condition where a prophet foretells something and it is fulfilled, if this seemingly true prophet encourages or desires allegiance to other gods, such as Baal, this prophet is not to be believed. Under such a circumstance, whole-hearted faithfulness to the Lord is being tested. But Crenshaw notes that this presupposed criterion is limited to prophets who are faithful to false gods—who would be appropriately considered false

---

66. Crenshaw, *Prophetic Conflict*, 54.
67. Crenshaw, *Prophetic Conflict*, 55.

prophets—however, the criterion is inadequate for prophets who are faithful to Yahweh but ignorantly serve Baal.

1.3.2 Crenshaw's criteria focusing upon the man

In terms of Crenshaw's second category of criteria relative to the human claimant to prophecy, the first criterion pertains to the prophetic office. In this supposed criterion, it is reasoned that prophets who are professional cultic officials are false prophets. But Crenshaw rightly rejects this assertion, for the OT witness does not support such a claim. In 1 Kings 22:1–28, for example, the cult prophet Micaiah faithfully spoke the word that the Lord had given him. And even if he did not, this "criterion" still would not be applicable to all who prophesy throughout history.

A second criterion suggests that true prophets are moral and false prophets are immoral.[68] A cursory glance at the OT would seem to affirm this criterion. Jeremiah 23:9–15, for example, denounces false prophets who were ungodly and prophesied by Baal. These false prophets were also adulterous, liars, and drunkards (Isa 28:7). But Crenshaw rightly finds this criterion to be limited because while flagrant immoral behavior can be a solid indicator of a false prophet, denouncing immoral behavior—as Jeremiah did—should not be considered a criterion for true prophecy.[69] This is because there were false prophets in which immoral behavior seemed to have been absent.[70] And there were true prophets who were guilty of immoral behavior.[71] Therefore, God can prophesy through immoral people, and holy people can be subject to deception.

The final criterion argues that true prophets have a conviction of being sent by Yahweh and false prophets do not share an experience of being called. This will be discussed in greater detail below in addressing McNamara's work. Suffice it to say, for now, that Crenshaw also considers this criterion to be limited because the conviction of having been sent by Yahweh cannot be "objectively" proven.[72]

Having considered the divine and human role in determining criteria, Crenshaw, in accord with other scholarship relative to prophetic criteria

---

68. Crenshaw, *Prophetic Conflict*, 56–60.

69. Crenshaw, *Prophetic Conflict*, 57. Cf. McNamara, "Discernment Criteria in Israel," 12.

70. E.g., Hananiah and the opponents of Micaiah.

71. For example, Hosea married a prostitute (Hos 1:2–3), and Micaiah often deceived the king before prophesying the word of the Lord (1 Kgs 22; 14–17).

72. Crenshaw, *Prophetic Conflict*, 11–12.

since Quell, concludes that there is no satisfactory criterion—by itself or among a group, neither divine nor prophet centered—that can always distinguish between true and false prophecy.[73]

1.4 Are There Different Criteria for Prophets and for the People?

After Crenshaw's work, and due to increased emphasis on revelatory claims brought on by the charismatic movement, however, Martin McNamara writes his "Discernment Criteria in Israel: True and False Prophets" out of a concern for proper guidance of the laity and the churches being able to discern true and false prophets. Crenshaw asserts there are no divine and human based criteria to authenticate prophecy. But, in his focus on OT prophecy, McNamara rightly notes that the subject is a rather complex phenomenon, and "it was evident that certain criteria were required for the discernment of true prophecy from false, both on the part of prophet and people."[74] Consequently, McNamara analyzes criteria that have been presupposed, for the prophet and for the people.

1.4.1 McNamara's criteria for the prophet

The major criterion for the prophet concerns a perceived call and a concomitant compulsion for the prophet to speak.[75] In fact, it has been expressed that the first criterion of a true prophet is being conscious of a call.[76] And a specific and personal call is featured in true prophets after Moses.[77] This belief is based on various OT texts where the prophet expresses an awareness of being sent or having had a special experience with Yahweh.[78] Such an experience, however, is not always unchallenged (Jer 43:1–3), and prophetic conflict has arisen because of conflicting claims of having such an experience with Yahweh. This is true of Hananiah and Jeremiah, who both claimed to be sent by the Lord despite having contradictory prophecies

---

73. Crenshaw, *Prophetic Conflict*, 61. Cf. Oswald, *Falsche Prophetie im Alten Testament*, 29.

74. McNamara, "Discernment Criteria in Israel," 6.

75. McNamara, "Discernment Criteria in Israel," 8. Crenshaw, *Prophetic Conflict*, 49, considers this criterion of call a divine message–centered criterion.

76. Albright, *Archaeology and the Religion of Israel*, 24.

77. Baker, "Prophecy, Prophets," 964.

78. Cf. Exod 3:1–4:17; Isa 6; Jer 1:4–19; Ezek 1–3; Hos 1:2; Amos 7:14–15; and Jon 1:1.

(Jer 28). Only one of these prophets could have been speaking the word of Yahweh, and the other is to be considered a false prophet. The possibility of there being such false claimants to prophecy is perhaps why the supposed criterion of a call is addressed in Jeremiah 23. There, in verse 18 Yahweh asks, "who has stood in the council of the Lord so as to see and to hear his word?" Then in verses 21–22 Yahweh adds, "I did not send the prophets, yet they ran; I did not speak to them, yet they prophesied. But if they had stood in my council, then they would have proclaimed my words to my people." To be sure, Jeremiah does not assert that the claimants to prophecy whom he attacks were not prophets. Indeed, they have many of the external experiences that true prophets exhibit. But such external experiences do not serve as criteria to determine which prophet is sent by Yahweh. Jeremiah's contention is that these prophets are prophesying what is on their own minds instead of a true word from Yahweh.

The compulsion aspect of the supposed criterion of call is articulated by Jeremiah when, in speaking of the word of Yahweh he has been given, he says, "if I say, 'I will not mention him, or speak any more in his name,' then within me there is something like a burning fire shut up in my bones; I am weary with holding it in, and I cannot" (Jer 20:9).[79] As has already been noted, the compelling force of the prophet's call is not to be equated with a loss of self-control. Rather, it is a criterion for the prophet that they have received the word of Yahweh.[80]

On this latter point, contrary to Mowinckel, McNamara is seemingly in agreement with Quell and the many scholars who declare that there are no criteria to discern between true and false prophecy. McNamara concludes that the prophetic call is essentially dependent on an internal experience of the prophet, and therefore no objective criteria can be given to authenticate it. He insists the most one can say is that there are criteria that can help a prophet determine that they are not sent by God.[81] McNamara therefore validates Crenshaw's conclusion that such a criterion of call is "outside the area of historical investigation,"[82] and there is no criterion by which a prophet, in particular, can authenticate prophecy.

---

79. The notion of having been called or having a special experience of Yahweh as a prophetic criterion is also evident, for example, in Amos 3:8 and Jer 23:18, 21–22.
80. Mowinckel, "Spirit' and the 'Word,'" 215.
81. McNamara, "Discernment Criteria in Israel," 10.
82. Crenshaw, *Prophetic Conflict*, 60.

1.4.2 McNamara's criteria for the people

Next, McNamara considers criteria for the people of Israel to discern true from false prophecy—several of which are similar to the divine message-centered criteria of Crenshaw that have already been discussed. Thus, the focus here will be on criteria that have not yet been discussed. McNamara's first criterion for the people is that of faithfulness to the central truth of Israelite religion. In this regard, he quickly concludes that this criterion is limited to the context for which it was intended.[83] McNamara reaches this conclusion because the true prophets of Israel did not always prophesy what seemed to be faithful to Israelite religion. For example, Micah predicted the destruction of Jerusalem (Mic 3:12) and Jeremiah prophesied that the temple and all of Jerusalem would be torn down (Jer 26:1–23). Because of the seeming contradiction of their prophecy to Israelite religion, these prophets were in danger of being put to death by the people. On the surface, this criterion appears to be like the moral criterion already discussed since both criteria concerns faithfulness to traditional beliefs. If this is the case, McNamara's findings would be contradictory to Mowinckel's claim that the inner content of the word of Yahweh is a criterion to authenticate prophecy.[84] But the moral criterion specifically relates to the person of God, as revealed in tradition, and not necessarily to everything pertaining to Israelite religious tradition.

McNamara's second and third criteria for the people relate respectively to fulfillment of prophecy and woe or welfare. But because nothing is added to the discussion above, his fourth criterion of the people will now be considered. This fourth criterion concerns the moral life of the prophet. In contrast to the first three criteria for the people presented by McNamara—which have all been considered limited in that their primary concern is predictive prophecy and were only valuable for the discernment of false prophecy—now McNamara introduces a criterion of discernment and personal living faith, which he considers to be more comprehensive in that it takes into account Israel's entire relationship with God. For McNamara, the realm of faith has not been considered in discussions of prophetic criteria. But without faith there can be no credible criterion for recognizing authentic prophecy, because faith was needed to accept as well as bring the prophecies to fruition.[85] McNamara's contribution here begs the question of whether faith is a sure criterion. After all, like the prophetic call—which was a limited criterion—the faith of the people of God also

---

83. McNamara, "Discernment Criteria in Israel," 10.
84. Mowinckel, "'Spirit' and the 'Word,'" 215–16.
85. McNamara, "Discernment Criteria in Israel," 12–13.

depends on an internal experience that cannot be objectified. Nevertheless, going forward, McNamara's conclusive comments are worthy to be taken into consideration. McNamara declares,

> it is no easy matter to discern who at any time is a genuine spokesman for God's plan, but discernment must be made in the light of the broad context of the divine mystery of salvation, now finally revealed in Christ, but intended to be ever more deeply understood and lived under the guidance of the Holy Spirit, the Spirit who spoke through the prophets of old and continues to make God's word a living reality.[86]

These words suggest that contexts may play a role in establishing criteria for authentic prophecy, so contextual considerations will now be explored.

1.5 Is There a Role for Tradition, Contexts, and Hermeneutics in Determining Criteria?

James Sanders, in his essay entitled "Canonical Hermeneutics: True and False Prophecy," argues that the problem of true and false prophecy in the OT can be better understood by considering ancient traditions (texts), situations (contexts), and hermeneutics. For Sanders, "texts" describes the "common authoritative traditions used by the prophet to bear upon the situation to which they spoke in antiquity."[87] The notion of "contexts" depicts "the historical, cultural, social, political, economic, national, and international situations to which prophets applied the 'texts.'"[88] And the term "hermeneutics" explains "the ancient theological mode, as well as literary technique, by which that application was made by the prophet, true or false—that is, how he or she read the 'texts' and 'contexts' and how he or she related them."[89]

In order to discern new criteria for distinguishing true and false prophecy, Sanders focuses his study on the hermeneutics of the disputation passages of the OT—especially those of Jeremiah 28, as well as Deuteronomy 13 and 18. In these disputation passages, prophets in the same respective contexts, who refer to the same respective tradition(s), address an issue but offer conflicting prophecies to resolve it. After careful study of such passages, Sanders concludes that the hermeneutic of the true and false prophets plays a critical role in the prophecy they deliver. This is because

---

86. McNamara, "Discernment Criteria in Israel," 13.
87. Sanders, "Canonical Hermeneutics," 89.
88. Sanders, "Canonical Hermeneutics," 89.
89. Sanders, "Canonical Hermeneutics," 89.

"whenever the freedom of God as Creator is forgotten or denied in adapting traditional 'text' to a given context, there is threat of falsehood."[90] In other words, in situations of dispute the false prophets' hermeneutic does not ascribe to the fundamental OT principle of God being Creator of all—both Israel and her opponents. Instead of this monotheizing principle of God as Creator of all people, the false prophets adopt a "text" or tradition to a "context" in a polytheizing manner by particularizing a God of Israel and a god(s) for other nations. This conclusion of Sanders does not explicitly deal with criteria for a true prophet. But his absolute assertion that whenever the principle of God as Creator of all is violated there is falsehood implies that authentic prophecy must evidence a God, who exacts justice and grace without respect of persons.

Nevertheless, in regards to the role of (texts), contexts, and hermeneutics in authenticating prophecy, or a prophet, Sanders affirms the previously mentioned studies of Quell, Oswald, and Crenshaw, which assert that "no single criterion of distinction between true and false prophecy can be emphasized . . . or any other criterion or combination of such."[91] This conclusion, however, begs the question of whether or not limiting his study to the disputation passages, while it benefits his overall purpose, perhaps also limits his findings. What if Sanders had considered other passages? Would he have identified other criteria or combination of criteria for authenticating prophecy? These questions are worthwhile because Sanders's affirmation is contrary, for example, to the studies by Mowinckel and McNamara—which are not limited to disputation passages. After considering OT prophecy in general, Mowinckel suggests a combination of the Spirit and a moral word of Yahweh—that is consistent with past revelation—as criteria for true prophecy. McNamara asserts that discernment and a personal living faith are criteria when determining authenticity. It is yet to be determined by this study if any combination of Sanders's or the latter two scholars' deductions are correct. However, coming to a resolution on the issue of OT criteria for prophecy, the final question of whether or not there is a model prophet from whom one can determine criteria will now be addressed.

---

90. Sanders, "Canonical Hermeneutics," 101.

91. Sanders, "Canonical Hermeneutics," 101. Cf. Crenshaw, *Prophetic Conflict*, 61; Oswald, *Falsche Prophetie im Alten Testament*, 29.

1.6 Is There a Model Prophet from Whom One Can Determine Criteria for True Prophecy?

In his "Diversity of OT Prophetic Phenomena and NT Prophecy," John Hilber seeks criteria for how God speaks to his people by analyzing OT prophecy and its implications for NT prophecy. Based on the text of Deuteronomy 18:15–22, Hilber says, "the ministry of all OT prophets meets the criteria set forth by the prophet Moses."[92] This conclusion has also been reached by other scholars. For example, McNamara states that true prophets are in succession to Moses (Hos 12:13; Amos 2:10–11).[93] And J. P. Baker comments that "OT prophecy received its normative form in the life and person of Moses, who constituted a standard of comparison for all future prophets (Deut 18:15–19; 34:10)—every feature of the true prophet was first found in Moses."[94]

To validate these claims, it is instructive to examine the supposed features of a true prophet that were evidenced in Moses. To begin, for Hilber, the true prophet was an intercessor, for both physical (1 Kings 13:6) and spiritual healing of individuals and the nation (Exod 32:10–32; Jer 42:4).[95] For the prophet to be an effective intercessor, however, he or she needs to maintain a close relationship with God. Thus, righteous "character is a prerequisite for the call as prophet."[96] While the significance of one's character can hardly be overstated, this criterion, however, must be limited, because, as has already been stated, God has called individuals to prophesy who did not necessarily have excellent character.[97]

Second, prophets after the manner of Moses deliver predictive (2 Sam 7:4–17), and comforting (Exod 6:6–9; 2 Chr 34:26–28; Isa 38:5–6) oracles to individuals. Such oracles can also be considered encouraging—even though they are not commonly perceived that way.[98] These oracles, however, can only be authenticated by the inward ecstatic experience of the prophet,[99] and therefore cannot be "objectively" discerned by all.

Third, true prophets in succession to Moses are characterized by ecstatic phenomena distinct enough for observers to recognize the act as

---

92. Hilber, "Diversity of OT Prophetic Phenomena," 244.
93. McNamara, "Discernment Criteria in Israel," 5.
94. Baker, "Prophecy, Prophets," 964.
95. Hilber, "Diversity of OT Prophetic Phenomena," 244–45.
96. Hilber, "Diversity of OT Prophetic Phenomena," 245. Cf. Jer 23:11, 14, 17, 21–22; Mic 3:5–11.
97. Cf., for example, Hos 1:2–3 and 1 Kgs 22:14–17.
98. Cf. Keown, "Prophet as Encourager," 156–61.
99. For example, Jeremiah waited ten days to discern a message from the Lord (Jer 42:7).

prophecy.[100] It is worth repeating that the ecstatic excesses discussed above are not necessarily characteristic of the Spirit of God, and there is not enough evidence to suggest that the ecstasy of the true prophet was not intelligible. In fact, prophecy is both verbal and nonverbal communication, and ecstatic behavior should not be viewed apart from a prophet's verbal declaration, otherwise the prophecy could be meaningless.[101] Hence, when the prophet declares "thus says the Lord," such verbal communication is not to be separated from, or considered to be of more importance than, the ecstatic activity that the prophet exhibits. The ecstatic Spirit as well as the word of Yahweh are integral to authoritative and authentic prophecy.[102]

Finally, just as the ecstatic Spirit should not be separated from the word of Yahweh, the word of Yahweh proclaimed by a true prophet in succession to Moses should not be contradictory of past revelation.[103] Thus, all prophecies should be examined and rejected if they contradict the word of Yahweh, even if they come from an established prophet. For where some criteria do not apply to every situation or one is unsure about them, God guards "the faithful [his people] and his word in such a way that a combination of tests provided an adequate means of validation."[104]

If there was a prophet who always evidenced a combination of attributes characteristic of God, then one could conclude that such a prophet is a model prophet from whom one can determine criteria for true prophecy. This prophet, as implied by Hilber, for example, would simultaneously be righteous, loving, edifying, can speak predictive words, evidence ecstatic manifestations, and be consistent with traditionally accepted revelations of God. But though there are, or can be, true prophets of God (cf. Amos 2:11), since human beings are fallible and prone to misrepresent God (Ps 14; 53; Rom 3:9–23), mere human beings cannot reliably be looked to as model prophets who always exhibit the criteria of authentic prophecy. Indeed, since the criteria for authentic prophecy must involve all that is characteristic of God, it can be deduced that God must be involved with the prophetic manifestation, and only God can fulfill the role of a model prophet from whom criteria can be determined. According to the NT, Jesus, who is both human and divine in nature, is that prophet "in

---

100. Hilber, "Diversity of OT Prophetic Phenomena," 246, 248. Cf. Exod 34:27–35.

101. Wilson, *Prophets and Society*, 87.

102. Hilber, "Diversity of OT Prophetic Phenomena," 250.

103. Van Winkle, "1 Kings XIII." Cf. Num 14:11–20.

104. Hilber, "Diversity of OT Prophetic Phenomena," 253–54. Cf. Exod 15:20; Num 12:1–15; 1 Sam 10:12, 19–24; 2 Kgs 3:17–20; Isa 7:11; 38:7, 22.

succession to Moses" whom one can look to for authenticating criteria of prophecy (Acts 3:20–26; Matt 21:11, 46).

1.7 Conclusion

This chapter has sought to answer the question of whether there are criteria for discerning the authenticity of prophecy in the OT by dialoguing with key contributors on the issue. Various scholars have approached the issue in different ways and posited various conclusions. For example, for Mowinckel, the observable outer experiences of ecstasy by the Spirit as well as a moral and religious word of Yahweh that is consistent with traditionally established revelation are criteria. Crenshaw disagrees with these findings and suggests that human limitation and divine sovereignty combine to create tension that renders it impossible to have criteria for authentic prophecy. But Crenshaw's assertion is based on assessing individual supposed criterion that rightfully were deemed limited. He did not consider that criteria could be inseparable and, when combined, could pass the various critical tests that individual criterion may have failed. For example, Mowinckel's criteria of the ecstatic Spirit and the word of Yahweh that is consistent with past revelation, despite being requisite for authentic prophecy, by themselves, cannot be considered criterion because of their subjective element. But they are inseparable components of prophecy that reinforce and authenticate the prophetic claim.

McNamara finds that there are no criteria specific to the prophet, but for the public there is a criterion of a discerning and personal living faith out of a relationship with God. For McNamara, then, divinity must be included in criteria for authenticating prophecy. This is because faith in God is needed for one to accept prophecy. But it is God alone who brings the prophecies to fruition. This criterion, however, is an inner experience that cannot be objectively authenticated. Thus, McNamara's proposed criterion—at least by itself—is not valid for the people to absolutely authenticate prophecy.

In considering the role of texts (traditions), contexts, and hermeneutics in determining criteria, Sanders suggest that hermeneutics can be considered a criterion to assess false prophecy, for such prophecy violates the principle that God is the Creator of all people and therefore is concerned with being just to all. Sanders also agree with Crenshaw that there is no criterion to assess authentic prophecy, and even adds that no combination of criteria can be authenticated. This is contrary to the earlier findings of Mowinckel, and leaves one questioning Sanders's limiting his study to three disputation passages instead of the entire prophetic corpus. Additionally, Sanders's very criterion for false prophecy—contrary to his assertion that there are no criteria for true prophecy—implicitly argues for a criterion for true prophecy being without respect of people and being applicable to all whom God created. This criterion, however, must be combined with others since false prophets can also present themselves without respect of persons.

Finally, Hilber suggests that true prophets are modeled after Moses and can be discerned because they possess a combination of the ecstatic Spirit and an inseparable word of God that is consistent with traditionally accepted revelation of God. This conclusion has come full circle with that of Mowinckel.

After considering the various arguments concerning criteria for authentic prophecy, therefore, it can be said that there are criteria for discerning authentic claims of divine revelatory experiences in the OT. Indeed, the combination of Spirit-led ecstasy and a hermeneutic consistent with the traditionally accepted word of God that is without respect of nations and individuals can serve as criteria for authenticating prophecy. By themselves, individual criteria are inadequate to authenticate genuine prophecy, even though they are always present in true prophecies. And while one may be able to find other combinations of criteria that are not included here, in the OT the Spirit-manifested word of God can serve as criteria(on) to distinguish between true and false prophecy, regardless of the situation, or to whom the prophecy is given. To gain further understanding of revelatory criteria, the apostle Paul's teachings on the subject will now be considered.

Part II

Authentic Spirituality in the New Testament

The purpose of the next four chapters is to dialogue with the apostle Paul concerning the issue of authentic spirituality, and how it is communicated in his pluralistic context. Understanding more about Paul's exhortations, in this regard, should provide clues about how to live and effectively communicate the things of God in our context. Towards this end, after examining the context of 1 Corinthians, the text of 1 Corinthians 12–14[1] will be exegeted. This study, therefore, is not claiming to represent the entirety of Pauline thought, for it is understood that 1 Corinthians is just one occasional document written by the apostle. This study, however, presupposes that, like the rest of the Christian Bible (OT and NT), 1 Corinthians is a timeless classic, significant, and, as is true for such texts, "speaks in such a way that it is not a statement about what is past . . . rather, it says something to the present as if it were said specifically to it."[2]

---

1. All quotations from this portion of Scripture are this author's own translation. All other biblical quotations, unless otherwise noted, are from the NRSV.
2. Gadamer, *Truth and Method*, 290.

Chapter 2

The Context of 1 Corinthians

2.1 Introduction

This chapter will focus on the context of 1 Corinthians—a prerequisite for our exegesis of 1 Corinthians 12–14. More specifically, we will now explore the first-century Graeco-Roman and Corinthian contexts, the history of the Corinthian Church and epistle, including the epistolary context, highlighting the issues relevant to our investigation of authentic spirituality.

2.2.1 First-century Graeco-Roman context

In his *Power Through Weakness: Paul's Understanding of the Christian Ministry in 2 Corinthians*, Timothy Savage seeks to understand Paul's paradoxical statement that "whenever I am weak, then I am strong" (2 Cor 12:10).[1] But to accomplish his objective, Savage conducts extensive archaeological and historical research and analysis of the first-century contexts of Graeco-Romans, in general, and Corinthians, in particular. His data on Graeco-Roman society is useful for assessing the evidence from Corinth—much of which has been damaged or loss. And it should be very helpful for elucidating Paul's writings concerning authentic spirituality in 1 Corinthians 12–14.

First-century Graeco-Roman society was comprised of two classes of people. The upper class, or the *honestiores*, made up about 1 percent of the population and included senators, equestrians, and decurions. These *honestiores* were highly esteemed, influential, and powerful individuals, who because of their status—gained either because of birth, character, office, or wealth—were never to be held in public prisons. The other 99 percent of the population were the *humiliores*, of whom two thirds were the working class or *plebs*—including freedmen or ex-slaves—and one third were slaves—whose status engendered scorn. Having moved up in status from being slaves,

---

1. Savage, *Power Through Weakness*, 1.

upward mobility was a passion for freedmen, who often pridefully displayed their achievements, and zeal for applause and esteem.[2]

Such upward mobility could be achieved in at least two ways. On the one hand, wealth, whether gained through inheritance or applying a trade or skill, increased one's status.[3] On the other hand, virtuous living could also lead to social respectability.[4] Freedmen, however, usually chose other—more immediate and easily recognizable—means of gaining status, for example, boasting about their city, religion, and athletic ability.

Being upwardly mobile was one of at least four significant aspects of first-century Graeco-Roman culture.[5] Perhaps this is because the majority of the population were freedmen or ex-slaves,[6] who were aware that their social mobility could move in either an upward or downward direction, based on a composite of various social indicators. For example, downward mobility could occur if one lost their fortune, or if they were convicted of crimes. On the other hand, it was a matter of upward mobility if one could visibly demonstrate that the Spirit of God was speaking through them.

This Graeco-Roman zeal for upward mobility was rampant in Corinth,[7] where social ascent was the goal. And this was also true in the church, where there were at least three factors important to the upwardly mobile. These status indicators included rhetorical ability, wealth and income, as well as religious qualifications like revelations, miracles, divine commissioning, and Jewish background.[8] But this upwardly mobile ethos had its consequences, for Corinthians continuously sought to show themselves better than others. This is evidenced in how they sought out applause and esteem. Corinthians were increasingly prideful and arrogant toward each other. Humility was scorned. And individuals became apathetic to the needs of their fellow citizens, focusing on themselves and their self-worth.

Second, first-century Graeco-Romans increasingly rejected the logic and learning associated with rationalism and scholarly doctrines.[9] Evidence of this in religion includes how Graeco-Romans increasingly sought out the supernatural activity associated with the gods, or the visible manifestation

---

2. Cf. Cicero, *De Officiis* 2.9.

3. Cicero, *Officiis* 75–76; Duff, *Freedmen in the Early Roman Empire*, 124; MacMullen, *Roman Social Relations*, 98–99; Savage, *Power Through Weakness*, 38.

4. Seneca, *Moral Essays (Dialogues)* 2.15.2–3 and 7.26.7.

5. MacMullen, *Roman Social Relations*, 109.

6. Cf. 1 Cor 1:26–29; Savage, *Power Through Weakness*, 52–53.

7. Barton, "Social Values and Structures," 1129.

8. Meeks, *First Urban Christians*, 72.

9. Peters, *Harvest of Hellenism*, 426–27.

of divine activity, instead of a rationalistic mindset. As with the quest for upward mobility, the rejection of rationalistic doctrines and the tendency toward the supernatural would be a more immediate and recognizable means by which the typical Graeco-Roman could gain status.

Third, *sōtēria* (salvation) was significant in first-century religion.[10] This concept, however, for the Graeco-Romans, was not primarily concerned with life after death, as it appeared for Christians (cf. 2 Tim 2:10; Heb 5:9; 1 Pet 1:5). Rather, *sōtēria*, to the Graeco-Roman, was both a political and religious idea. *Sōtēria* is political because it concerns a yearning for the emperor to provide things beneficial to the present life, such as good health, sustenance, and protection.[11] This yearning can also be considered religious, because, along with the imperial cult, the emperor, being asked to provide for the present needs of the people, considered himself deity. Indeed, Caesar considered himself to be the savior of the world.[12] The imperial cult sentiment that Caesar is "filled with virtue to the good of the human race, as the savior for us and for our descendants, the man who ends war and creates peace . . . he has not only towered over all the benefactors who lived before him, but has also robbed all future benefactors of the hope of doing more than he has done," also evidences that Caesar was looked to for salvation as a god.[13]

For Paul, however, *sōtēria* is a religious phenomenon that concerns being saved from the eschatological wrath of God (cf. Rom 1:16-18). Paul's soteriology, or doctrine of salvation, is inseparably linked to the revelation and gospel (Rom 1:16) of his Lord, Jesus Christ (Rom 10:13; 1 Thess 5:9).[14] And "no one is able to say Jesus is Lord except by the Holy Spirit" (1 Cor 12:3). For Paul, then, *sōtēria* involves the triune God, and the personal confession that Jesus is Lord (1 Cor 8:5-6). Pauline *sōtēria* does not involve deifying the emperor.

Finally, Graeco-Roman society was religiously tolerant. Despite the presence of numerous cults with varying doctrines and philosophies (cf. 1 Cor 8:5), in Corinth, for example, there was little tension among religious adherents of pagan cults. Inclusivity and harmony were emphasized. Ironically, the prevailing ethos of rejecting philosophies and doctrines, which has already been discussed, may have been a contributing factor to this

10. Savage, *Power Through Weakness*, 27–28.

11. Nilsson, "Problems of the History of Greek Religion," 259; cf. MacMullen, *Paganism in the Roman Empire*, 55, 172.

12. Cf. Schnelle, *Apostle Paul*, 485.

13. This is an excerpt (lines 32–41) from a letter of proconsul Paullus Fabius Maximus; cf. Latte, *Religion der Römer*, 24.

14. Helyer, *Witness of Jesus, Paul and John*, 385; Fee, *Pauline Christology*, 1.

tolerance of the supernatural, for if doctrines were taken seriously, differences, perhaps, would have led to divisiveness.

Such tolerance among the pagan cults, however, does not mean that converts were spiritually transformed, for rather than criticizing or being convicting of Graeco-Roman life, religion functioned as a sanctioning agent for it. Perhaps this is why, on the one hand, it has been said that the religious pluralism and tolerance in first-century Graeco-Roman culture contributed to the spread of Christianity.[15] On the other hand, however, it can also be argued that intolerance—evidenced by the persecution, and the concomitant dispersing of Christians—was a major factor in the spreading of Christianity (cf. Acts 8:1; 11:19; 2 Tim 3:1). For, it seems like Graeco-Roman tolerance applied to pagan cults, but not to advocates of only one religion, or system of doctrine. Certainly Christians were often not tolerated, but were abused and ridiculed.[16]

Unlike the supposed tolerance of their Graeco-Roman counterparts, Christians exclusively claimed Jesus as their Lord (1 Cor 8:6), a claim that was the basis for Christian unity. This does not mean that Christians were intolerant of non-believers. In fact, Christians were more inclusive, in terms of social stratification, than pagan society was. Social stratification in Graeco-Roman society was determined by economic class, status, and power, all of which were gained primarily through birth and legal status. For Christians, however, because of the same Spirit that dwells within them, "there is neither Jew nor Greek, there is neither bond nor free, there is neither male nor female: for all are one in Christ Jesus" (Gal 3:28; cf. 1 Cor 12:13). Therefore, despite being mistreated because of their exclusive claim to Jesus as the Lord, and/or perhaps because of it, first-century Christianity grew in adherents.

Having highlighted these four significant aspects of Graeco-Roman life, it is important to note that operating in the gifts (*charismata*) of the Spirit could provide the upwardly mobile with applause and esteem given to those visibly manifesting divine activity. And while charismatic phenomena are inconsistent with rationalistic philosophy, it is consistent with the first-century Graeco-Roman focus on the practical. Further, the *charismata* of healing (1 Cor 12:9) could provide the present-life *sōtēria* valued by first-century Graeco-Roman society. Moreover, operating in the *charismata* would satisfy the religious appetite of the people without being exclusive since "*charismata*" was not limited to particular religious groups.[17] Thus, in order to live and

---

15. Schnelle, *Apostle Paul*, 141.
16. Cf. Apuleius, *Metamorphoses* 9.14.
17. Hutton, *Charisma and Authority*, 107.

communicate authentically spiritual in a pluralistic context where values were in conflict with Christianity, but citizens could benefit from exercising the *charismata*, as Christians do, criteria for authentic spirituality was needed in Corinth. So, our focus will now shift from the general first-century Graeco-Roman context to the specific context of Corinth.

2.2.2 First-century Corinthian context

The city of Corinth was destroyed by Lucius Mummius, the Roman General, in 146 B.C.E. when he defeated Greek forces at Leucopetra on the Isthmus of Corinth. According to the Greek geographer Strabo, in 44 B.C.E. Julius Caesar ordered the re-establishment of Corinth and colonized it with mostly freedmen.[18] This was to rid Rome of the potential trouble of being overpopulated with ex-slaves, and it made the population of Corinth consistent with that of the larger Graeco-Roman culture. Moreover, soldiers were among the early settlers in Corinth.[19] Jews (cf. Acts 18:1–16), Syrians,[20] and Egyptians came later.[21] This influx of people led to Corinth being the most cosmopolitan of all Mediterranean cities except Rome,[22] and freedmen continued to dominate the culture.

These freedmen were essential in the burst of construction in 14–44 C.E. that made Corinth perhaps the most impressive of cities. It is therefore not surprising that freedmen boasted in their Corinthian citizenship as a means of gaining status. But most of these ex-slaves, for whom social ascent was the goal,[23] gained status as a result of employing the trade they learned as a slave. Such self-made freedmen were often prideful and boasted in their accomplishments.

These accomplishments were one factor stimulating the Corinthian economy. Perhaps the most significant economic boost to Corinth, however, was due to its location on the Isthmus of Greece, which rendered the city a "global" marketplace. Corinth was a master of two harbors, "a meeting

---

18. Strabo, *Geographica* 8.6.23; cf. Crinagorus, *Anthologia Graeca* 9.284.
19. Strabo, *Geographica* 17.3.15.
20. Wiseman, "Corinth and Rome I," 497.
21. Cf. Acts 18:24; Smith, "Egyptian Cults at Corinth."
22. Corinth's diversity is also evident by the people Paul mentions relative to the Corinthian church. Indeed, Aquila, Priscilla, and Crispus were Jewish; Fortunatas, Quartas, Gaius, Titius, and Justus were probably Roman; and Stephanas, Achaicus, and Erastus were Greek (Fee, *First Corinthians*, 3).
23. Chrysostom, *Orations*, 9.21.

place for Asia and Greece,"[24] and "a passage for all mankind."[25] Consequently, Corinth became a maritime center of trade, banking, and entertainment. Unfortunately, some of this entertainment involved sexual debauchery, which led the Graeco-Roman philosopher Favorinus to describe Corinth as "a city of aphroditic-type pleasure beyond all that are, or ever have been."[26] There was an absence of sexual restraint in the city. And while this excessive claim of immorality in Corinth may be in regards to Old Corinth (prior to 146 B.C.E.), "there can be little question that Corinth had a history of being an exceptionally immoral city, and it was still filled with immorality in Paul's day."[27] Perhaps, more positively, however, the cosmopolitan also generated great revenues from entertaining the crowds of the Isthmian Games.

Of the more than three hundred athletic games in Greece, the Isthmian Games was second only to the Olympics. Crowds came from all over the Graeco-Roman world, stimulating the Corinthian economy, idolizing the victorious athletes and those who displayed their dominance.[28] Such praise increased one's status and simultaneously contributed to the Corinthian's competitive drive. This acclamation became an incentive for individuals to show themselves better than others. And this led to a selfish coveting of eloquence, and manifestations of the Spirit (*charismata*), from which they could profit.[29]

Accordingly, religious life was also integral to the economy of Corinth. And the Isthmian Games were religious occasions.[30] In fact, Corinth epitomized the religious character of the Graeco-Roman world. Archaeological and literary sources reveal as many as thirty-four deities in Corinth.[31] But, as with the rest of the Graeco-Roman world, Corinthians focused on what they could get from religion, such as healing and powerful displays, instead of being truly transformed. There was also great tolerance for multiple cults, because Corinth stressed harmony, not exclusivity.[32] Moreover, Corinthians generally expected cults to affirm their present lives, not to transform them for eternity. These cults were central to the economy of the

24. Livy 33.32.2.
25. Aristides, *Orations* 46.27.
26. Chrysostom, *Orations* 37.34.
27. McRay, "Corinth," 228–29.
28. Moretti, *Inscrizioni Agonistiche Greche*, 58–59, 65, 69.
29. Cf. 1 Cor 12:7, 31; 14:1, 12, 39.
30. Brooner, *Isthmia*, 103.
31. Savage, *Power Through Weakness*, 49; cf. 1 Cor 8:5.
32. Ironically, this harmony or inclusivity would be intolerant of Christianity's supposed exclusive claim (1 Cor 12:1–3) and mandate to be transformed into the image of Christ (Rom 12:2).

city, because they were the locus of fine culture. Temples and shops were even located together.

Therefore, one can conclude that Corinth, like the larger Graeco-Roman world, was primarily comprised of freedmen eager to win respectability, power, and social prominence. This upwardly mobile ethos rendered the Corinthians especially susceptible to various spiritual issues relative to self-display, personal power, and boasting—all of which could come about through a misuse of the *charismata*. Further, in Corinth there existed a tension between an upwardly mobile, pluralistic, "global" Graeco-Roman culture and authentic Christianity. Corinth's context was one in which criteria for authentic spirituality was needed. And this was true even in the Corinthian church.

2.2.3 History of the Corinthian church and epistle

The founding of the cosmopolitan church of Corinth is chronicled in Acts 18. Evidently, Paul spent eighteen months teaching the word of God among the Corinthians before leaving for Ephesus (Acts 18:1–19). Paul later sent a now-lost letter (1 Cor 5:9), learned of factions at Corinth (1 Cor 1:11), received a letter with questions (cf. 7:1), and responded to such "spiritual things" in the First Epistle to the Corinthians. This response includes providing his criteria for what is authentically spiritual (1 Cor 12–14).[33]

2.2.4 The 1 Corinthians epistolary context

An overview of the 1 Corinthians epistle makes clear that Paul was addressing various "spiritual things." And he was doing so out of his authority as one who received the revelation of Jesus Christ through the Spirit (1 Cor 2:10–13). It became necessary for Paul to discuss "spiritual things" because the Corinthian believers continued to be influenced by their pagan background, even to the extent of questioning Paul's spiritual authority over them (9:11–15). Such behavior led Paul to say, "I could not speak to you [Corinthian believers] as spiritual people, but rather as people of the flesh" (Cor 3:1). Paul's speaking to the spiritual issues of the Corinthians, then, was an attempt to alleviate the threat to authentic Christian living brought on by their pagan background. These threats, as already highlighted, includes the consequences of a zeal for upward mobility, a rejection of rationalism and a seeking out of visible manifestations of divine activity, *sōtēria* which comes from deity providing

---

33. Cf. Conzelmann, *1 Corinthians*, 15; Thiselton, *First Corinthians*, 910.

such things as good health (physical healing) and miraculous protection in this life. Additionally, there was an inclusive and tolerant religious ethos that sanctioned their pagan influenced lifestyle.

As already alluded to, these threats, or spiritual issues, facing the Corinthians could all be associated with an abuse of the *charismata*. And the Corinthians were modifying the gospel, including the proper exercise of the *charismata*, towards Hellenism, to reconcile the competing claims of Graeco-Roman society and authentic Christianity. Indeed, the Corinthian church reflected the social, religious, and cultural pluralism of Corinth and the broader Graeco-Roman world. Their assimilation of secular culture caused truth and tradition—especially as related to the gospel message—to be devalued. Consequently, after his salutation (1 Cor 1:1–9), in which he affirms that he and the Corinthian church—"Jews or Greeks, slaves or freedmen" (1 Cor 12:13)—are called of God unto Jesus Christ (1:1–2, 9, 24), and thanks God that the same church is enriched in all grace and all knowledge, and come behind in no gift (1:4–7), Paul proceeds to address various "spiritual things"—including criteria for what is authentically spiritual.

The first spiritual thing Paul addresses is division in the church (1 Cor 1:10—4:21; 11:18–19). The Corinthians were divided on at least two related fronts. On the one hand, they were divided between Paul, who was called to proclaim Christ to the Gentiles (cf. Rom 15:16; Gal 2:2, 8); Apollos, a Jewish Christian skilled in Greek rhetoric; Cephas, an apostle to the Jews;[34] and Christ (1:12). In other words, the Corinthians, being primarily upwardly mobile freedmen, were exhibiting the Graeco-Roman competitive spirit, separating themselves, boasting pride fully and arrogantly towards each other based on ethnicity (Jew or Greek) and zeal for status. Jewish versus Greek ethnic division is probably because the Jews—being more experiential or spiritual in their outlook—require a sign, while the Greeks—being more of a rational or philosophical mindset—seek wisdom (1:22). The Corinthians' zeal for status is evident, for example, in their desire for the eloquence of Apollos, or perhaps for the charismatic ability of Paul (cf. 1 Cor 3:4; 14:18; Acts 18:24). Because of selfish divisions, Paul encourages the church,

> Consider your own call, brothers and sisters: not many of you were wise by human standards, not many were powerful, not many were of noble birth. But God chose what is foolish in the world to shame the wise; God chose what is weak in the world to shame the strong; God chose what is low and despised in the

---

34. It is noteworthy that the name Cephas is in the Aramaic language common to Jews and is used here rather than the Greek *Petros*, or Peter.

world, things that are not, to reduce to nothing things that are, so that no one might boast in the presence of God. (1 Cor 1:26–29)

... so that none of you will be puffed up in favor of one against another. For who sees anything different in you? What do you have that you did not receive? And if you received it, why do you boast as if it were not a gift? (1 Cor 4:6b–7)

To Paul, then, regardless of ethnicity or socioeconomic status, as Christians possessing the Holy Spirit of God, the Corinthians are all special, chosen by God, and have been given *charismata* enabling them, in their context, to do great things for God's glory. Therefore, when the activity of the Spirit is manifested in their lives it is simply because of what God is doing. And, there is no basis for selfish boasting.

On the other hand, the Corinthians were divided because they were being enticed by human wisdom, or a self-exalting ethos that glories in humans and undermines the power of God, which the Holy Spirit teaches (1:17—2:15). To be sure, some commentators suggest that the "human wisdom" that Paul is speaking against is excessive rhetoric,[35] or pneumatic utterance.[36] But based on the 1 Corinthians context already discussed, it is more appropriate to agree with Savage and Heinrich Schlier that Paul is offering a corrective to divisive speech marked by arrogance and pride.[37] For Paul, such human wisdom is divisive because it is carnal and not of the Spirit (3:1–23), it could lead to faulty judgment of the ministers of Christ (4:1–21), and is a result of heresies in the church (11:18–19).

The second concern that Paul addresses is unrighteousness (1 Cor 5:1—6:20). The Corinthians were involved in sexual immorality—including fornication and prostitution (cf. 5:1, 11; 6:13–20)—as well as arrogant boasting (5:6). For Paul, those who consider themselves Christians but participate in such unrighteousness should be purged from (5:7, 11–13) and judged by the congregation, rather than by a court of unbelievers (5:12—6:8). Instead of living in unrighteousness, Corinthian Christians should exercise self-control (6:9–12) by avoiding and abandoning acts like fornication that do not glorify God in their body and spirit (6:13–20). Furthermore, unrighteous boasting, regardless of how insignificant it may seem, is not without devastating consequences (5:6–7). And, considering

---

35. Cf. Munck, *Paul and the Salvation of Mankind*, 153; Mofatt, *First Corinthians*, 22–23.
36. Painter, "Paul and the Πνευματικοι," 241; Wilckens, "Σοφια," 523.
37. Schlier, *Zeit der Kirche*, 223–24.

the sacrificial and selfless death of Christ (5:7), the Corinthians are encouraged to be sincere and truthful people (5:8).

Paul's third concern is related to the unrighteousness just discussed, for it concerns the sexual immorality relative to marriage (1 Cor 7:1–40). Probably motivated by a belief in the imminent return of Christ (7:29), Paul recommends and considers it good for widows to remain chaste—and unmarried if they are so called, or gifted, to remain as he is, for they are married to the Lord (7:1, 8–9, 25–40). In other words, those without spouses do not need to seek the status that may come from being married. Instead, they are to focus on the things of God, for Christ is returning soon. However, if one is already married, to avoid fornication—and being found in sin at Christ's return—Paul recommends there should be a mutual coming together of spouses, unless both consent to be chaste for a time (7:2–7). Additionally, believing spouses should not separate or leave each other (7:10–11). Likewise, Christians should not put away unbelieving spouses. But if the unbeliever departs, the believer is not under bondage in such cases (7:12–16). Moreover, everyone should live according to their calling or gift of God (7:17–40). That is, whatever abilities or identity one may have—including their socioeconomic (rich or poor, slave or free), athletic, or ethnic status (Jew or Gentile)—they should behave in good order as faithful to the Lord, and not succumb or fall prey to the prevailing Graeco-Roman ethos. Thus, considering an imminent return of Christ, whether one is married or not, they should be faithful to God and each other. The unmarried should not fornicate, but be faithful to the Lord (7:25–27, 32, and 34). And the married should be faithful to their spouse (7:27, 33–34). If the unmarried chooses to marry, that is fine if it is "in the Lord" (7:28, 36, 39).

Next, Paul addresses the concern over things offered to idols (1 Cor 8:1—11:1). He exhorts that, out of love and the need for edification, one should not eat meat offered unto idols if it might be an offense or stumbling block to an onlooker (8:1–13). This advice was contrary to Graeco-Roman ethos, which was self-exalting and apathetic to the needs of others. So, to effectively communicate his point, Paul refers, both to his example of being with the Corinthians as well as the example of his forefathers, or Jewish tradition (9:1—10:15). He reminds his audience that in order not to be a stumbling block, he labors amongst them without accepting compensation that was duly his (9:1–18). Though it is often thought that because of Paul's refusal of support he is simply defending his apostleship or right to receive such support,[38] Paul is perhaps, more importantly, stressing that individual

---

38. Cf., for example, Barrett, "Paul's Opponents in II Corinthians"; Dahl, *Studies in Paul*, 33; Meeks, *First Urban Christians*, 72.

rights, personal status, or gifts, should not be exercised or sought out at the expense of, or without concern for others. That is why Paul considers the needs of the Corinthian people and adopts a lifestyle that is edifying to them and to himself (9:19-27).

Paul also reminds the Corinthians of the forefathers of Jewish—and now Christian—tradition (10:1-15). Some of the Jewish forefathers were idolaters and fornicators; they tempted and they murmured against God. For these idolatrous acts, God punished them. But the lessons of the forefathers are not just for Israel; they are examples for the church that they are not to participate in idolatrous behavior. Thus, Paul emphasizes to the Corinthian church that all things should be done for the glory of God and the edification or the benefit of others (10:16—11:1).

The fifth spiritual thing that Paul addresses is ordinances concerning corporate worship (1 Cor 11:2-34). Paul prefaces his remarks on this issue by commending the maintenance and handing down of traditions (11:2), by saying that the Corinthians should follow the ordinances he has prescribed, but know that God is head over all (11:2-3). As one who speaks God's words, Paul never wants himself to be exalted above God and the things of God that have been faithfully handed down to generations over time.

In terms of corporate worship, Paul allows for both men and women to pray and prophesy, but in the Corinthian context he suggests that men should have their head uncovered and women should cover their heads (11:4-16). Paul's prescription for women is probably due to the Roman cultural influence on Corinth, in which women without head covering in public signaled a lack of respectability and sexual availability.[39] This prescription would probably also serve to guard against any hint of sexual immorality in a church struggling with the issue (1 Cor 5:1).

Despite this distinction between men and women in terms of corporate worship in Corinth, it is evident that, for Paul, all Corinthian saints—whether male or female, bond or free—can exercise the *charismata*. Paul makes it clear that there should be an inclusive mutuality and reciprocity among the sexes in the church. This is ironic, on the one hand, in a culture that valued "religious tolerance" and inclusivity—except for the Christian faith, because of its exclusive claim of Jesus as Lord—but operated with respect of persons and excluded, favored, and even devalued individuals based, for example, on ethnic or socioeconomic status. Christianity, on the other hand, advocated equal value for all (1 Cor 12:13), and proclaimed that the basic social distinctions of Graeco-Roman society are eradicated in Christ. Therefore, Paul recommends that all should examine

---

39. Rousselle, "Body Politics in Ancient Rome."

themselves and consider others before taking the Lord's Supper in the congregation (11:17–34).

The sixth concern that Paul is addressing is knowledge of "spiritual things," or criteria for discerning what is authentically revelatory of God (1 Cor 12:1—14:40). Since this pericope (12:1—14:40) will be focused on in the following chapters, extensive comments in this regard will be reserved until later. Suffice it to say here, as already indicated, among other things, the Corinthians were engendering an abuse of the *charismata*, making it necessary for Paul to inform the church of various criteria for being authentically spiritual, including the proper functioning of the *charismata*.

Next, Paul addresses questions concerning the resurrection of Jesus Christ (1 Cor 15:1–58). He exhorts the Corinthians not to be as some who do not have knowledge of God and think Christ was not resurrected (15:33–34)—a direct reference to the religious tolerance and pluralism of their Graeco-Roman background, which does not value the exclusive claims of Christianity, like the idea of the resurrected Christ as the true God, but seeks to make different religions compatible. For Paul, however, because there is a resurrection, one can be truly "spiritual"—not just focusing on the benefits they can obtain from religion, such as those evident in the manifestation of divine activity through the *charismata*—and it will not be in vain (15:58). One does not have to give in to the cultural influences around them. Instead, they can be transformed and renewed according to the will of God (Rom 12:2).

The final "spiritual thing" concerning the Corinthian church that Paul addresses is a collection for the saints in Jerusalem (1 Cor 16:1–4). Paul directs the relatively wealthy Corinthians to contribute to the needs of others—specifically those in Jerusalem—based upon how God has prospered them. The Corinthians are not simply to focus on themselves and treat others as competitors by accumulating their resources in a quest for personal wealth and status. Instead, they should consider the very real need of others and help as they are able to. After addressing the various "spiritual things" he intended, Paul concludes the 1 Corinthians epistle stating how he plans to revisit Corinth (16:5–12), and offers final encouraging remarks and farewell salutations. (16:13–24).

2.3 Conclusion

The Graeco-Roman, Corinthian, and epistolary context all suggest the Corinthians were primarily former slaves (freed men) who, because of their servile background, "placed a higher premium on social prominence and self-display, on personal power and boasting."[40] All of these means of attaining status in the Graeco-Roman context could be realized through the display of the *charismata*, which the Corinthians sought.[41] These values, however, were also at odds with the transformative and renewal teachings of their Christian faith. Being aware of the two competing claims, and the tendency for Graeco-Romans to focus on how they could benefit from "religion" (e.g., healing and powerful displays) instead of how "religion" could transform them, Paul addresses various spiritual things to inform, answer questions, and effectively communicate to the Corinthian church about what it means to live authentically Christian in a pluralistic setting. This notion of "spiritual things" will now be elucidated.

---

40. Savage, *Power Through Weakness*, 52.
41. Cf. 1 Cor 12:7, 31; 14:1, 12, 39.

Chapter 3

Spiritual Things

3.1 Introduction

In 1 Corinthians 12:1, Paul's use of the phrase "now concerning" (*peri de*) makes clear that he is starting a new topic of discussion.[1] Paul is continuing to talk about "spiritual things," but now he is going to specifically address knowledge of, or the criteria(on) by which one can discern what is truly revelatory of God. In light of the various spiritual challenges the Corinthian believers were wrestling with, Paul does not want them to be ignorant of what is authentically spiritual.

It is important to note, however, that most scholars have narrowly viewed this passage as focusing on spiritual gifts (*charismata*)—instead of revelatory criteria. To be sure, except for Bezuidenhout's work,[2] while the subject of criteria is mentioned, the discussion is usually limited to the criteria of the confession of Jesus as Lord (12:3), love (ch. 13), and edification of the church (ch. 14).[3] Moreover, despite the focus on gifts of the Spirit, these studies have been christocentric in that they do not recognize manifestations of the Spirit as integral to a criterion for authentic revelatory experiences.[4] Siegfried Schatzmann, for example, considers the christological criterion as "the supreme test for all claims to pneumatic endowment."[5] Consequently, there has been a de-emphasis of the various other "spiritual things" that Paul prescribes as criteria for authentic spirituality.

---

1. Thiselton, *First Corinthians*, 909. Cf. 1 Cor 7:1, 25; 8:1; 16:1, 12. Herein it is important to note that quotations from 1 Corinthians 12–14 are this author's own translation. All other biblical quotations, unless otherwise noted, are from the NRSV.

2. Bezuidenhout, *Pauliniese kriteria ten opsigte*.

3. Cf., for example, Dunn, *Jesus and the Spirit*, 293–96.

4. Cf. Dunn, *Jesus and the Spirit*, 293–97; Thiselton, *First Corinthians*, 916; Fee, *First Corinthians*, 574–82.

5. Schatzmann, *Pauline Theology of the Charismata*, 31.

3.2 Spiritual Things in 1 Corinthians 12–14

Now concerning spiritual gifts,[6] most commentators—evidenced from their translation of *tōn pneumatikōn* (1 Cor 12:1) as "spiritual gifts," as well as their equating of *pneumatikōn* with *charismatōn* (12:4)—believe that 1 Corinthians 12–14 is about the proper use of "spiritual gifts," or what should be properly called "gifts from the Spirit."[7] These commentators include, for example, the church father Tertullian,[8] but also scholars like Hans Conzelmann,[9] James Dunn,[10] Marthinus Bezuidenhout,[11] Gerald Bray,[12] Andreas Lindemann,[13] Craig Keener,[14] and Joseph Fitzmyer.[15] Additionally, various Bible translations, including the KJV, RSV, NRSV, and NIV, translate *pneumatikōn* as "spiritual gifts."

Fitzmyer's translation of *pneumatikōn* as "spiritual gifts" appears ambiguous. Thus, it would be instructive to examine the Jesuit priest's comments on this subject. For Fitzmyer, in 1 Corinthians 12–14 Paul is dealing with "problems caused by charismatics in the Body of Christ," and is now addressing the issue of "spiritual gifts."[16] To be clear, Fitzmyer considers *pneumatikōn* to be external manifestations of "spiritual gifts," which are bestowed by the Spirit,[17] for *pneumatika* comes from the Spirit.[18] There are at least three reasons—all related to each other—why Fitzmyer's comments can be considered ambiguous. If charismatics are those who exercise the *charismata*, and "*pneumatika* are not simply to be equated with *charismata*" since the former deals with other specific endowments,[19]

---

6. Note the intended pun to begin this paragraph. This is exactly how most commentators translate the apostle Paul's words beginning the 1 Cor 12–14 pericope.

7. It will be fully elaborated on below that the τῶν πνευματικῶν are inclusive of the *charismata*, but are distinct realities to Paul. The latter term describes "gifts" that are specifically related to the Spirit. And the former describes various "spiritual" realities characteristic of the triune God (Father, Son, and Spirit).

8. Tertullian, *Against Marcion* 5.8.

9. Conzelmann, *1 Corinthians*, 204.

10. Dunn, *Jesus and the Spirit*, 208.

11. Bezuidenhout, "Trinitarian Nature."

12. Bray, *1–2 Corinthians*, 117.

13. Lindemann, *Erste Korintherbrief*, 261.

14. Keener, *1–2 Corinthians*, 9, 100.

15. Fitzmyer, *First Corinthians*, 13, 80, 453.

16. Fitzmyer, *First Corinthians*, 453.

17. Fitzmyer, *First Corinthians*, 80, 463.

18. Fitzmyer, *First Corinthians*, 457.

19. Fitzmyer, *First Corinthians*, 457.

it is unclear if *pneumatikōn* is specifically to be considered "spiritual gifts," or if it is inclusive of other spiritual concerns. A second point of ambiguity is evident, because though he translates *pneumatikōn* as "spiritual gifts," and asserts that Paul is reacting against the abuse of gifts, Fitzmyer also suggests that Paul is dealing with "spiritual things," "seeking to put all πνευματικά 'spiritual things,' especially the endowments of the Spirit, in a proper perspective."[20] Fitzmyer also makes it clear that "πνευματικά can refer to names of persons, abstract abilities, or actions."[21] The third point of ambiguity relates to the source of *pneumatikōn*. Fitzmyer considers *pneumatikōn* to be "those aspects or factors of Christian community life that stem from the influence of the Spirit."[22] In other words, *pneumatikōn* are bestowed by, and come from the Spirit. But Fitzmyer also ascribes the source of *pneumatikōn* to be triadic,[23] being from the "same Spirit," "same Lord," and "same God."[24] In brief, Fitzmyer is ambiguous in his employment of the term *pneumatikōn*. For him, this concept has its source specifically in the Spirit, but also in the triune God. And the term is used to refer to both "spiritual gifts" and "spiritual things."

Unlike the apparent ambiguity in Fitzmyer's work, and contrary to the scholarship that considers *pneumatikōn* to be spiritual gifts, some scholars explicitly argue that *pneumatikōn* is not to be translated as "spiritual gifts." D. W. Robinson's work is an example of such scholarship. In his brief article entitled "*Charismata* versus *Pneumatika*: Paul's Method of Discussion," Robinson argues that in the 1 Corinthians 12–14 pericope, Paul never uses *pneumatikōn* to simply mean spiritual gifts. Rather, *pneumatikōn* refers specifically to "speaking in spirit" by tongues and other ecstatic utterances such as words of wisdom, words of knowledge, prophecy, and interpretation of tongues. Hence, the translation of *pneumatikōn* as "spiritual gifts" takes for granted that Paul is already using it (*pneumatikōn*) to describe *charismata* (gifts from the Spirit), for all *charismata* are *pneumatikōn*, since *pneumatikōn* is a wide term that addresses things representative of the Holy Spirit.[25] In fact, there is no expression in the Greek NT that can be translated as "spiritual gifts." Technically, the term "spiritual gifts" would be *charismata pneumatikōn*. The closest rendering of this is in Romans 1:11, where Paul longs to see the

---

20. Fitzmyer, *First Corinthians*, 454–55.
21. Fitzmyer, *First Corinthians*, 463.
22. Fitzmyer, *First Corinthians*, 455.
23. Fitzmyer, *First Corinthians*, 464.
24. Fitzmyer, *First Corinthians*, 80.
25. Robinson, "Charismata versus Pneumatika," 50–53.

Romans, for he wants to share some spiritual gift (*charisma pneumatikōn*) with them so that they might be strengthened.

Robinson is right that *pneumatikōn* is inclusive of *charismata*. Unfortunately, however, he limits the latter to what are commonly called revelatory gifts.[26] There are at least two reasons why this assumption is inappropriate. In the first place, Robinson fails to wrestle with the implications of Paul ascribing *charismata* as gifts from the Spirit (1 Cor 12:4). Though Paul does not use the terms *charismata pneumatikōn* together, the Corinthian context makes it clear that *charismata* are derived from the Spirit and are therefore "spiritual gifts." The *charismata*, then, are manifestations of the Spirit, but they are not limited to "speaking in spirit," for such manifestations also include gifts like faith, healing, and works of power (cf. 12:7-11, especially vv. 9-10).

The other reason why Robinson's limiting of *pneumatikōn* to revelatory gifts is inappropriate is that while he appropriately recognizes that revelatory gifts were being abused at Corinth—in that Paul was seeking to affirm and provide guidelines for "spiritual things" (*pneumatikōn*), or ethical issues,[27] without quenching the work of the Spirit—such abuse, however, was not the only "spiritual thing" that Paul was addressing in 1 Corinthians 12:1. This latter statement becomes clear when one considers that the new subject Paul addresses in the pericope of 1 Corinthians 12-14 is criteria for what is authentically spiritual (cf. 12:1).[28] The repetition of words dealing with the Spirit (*pneuma*), or what is spiritual, in these chapters evidences this claim. For example, in 14:1 Paul commands the pursuit of love and "spiritual things" (*pneumatika*)—including, but not limited to, the *charismata*. Since the Corinthians are zealous of "spiritual things" (*pneumatōn*), they should seek to excel in what is edifying to the church (14:12). And those who consider themselves to be spiritual (*pneumatikos*) should acknowledge the exhortations of Paul (14:37).

Paul's emphasis on "spiritual things" is also indicated throughout the 1 Corinthians epistle. In light of his revelation of Jesus Christ, through the Spirit (1 Cor 2:10), Paul has the authority to communicate "spiritual

---

26. This term "revelatory gifts" usually pertains to *charismata* such as words of wisdom, words of knowledge, prophecy, and interpretation of tongues, where the word of God is verbally communicated. But it is the presupposition of this work that all the *charismata* are revelatory gifts since they are manifestations of the Spirit, or divine energies that, while they do not reveal the essence of God, always reveal something about the triune God.

27. Wolter, "Pauline Ethics according to 1 Corinthians," 203.

28. Cf. Conzelmann, *1 Corinthians*, 15; Thiselton, *First Corinthians*, 910. This suggests that the main concern of 1 Cor 12-14, rather than being "spiritual gifts," is actually criteria for authentic spirituality ("spiritual things"). Obviously, this includes criteria for the functioning of the *charismata*.

things" (*pneumatika*).²⁹ Because of their immaturity in the things concerning Christ, and perhaps because of their continuous associating with, and concomitant influence of, their pagan background in Graeco-Roman culture, the Corinthians continue to live in a way that is not authentically spiritual (*pneumatikois*).³⁰ And this influence even causes them to question Paul's apostolic authority to communicate spiritual things (*pneumatika*) to them (9:11–15).

If *pneumatikōn* relates to all that is characteristic of the triune God,³¹ the discussion of "spiritual things"—as will be elaborated on below—should not be limited to occasions when the *pneuma* root is employed by Paul. From this perspective, the various issues of the Corinthians that Paul is addressing can also be considered "spiritual things," for Paul is addressing such issues by communicating behavior that is truly representative of the triune God. He wants the Corinthians to know, for example, that Christian ethos, or behaviors that are authentically spiritual, do not include divisiveness (1 Cor 1:10—4:21; 11:18–19), unrighteousness (1 5:1—6:20), sexual immorality relative to marriage (7:1–40), or the offering of things to idols (8:1—11:1). Another spiritual thing being addressed by Paul is the resurrection of Jesus Christ (15:1–58).³² Summarily, Paul wants the Corinthians to seek to be spiritual, or what is spiritual (this includes manifesting spiritual gifts), by guarding their associations, doing what is loving, edifying, and consistent with traditionally accepted word of God.

Considering this discussion, then, it should be abundantly clear that Robinson's limiting of *pneumatikōn* to revelatory gifts is an oversimplification of the Pauline context. Neil Chambers rightfully agrees with Robinson, however, that for the sake of clarity the terms *pneumatikos* and *charismata* should be kept distinct and maintain their different emphasis.³³ For Chambers,

> the term "spiritual gift" is a misnomer, resulting from an identification of pneumatika ("spiritual things/people") with *charismata* ("gifts") in 1 Corinthians 12–14. This has restricted the perception of the breadth of Paul's teaching on gifts (*charismata*) and its close integration with the dominant motifs of

---

29. Cf. 1 Cor 2:13.
30. Cf. 1 Cor 3:1.
31. Kleinknecht, "πνευματικων," 346.
32. The various excursions on spiritual concerns addressed by Paul that are listed in Lindemann's *Der Erste Korintherbrief*, ix, attests to the notion that in 1 Cor 12–14, and throughout 1 Corinthians, Paul is addressing much more than spiritual gifts.
33. Chambers, "Spiritual Gifts," 118, 125, 126.

his understanding of congregational life, as well as fostering an unhealthy preoccupation with some of the more spectacular phenomena mentioned by Paul.[34]

Thus, *charismata* should be translated as "gifts of the Spirit" and *pneumatika* as "spirituals" or "spiritual things."[35] Even Fitzmyer seems to affirm this understanding when he says, "*charismata* are specific forms of *pneumatika*, distinct from those to be mentioned in vv. 5–6 . . . if they were interchangeable, why does Paul separate them, ascribe them to different sources, and in each case use *to auto* or *ho autos* [same]?"[36]

According to Gordon Fee, there is a relatively weak distinction between the terms *charismata* and *pneumatika*, for

> Paul's immediate—and overall—concern has to do with what comes from "the Spirit of God" (1 Cor 12:3). Moreover, elsewhere in chap. 12 he uses *charismata* for the specific manifestations of the Spirit' activity. It seems likely therefore that even though at points the two words are nearly interchangeable (as 12:31 and 14:1 would imply), the emphasis in each case reflects the root word (*pneuma*, Spirit; *charis*, grace). When the emphasis is on the manifestation, the "gifts" as such, Paul speaks of *charismata*; when the emphasis is on the Spirit, he speaks of *pneumatika*. If so, then both here (at 12:1) and in 14:1 the better translation might be "the things of the Spirit," which would refer primarily to spiritual manifestations, from the perspective of the Spirit's endowment; at the same time it would point toward those who are so endowed.[37]

Fee is right about the near interchangeability of *pneumatika* and *charismata*, because both are "spiritual things." The latter is a more specific case of a general category relative to things that are characteristic of the triune God. Thus, while the immediate context of 12:3–4 deals with what comes from the Spirit of God, the overall context of 1 Corinthians 12–14 pertains to things typical of the triune God.

Perhaps this is why Anders Eriksson argues that 1 Corinthians is "a discussion about spiritual things or spiritual people."[38] And the new topic introduced in 12:1 concerns more than just spiritual gifts, but also includes,

---

34. Chambers, "Spiritual Gifts," 117.
35. Chambers, "Spiritual Gifts," 118.
36. Fitzmyer, *First Corinthians*, 464–65.
37. Fee, *First Corinthians*, 576.
38. Eriksson, *Traditions as Rhetorical Proof*, 110.

for example, the body of Christ, worship service, and the role of women.[39] Eriksson is right that in 1 Corinthians 12–14 Paul is discussing a variety of spiritual concerns. But, Eriksson also fails to recognize that the new subject introduced in 12:1 is more than just "spiritual things," and is in fact criteria for what is authentically spiritual.[40]

David Garland agrees that *pneumatikōn* is more than just "spiritual gifts." In his *1 Corinthians*, he states that in 1 Corinthians 12–14 *pneumatikōn* concerns spiritual persons.[41] Seemingly paradoxical, this study affirms both the views of the commentators (who translate *pneumatikōn* as "spiritual gifts") as well as that of Garland (spiritual persons). This is because, based on the context of the 1 Corinthians 12–14 pericope, the commentators have appropriately chosen to parse the word *pneumatikōn* as neuter plural genitive (NPG) instead of the alternative masculine plural genitive (MPG)—even though MPG is also a possible parsing since MPG and NPG share the same Greek ending, making it virtually impossible to choose one or the other. This difficult choice is also because, on the one hand, "spiritual people" (MPG) have "spiritual gifts" (NPG). On the other hand, the translation of *pneumatikōn* as "spiritual things" (NPG) does not exclude "spiritual gifts," persons, or any other subject relative to what characterizes God; and Paul is thinking about people who exercised the gifts.[42] To the contrary, the MPG parsing limits the subject of Paul's discourse to male persons. Thus, the MPG parsing is not always inappropriate, but the NPG parsing of "spiritual things" does not exclude spiritual people.

To further elaborate on the translation of *pneumatikōn*, a thorough exegesis suggests that, for Paul, *pneumatikōn* is concerned with more than just criteria for being spiritual people (male).[43] In fact, *pneumatikōn* concerns things that are characteristic of experience of the triune God,[44] spiritual things, or things pertaining to transcendent or divine influence.[45] Therefore, *pneumatikōn* is not simply concerned with "things bestowed by the Spirit," or the third "person" of the Trinity, as is the case with *charismata* ("gifts from the Spirit").

In his book *A Pauline Theology of the Charismata*, Siegfried Schatzmann, after thorough exegesis, defines *charismata* as

---

39. Eriksson, *Traditions as Rhetorical Proof*, 196.
40. Cf. Thiselton, *First Corinthians*, 901; Conzelmann, *1 Corinthians*, 15.
41. Garland, *1 Corinthians*, 561–62, 564.
42. Morris, *1 Corinthians*, 166.
43. Cf. 1 Cor 14:1.
44. Kleinknecht, "πνευματικων," 346.
45. BAGD, 837.

a diversity of experienced concretions (sum) of the grace of God, sovereignly bestowed by the Spirit upon members of the community of believers and functioning interdependently for the purpose of the upbuilding of the church in love, thereby demonstrating the lordship of Christ.[46]

Schatzmann's definition highlights the mysterious *perichoretic* unity of the Godhead, because *charismata* are "concretions of the grace of God." Additionally, however, the hypostatic diversity of the Trinity is also evident because, for Schatzmann, *charismata* are bestowed by the Spirit. To the contrary, *pneumatikōn* includes all that is characteristic of the triune God—Father, Son, and Spirit—and includes more than spiritual gifts and/or persons.

Though he agrees that the key issue of 1 Corinthians 12–14 concerns criteria for "specific people or specific gifts" to be considered authentic, Thiselton also asserts, based on the 1 Corinthians context, that *pneumatikōn* concerns more than spiritual gifts and/or persons. This is clear when he says,

> too many writers treat 12:1—14:40 as if it were simply an ad hoc response to questions about spiritual gifts (or spiritual persons) rather than an address to this topic [things that come from the Spirit] within the broader framework of 11:2—14:40 in deliberate continuity with 8:1—11:1, and indeed ultimately with 1:1—4:21.[47]

To be sure, Thiselton specifically translates *pneumatikōn* as "things that come from the Spirit,"[48] "a formation, gift, or phenomenon that reflects the agency, operation, and presence of the Holy Spirit."[49] But this statement—while it recognizes that 1 Corinthians addresses various "spiritual things," and *pneumatikōn* concerns more than just spiritual gifts—limits *pneumatikōn* to being from the Spirit, and does not seem to allow for activity of the Father and Son. So Thiselton does not convey the Trinitarian motif that Fitzmyer noted, which, as will be shown in this study, is integral to the way Paul is communicating his message in this entire pericope. Therefore, in discussing spiritual gifts (*charismata*), one could say that Thiselton subordinates Christology and theology to his pneumatology.

---

46. Schatzmann, *Pauline Theology*, 51–52.

47. Thiselton, *First Corinthians*, 900.

48. Thiselton, *First Corinthians*, 907, 910. As will be shown below, spiritual things refer to more than things that come the Spirit, for things that are truly spiritual cannot be separated from the entire Godhead.

49. Thiselton, *First Corinthians*, 1107.

Further, Thiselton's interpreting *pneumatikōn* to be things coming from the Spirit seems to be at odds with his further statement that

> God is essentially one, as an "ordered" being, but manifests himself in acts of the Spirit, acts of the Lord, and acts of God, both jointly and in differentiated ways. Any account of "spiritual gifts" which is merely Spirit-centered rather than Christomorphic (12:3) and Trinitarian (12:4-6) is untrue to Paul.[50]

The notion that the triune God is manifested both jointly and in differentiated ways is a reference to the Cappadocian Fathers' reasoning that God is of one essence (*ousia*) and three "persons" (*hypostases*). And there is a *perichoretic* nature within the Godhead, for there is mutual participation of each "persons" of the Godhead in the acts of each other.[51] Leonardo Boff well articulates this Trinitarianism in the contemporary context when he says,

> speaking of God must always mean the Father, Son, and Holy Spirit in the presence of one another, in total reciprocity, in immediacy of loving relationship, being one for another, by another, in another, and with another. No divine Person exists alone for its own; they are always and eternally in relationship with one another.[52]

But there are at least two other reasons suggesting that most scholarship concerning 1 Corinthians 12–14 neglects Paul's Trinitarian motif while overemphasizing gifts from the Spirit (*charismata*). In the first place, as Thiselton alluded to, the 1 Corinthians context makes it clear that Paul is involved in a discussion of "spiritual things" throughout the entire book, including in this focal pericope of 1 Corinthians 12–14, where he focuses on criteria for what is authentically spiritual (including the proper functioning of the *charismata*). Indeed, Paul implies that he is discussing "spiritual things" when he says, "I could not speak to you as spiritual people, but rather as people of the flesh" (3:1). Paul wants to talk about what is authentically spiritual as a corrective to the lack thereof amongst the Corinthians.

As already alluded to, one evidence, for Paul, that the Corinthians are not truly spiritual is their divisiveness. This division in the church (1 Cor 1:10—4:21; 11:18–19) is also one of the various "spiritual things" that Paul is addressing. Other spiritual things being addressed by Paul include: unrighteousness (5:1—6:20), sexual immorality (7:1–40), the offering of things to idols (8:1—11:1), ordinances concerning corporate worship (11:2–34),

---

50. Thiselton, *First Corinthians*, 989.
51. Gregory of Nyssa, *On "Not Three Gods"* 4.84.
52. Boff, *Trinity and Society*, 133.

knowledge of or criteria for "spiritual things"—including gifts of the Spirit (12:1—14:40), questions concerning the resurrection of Jesus Christ (Cor 15:1–58), and a collection for the saints in Jerusalem (16:1–4).[53]

Relative to the 1 Corinthians 12–14 context, Paul explicitly states that he is addressing knowledge of or criteria for "spiritual things"—*pneumatikōn* (1 Cor 12:1).[54] In other words, Paul is discussing "what constitutes the shape of the Corinthian church,"[55] or the Corinthians' understanding of what it means to be "spiritual."[56] Some of the *pneumatikōn* or "spiritual things" Paul addresses include, for example, *diaireseis charismatōn*, or varieties of gifts from the Spirit (12:4, 7–11); persons (12:21–26, 28; 14:2-4, 37); the *ekklēsia/soma christou*, or the church/body of Christ (12:12–28)—of which "perhaps the greatest theological contribution . . . to the Christian faith is Paul's understanding of the nature of the church."[57] H. Schlier even suggests that the church is the main concern in 1 Corinthians 12–14.[58] Other "spiritual things" being addressed include soteriology (12:3, 13); eschatology (13:8–10, 12); ethics;[59] *diaireseis diakoniōn*, or varieties of services from the Lord (12:5); *diaireseis energamatōn*, or varieties of works from God (12:6); love (ch. 13); and spiritual edification (ch. 14).[60]

Because of his translation of *pneumatikōn* as "gifts of the Spirit," Lindemann considers such "spiritual things" as excursions in Paul's argument.[61] And in 1 Corinthians 12–14 these "excursions" include the community as body (12:27), the necessity of the *charismata* to be exercised in love (13:3), *glossolalia* (14:2ff.), and the silent command against women (14:35). Such speaking to the spiritual issues of the Corinthians by Paul was an attempt to alleviate the threat to authentic Christian living brought on by Hellenization and the influence of their pagan background by positing

---

53. Cf. Fitzmyer, *First Corinthians*, 52, 69. Meeks, *First Urban Christians*, 166.
54. Cf. Conzelmann, *1 Corinthians*, 15; Thiselton, *First Corinthians*, 910.
55. Fitzmyer, *First Corinthians*, 454.
56. Fee, *First Corinthians*, 6.
57. Fee, *First Corinthians*, 18–20.
58. Schlier, "Uber das Hauptanliegen des 1," in *Zeit der Kirche*.
59. Cf. 1 Cor 12:7, 25–26; 13:1–3; 14:1, 26–36, 39–40.
60. Though he is right that 1 Cor 12–14 is a discussion of criteria, Aune, however, seems to have inappropriately limited Paul's exhortations to criteria for the functioning of the charismata when he suggests that Paul is discussing criteria for all forms of religious communication in the worship service (cf. Aune, *Prophecy in Early Christianity*, 220). It would be a mistake to infer that this work is suggesting that Paul is limited to the same subject in 1 Cor 12–14. In this regard, this work agrees with Conzelmann, *1 Corinthians*, 15; and Thiselton, *First Corinthians*, 910.
61. Lindemann, *Erste Korintherbrief*, ix.

criteria for Christian behavior.⁶² The Corinthians were modifying the gospel towards Hellenism, in an attempt to reconcile the competing claims of Greek philosophy and the Christian religion.

In 1 Corinthians 12–14, Paul is therefore giving the Corinthians some spiritual teaching. However, most scholars overemphasize the *charismata* (12:4) to the relative neglect of other "spiritual things" that are of concern to Paul and the triune God. For example, Schatzmann and Dunn consider *charismata* to be synonymous with πνευματικῶν,⁶³ and the former is introduced by Paul as a corrective to what the Corinthians considered authentic spiritual gifts.⁶⁴ But while it may be true that Paul is positing a corrective for the misuse of spiritual gifts,⁶⁵ this understanding does not seem to consider the context of the pericope, in which it could also be said, for example, that *pneumatikōn* is synonymous with other "spiritual things" such as *diakonia* and *energēmata* (12:5–6). For Paul is also offering a corrective, and providing criteria for such spiritual deficiencies among the Corinthians. Moreover, "*pneumatika* are not simply to be equated with *charismata*."⁶⁶ And it will become clear through a thorough exegesis of the 1 Corinthians 12–14 text that the decisive question that Paul is addressing concerns criteria for authentic spirituality.

---

62. Betz and Mitchell, "Corinthians, First Epistle," 1146.
63. Schatzmann, *Pauline Theology*, 34; Dunn, *Jesus and the Spirit*, 208.
64. Schatzmann, *Pauline Theology*, 4, 30.
65. The fact that Paul is offering criteria for what is authentically revelatory of God suggests that there was a need for some correction.
66. Fitzmyer, *First Corinthians*, 457.

Chapter 4

The Criterion of the Manifestation of the Spirit (1 Cor 12:1–31)

4.1 The Confessional Criterion (12:1–3)

In 1 Corinthians 12:1–3 Paul posits a basic criterion for distinguishing between what belongs to the Spirit and what does not.[1] This is considered the "confessional criterion." Because the Corinthians used to be pagan idolaters, and to guard against the threat to authentic Christian living posed by the continuing influence of their Graeco-Roman context, the apostle to the Gentiles wants the Corinthians to know that "no one while talking by the Spirit of God says, 'Jesus is a curse,' and no one is able to say Jesus is Lord, except by the Holy Spirit" (1 Cor 12:3).

Most scholars consider this confession as the christological criterion for authentic spirituality because of the requisite exaltation of Jesus.[2] But here it must be said, again, that this is a limiting view. For while the verse is obviously christological, it is more appropriately triune—or at least binary (Jesus and the Spirit)—and will be shown to be typical of a "Trinitarian" and *perichoretic* hermeneutic that Paul employs in his discourses concerning God.

The Trinitarian nature of this criterion is affirmed by Bezuidenhout, who, seemingly paradoxically, also adds that "the emphasis is on Jesus as Lord."[3] This begs the question, can a concept be considered Trinitarian and at the same time be focused on the second "person" of the Trinity? The answer to this question will be reserved until further exegesis is conducted. But it is interesting to note here that in Paul's first-century Graeco-Roman context the confession of Jesus as Lord is an obvious political statement, because if Jesus is Lord, Caesar is not. And such an admission could have dire consequences

---

1. Fee, *First Corinthians*, 571–72, 582.

2. Cf. for example, Dunn, *Jesus and the Spirit*, 293; Thiselton, *First Corinthians*, 916. Fee, *First Corinthians*, 574–82.

3. Bezuidenhout, "Trinitarian Nature," 96.

for the confessor. Perhaps this is also why Paul's exaltation of Jesus is embedded in pneumatological and Trinitarian language. With such consequences, it is not surprising that Paul tells the Corinthians that "no one is able to say Jesus is Lord except by the Holy Spirit" (1 Cor 12:3).

In regards to the emphasis of 1 Corinthians 12:3, this study is in slight disagreement with Bezuidenhout, for, as will be shown below, with thorough exegesis of the 1 Corinthians 12–14 pericope, the criteria Paul discusses in chapter 12 are focused on the Spirit, and the real christological criterion is that of love (ch. 13).[4] In this way of thinking, Bezuidenhout's christocentric conclusion regarding 1 Corinthians 12:1–3, then, epitomizes much of modern scholarship that subordinates pneumatology to Christology. Bezuidenhout could have relied more on the immediate context of the 1 Corinthians 12–14 pericope instead of just evidence from the general Pauline corpus.[5] But, as Bezuidenhout rightly notes, one who exalts Jesus does so by the Spirit of God, or is manifesting a gift of the Spirit—perhaps a prophetic word, or even some form of tongues—either interpreted or uninterpreted.[6]

Having confessed Jesus as Lord, Corinthian believers are now possessors of the Spirit of God. They therefore cannot be justifiably prideful, since whatever spiritual gifts or divine manifestations evident in their life are not of their own doing (1 Cor 12:6, 11). Rather, the *charismata* are the work of one and the same Spirit (12:4, 11), for the common good (12:7). Instead of being concerned about the relative superiority of various gifts, all of which are essential to the proper functioning of the body of Christ (12:14–26), more appropriate concerns should revolve around criteria for their functioning (12:1; 14:40). For example, can it be discerned when one authentically possesses the Spirit? And, are all revelatory claims of possessors of the Spirit to be considered authentic? This study is seeking answers to such questions. For now, based on the revelatory criteria from the OT and the confessional criterion mentioned above, it can be said that the answer to the former question is yes. That is, if there is ecstatic phenomenon coupled with a traditionally accepted word of God that is edifying for humanity. The answer to the latter question is no, however, because of the subjectivity of the Spirit and the fallibility associated with the human witness (cf. 12:11; 14:32). Being a believer, then, is not an absolute way to verify that

---

4. The christological criterion of love will also be discussed in the section on the "Trinitarian" theology of Paul, and in chapter 5 on the criterion of love (1 Cor 13).

5. Bezuidenhout, "Trinitarian Nature," 96–97. Reference is made to texts from the Pauline corpus such as Rom 1:3–4; Phil 2:9–11; Col 1:15–18.

6. Bezuidenhout, "Trinitarian Nature," 95. Later, Paul will make it clear that uninterpreted tongues exalt God (1 Cor 14:2, 17)—this is inclusive of Jesus.

one's revelatory claim is authentic. Indeed, spiritual gifts, for example, occur among Jews and other non-Christians.

In brief, the charismatic exaltation of Jesus that is considered the confessional criterion is vital in authentic Christian living. But such a confession, at least by itself—as Garland agrees,[7] and contrary to Bezuidenhout, who considers it "an infallible norm"[8]—should not be considered a criterion for an authentic revelatory claim. For Garland, this is a confession made by all Christians as they receive the Holy Spirit, and it is more appropriately to be considered in terms of a criterion for discerning who is a Christian, rather than for the functioning of the *charismata* or authentic spirituality. It will be informative, however, to examine how Paul communicates this Christian principle, and perhaps other criteria for authentic spirituality by addressing our first hermeneutical consideration.

4.2 Excursion 1: Paul's Trinitarian Theology

If it is true that this so-called confessional criterion is a vital principle in authentic Christian living, then it would be instructive to examine the hermeneutical principle Paul employs in communicating it to the believers in the pluralistic Corinthian context, and why he has chosen that means of communication. What is the hermeneutical consideration at the heart of Paul's "confessional criterion"? This excursion will first analyze the "confessional criterion" for a hermeneutical style of communicating, and then examine the rest of the 1 Corinthians 12–14 pericope to see to what extent such a hermeneutical style can be considered a Pauline theological motif. This supposed motif will also be filtered through the lens of Paul's Corinthian context to answer the question of why Paul communicates in this way.

4.2.1 What is the hermeneutical consideration behind the "confessional criterion"?

The immediate context of the "confessional criterion" is 1 Corinthians 12:1–6, and these first verses are important for comprehending Paul's purpose in writing this entire pericope. In 12:1, Paul begins his communication by making it clear that he is now addressing *tōn pneumatikōn*, or "spiritual things," characteristic of experience of the triune God.[9] Paul's use of

---

7. Cf. Garland, *1 Corinthians*, 567, 572.
8. Bezuidenhout, "Trinitarian Nature," 96.
9. Kleinknecht, "πνεῦμα, πνεῦμα τικός," 6:346.

pneumatikōn, then, is an example of "proto-Trinitarianism."[10] But why is it important for Paul to communicate this way?

One reason is that these verses evidence the earliest "clear" Trinitarian language from which later theological constructs are correctly derived. Such Trinitarian language, being monotheistic and centered on the Judeo-Christian God, is contrary to the Corinthians' pagan background of being tolerant of multiple gods or idols (12:2). On the other hand, Trinitarian language, indeed, things that are characteristic of the triune God, demonstrates the principle of unity in diversity. That is, though there are three distinct *hypostases* in the Godhead, there is a *perichoretic* unity of the Father, Son, and Spirit. For the pluralistic Corinthians, this suggests that despite varying socioeconomic, ethnic, and gender status, for example, they can be united as people of God (1 Cor 12:13; Gal 3:28). In other words, based on his divine revelation (1 Cor 2:10), Paul is advocating things that are characteristic of "the true God" (12:1), whose *hypostases* are inseparably linked and mutually participate in the life of the other two (12:3). This unity in diversity, then, can serve as an effective bridge to what Paul considers authentically spiritual. As already noted, Thiselton affirms such a Trinitarian and *perichoretic* motif when he says, "any account of 'spiritual gifts' which is merely Spirit-centered rather than Christomorphic (12:3) and Trinitarian (12:4–6) is untrue to Paul."[11] Bezuidenhout has also noted that the ensuing "confessional criterion" is by nature Trinitarian.[12]

Indeed, a Trinitarian and *perichoretic* motif is also evident in 1 Corinthians 12:4–6. In those verses, Paul says, "Now, there are varieties of gifts, but the same *Spirit*. Also, there are varieties of services, and the same *Lord*. And there are varieties of works, but the same *God* who works them all in everyone." Keener, for example, says the verses are "a proto-Trinitarian

---

10. The term "proto-Trinitarianism" is used here to acknowledge that in Paul's writings there is a definite background for a later Christian Trinitarianism (cf. Keener, *1–2 Corinthians*, 100). Herein, this notion will be referred to simply as being Trinitarian. But it is understood that language of "Trinitarian"—and "perichoretic"—is anachronistic to Paul. Trinitarian language was fully developed in the fourth century by the Cappadocian Fathers, Basil the Great (329–79 C.E.), Gregory of Nyssa (335–94 C. E), and Gregory of Nazianzen (330–90 C.E.). Their formulation was accepted as part of the Nicean-Constantinopolitan Creed (381 C.E.) and has been the basis of orthodox Christian thought ever since. The Cappadocians reasoned that God was of one essence (*ousia*) and three persons (*hypostases*). The perichoretic nature of God describes the mutual participation of each "persons" of the Godhead in the life of the other two. The argument here is that Paul communicates the triune and perichoretic nature of God throughout the entire pericope of 1 Cor 12–14, beginning in 12:1–3.

11. Thiselton, *First Corinthians*, 989.

12. Bezuidenhout, "Trinitarian Nature," 93–94.

perspective."[13] To Schatzmann, this "Trinitarian" formula is artless and unconscious—but not "likely unintentional."[14] If Schatzmann is correct, this would suggest that Paul is consciously communicating concepts, or in a manner, that he considers will be effective in getting his point across to his Corinthian audience. Additionally, for Thiselton, these verses mark the only place where Paul places *pneuma* (Spirit), *christos* (Son), *and Theos* (God the Father) in consecutive and closely parallel statements. This is correct in terms of talk about the Trinity. But relative to the second person of the Trinity (the Son), Paul used the term *kurios* (Lord) instead of the *christos* Thiselton mentions. Further, Thiselton fails to note that the three "persons" or *hypostases* of the Godhead are also mentioned—in consecutive order—together in the single verse of 12:3, where Paul says, "Therefore, I am making known to you that no one while talking by the Spirit of *God* says, '*Jesus* is a curse,' and no one is able to say *Jesus* is Lord, except by the *Holy Spirit*."[15] Thiselton, however, correctly notes the *perichoretic* relationship that exists in the Godhead when he says that in 12:3-6, "God is essentially one, as an 'ordered' being, but manifests himself in acts of the Spirit, acts of the Lord, and acts of God, both jointly and in differentiated ways."[16]

Implicit in Thiselton's statement is the idea that 1 Corinthians 12:3 explicitly introduce the three "persons" of the Trinity, who are one in essence. Bezuidenhout affirms this assessment when he says, "the interchange of 'Spirit of God' and 'Holy Spirit' is not only a stylistic variation, but a deliberate qualification of the Trinitarian character of the criterion."[17] In light of this Trinitarianism in 12:3, it is fair to conclude that 12:4-6 expounds and highlights the diversity of each *hypostasis* being affiliated, respectively, with various gifts, services, and activities, as well as the unity behind such divine energy being issued from one God. Paul writes that there are a variety of gifts (*charismata*), but these varied gifts have one thing in common, that is, they are all from the same Spirit (12:4, 11). The *charismata* are a manifestation of the sovereign grace of God the Spirit upon believers in order to edify the church while demonstrating the love of Christ. Thus, though the *charismata* are specifically from the Spirit, charismatic activity cannot be

---

13. Keener, *1-2 Corinthians*, 100.

14. Schatzmann, *Pauline Theology*, 35. Paul's "Trinitarian" hermeneutic will be discussed below.

15. Italics added.

16. Thiselton, *First Corinthians*, 989.

17. Bezuidenhout, "Trinitarian Nature," 96.

separated from the very presence and personal action of the triune God, who activates them in everyone.[18]

For Dunn, the *charismata* reveal the Spirit in that they are a demonstration of the Spirit's presence and activity.[19] Through the *charismata*, God, or something about God, can be known. But how is this possible, if God is ineffable? In his book *The Triads*, Gregory Palamas (1296–1359 C.E.) addressed this very question,[20] and came to a similar conclusion as Dunn. Palamas had been engaged in a prolonged debate with the Greek-Italian philosopher Barlaam the Calabrian over the issue of whether humans could directly experience God. The rationalistic Barlaam insisted, contrary to the Hesychasts—who claimed visions of God and taught that one can experience God through true prayer (the Jesus prayer)—that only a secular education around the acquisition of wisdom could lead to a true knowledge of God. Palamas, on the one hand, recognized a seeming inconsistency between Hesychasm and the absolute transcendence of God, and, on the other hand, Barlaam and the immanence of God, and sought a middle ground. Palamas constructively suggested that God cannot be known, communicated, and participated in as he is in essence—which is infinite and unknowable—but God can be known, communicated, and participated in as he is in his energies—which concerns the immanence of God, which can be known and experienced. The energies of God are possessed and exercised in common by all three persons of the Godhead.

So, Dunn has appropriately said that the *charismata* reveal the Spirit. In other words, genuine charismatic activity represents knowledge of, participation in, and communication of things of the Spirit. It reveals, for example, that God is wise, knowledgeable, a healer, faithful, a miracle worker, prophetic, a discerner of spirits, speaks whatever language we do, and can interpret our every thought.

There is yet before us a definitive answer as to how or whether charismatic activity can be authenticated. For the personal experience of the Holy Spirit, at best, is difficult to clearly authenticate. In fact, even the charismatic with their experience of the divine energy do not attain the full vision of God in this world. What can be definitively stated for now, however, is that while there can be great zeal for charismatic activity, the desire for "spirituality" is

---

18. Cf. 1 Cor 12:6. The varieties of *charismata* Paul mentions will be discussed in greater detail below, and tongues and prophecy will be particularly highlighted in the section on ch. 14.

19. Dunn, *Jesus and the Spirit*, 212.

20. Palamas, *Triads*.

no religious technique, but experience of the Spirit, and being authentically spiritual, depends on the activity of the triune God.[21]

Paul speaks of another activity, or divine energy, when he says, "there are varieties of services [*diakonia*] and the same Lord" (1 Cor 12:5). His use of *diakonia* conveys a variety of related ideas. Among them is that of acting or serving in an intermediary capacity, an office, and serving on behalf of a larger public. Also, *diakonia* refers to the work of mediating divine revelation.[22] The author of Ephesians provides examples of such mediators and mediation of the ascension gifts of Christ (*doreas tou christou*).[23] These mediators of divine revelation include the apostle, prophet, evangelist, pastor, and teacher (Eph 4:7–13).[24] Their "gifts" are specifically from the risen Lord, Jesus Christ, and are for the edification of the body of Christ.

Likewise, there are varieties of works (*energēmata*), but they are all from the same God (12:6). Paul's use of *energēmata* refers to activity that impacts others (such as miracles). God's *energēmata* takes place within the community, including in individuals, for their edification. Furthermore, as divine energies, the *energēmata* are synonymous with the *charismata*, and *diakonia*—all of which are "spiritual gifts" since they are revelatory of, inseparably linked to, and activated by the *hypostases* of the triune God.

A third instance of Paul's Trinitarianism can be seen in how he discusses the sovereign work of the Godhead. Certainly, the different *charismata* are given to individuals "as the same Spirit wills" (1 Cor 12:7–11), and the body of Christ has many members *in Christ* (12:12). Paul's identification of members with Christ is metonymous, for the members are to be so closely associated with Christ that it will be apparent that they are "in him," operating in their gifts, serving each other, and doing the work of ministry according to the will of Christ. Additionally, it is God who places each member of the body *as he pleases* (12:18, 24, 28). Thus, God the Father, the Son, and the Spirit sovereignly operate in the lives of individual members of the body of Christ.

Another way in which the triune and *perichoretic* nature of God is communicated by Paul can be seen in how he uses 1 Corinthians 12:7–11 to explain the variety of gifts (*charismata*) he mentions in 12:4. Subsequently, 12:12–17 explains the varieties of services, from the same Lord (12:5), or

21. Thiselton, *First Corinthians*, 915.
22. Collins, "Mediatorial Aspect."
23. Here it is important to note that the term "gift," relative to Christ, is not translated from χαρίσματα, as Paul employs in 1 Corinthians. The author of Ephesians uses the term δορεᾶς for "gifts" from Jesus. Paul uses χαρίσματα to specifically reference gifts of the Spirit.
24. Beyer, "διακονία," 87, 92.

how the body of Christ is administered. Regardless of the services that the various members of Christ's body participate in, they are essential, for they are needed for the optimal function of the body of Christ. Finally, 12:18–26 explains the variety of works from the same God that is referred to in 12:6. God operates through every member of the body regardless of how insignificant some members may consider themselves to be. God operates this way to prevent schisms among the members of the body. Summarily, 1 Corinthians 12:7–26 evidences that Paul is continuously explaining and reinforcing the unity in diversity that is characteristic of, and therefore inseparably linked to, the triune God.

The fifth example of Pauline Trinitarianism is evident in 1 Corinthians 12:27–30, where it is highlighted that God places the members of the church (v. 28), who are Christ's body (v. 27)—including those with the variety of services of Christ, such as apostles, prophets, and teachers (vv. 28–29)—and the various gifts apportioned by the Spirit, such as gifts of healings, kinds of tongues, and interpretation of tongues (vv. 28, 30).

Finally, Paul depicts the triune and *perichoretic* nature of God in the structural emphases of 1 Corinthians 12–14. These chapters focus on the requisite criteria for revelation that is authentically spiritual or characteristic of the triune God. 1 Corinthians 12 focuses on the manifestation of the gifts of the Spirit—though it is not limited to this concern. Then 1 Corinthians 13 focuses on the more excellent way of love—exemplified by the person and ministry of Jesus Christ, the Son of God. And 1 Corinthians 14 focuses on edification that reveals God, as well as members of the accountable community appointed by God.[25] Like the Godhead, therefore, these three foci are to be considered complementary and inseparable linked to each other. Therefore, *charismata* evidence the presence of the Spirit, but there is need for discernment since pagans also manifest "charismatic" behavior. Because of this possible ambiguity, it is requisite that genuine *charismata* also evidence the love of Christ and represent godly edification (14:1).

Having highlighted the Trinitarian motif in Paul's "confessional criterion," it has repeatedly been shown that this Trinitarianism is important in how Paul is communicating the criteria for authentic spirituality to the Corinthians. Thus, a Trinitarian motif is fundamental to Paul's theology,[26] and is at least one hermeneutical consideration for Paul in his communicating with the pluralistic church.

---

25. Cf. 12:18; 14:3–5, 12, 25–26, 36.
26. Fee, *God's Empowering Presence*, 898.

4.2.2 Why does Paul employ a Trinitarian hermeneutic?

With regards to why Paul communicates in Trinitarian language, several reasons can be posited. First, Paul's theology is based on compelling revelation from the triune God. His hermeneutic is a demonstration of the Spirit working in him (1 Cor 2:2–5) and is a "command of the Lord" (14:37), for it is based in his revelation of Jesus Christ, by God (Gal 1:12, 15–16; 2:2; cf. Rom 16:25–26).

With this hermeneutical basis in mind, then, it stands to reason, second, that Paul is simply conveying the reality of who God is and how he operates. This is important, for in a pluralistic Corinthian culture where many gods are accepted, Christ may be a stumbling block, but for Paul there is but one God, who is revealed as three distinct *hypostases*, mysteriously participating in different acts which are also inseparably linked to all three "persons." Hence, there is a unity in diversity relative to the Godhead, which serves as the ideal model of how Christians, in all their diversities, should be united in Christ. That is, despite the influence of the surrounding culture, the Corinthian believers should stand fast in the things of Christ (1 Cor 15:58). And since the culture is intolerant of Christians, true tolerance can be found in the unity in diversity found in the Christian ethos, where all are accepted in Christ regardless of their ethnicity, gender, or socioeconomic background.

Finally, rather than succumbing to the prevailing self-exalting ethos of their culture, Paul wants the Corinthians to be united—even as the triune God is—and focus on things characteristic of the triune God. Individual members of the congregation may have different gifts, but they should not seek individual profit from the gifts; rather, *charismata* are for the common good and according to the will of the Spirit.

4.3 The Criterion of Common Benefit (12:4–11)

Bezuidenhout considers the various *charismata*, *diakonia*, and *energēmata* mentioned in 1 Corinthians 12:4–6 to be interchangeable terms depicting gifts of the Spirit (*charismata*).[27] This assertion is based on the interpretation that the *charismata* mentioned in 12:31 include all the "gifts" listed in 12:28–30. These "gifts" include being an apostle, prophet, and teacher, as well as workers of miracles, healings, tongues, and interpretation of tongues. But based on the context of 1 Corinthians, the list of "gifts" can only be considered spiritual gifts because they were given by the triune God. These spiritual gifts

---

27. Bezuidenhout, "Trinitarian Nature," 97.

are inclusive of, but not limited to, *charismata* (gifts of the Spirit), for gifts of Christ (*diakonia*) such as being an apostle, prophet, and teacher are also included. Hence, Paul's use of *charismata* in 12:31 was only about the latter three gifts of the Spirit (healings, tongues, and interpretation of tongues), which are consistent with the *charismata* listed in 12:8–10. And this makes sense, because *charismata* such as prophecy and tongues were at the forefront of the spiritual things, or gifts, being abused in the Corinthian church.

Furthermore, the claim that the gifts of Romans 12:6–8 are also called *charismata* is inconsistent with the context of Romans 12, where Paul is discussing the unity in diversity of the body of Christ (Rom 12:5). In this context, members have been given "spiritual gifts" or divine energies from the triune God. This includes the *charismata* of prophecy and faith (Rom 12:6)—from the Spirit, διακονία, such as teaching (Rom 12:7)—from the Lord, or exhortations (Rom 12:8). *Charismata*, then, can be associated with *diakonia*, for example, in that they are divine energies that have their source in the Godhead. But the two "spiritual things" (*tōn pneumatikōn*) are distinct in that they are distributed by a different *hypostasis* of the Trinity. Therefore, Bezuidenhout's conflation of the divine energies of 1 Corinthians 12:4–6 is inappropriate, especially since he agrees that Paul is emphasizing the unity and diversity of the triune God.[28] On the one hand, the South African scholar appropriately affirms the unity of the Godhead. But such unity is not based on the various activities or energies of the Godhead being depicted as gifts of the Spirit. Instead, the unity Paul communicates is based on the essence of God as one being who activates spiritual gifts.

On the other hand, Bezuidenhout minimizes his argument for Paul's Trinitarian hermeneutic by not considering the diversity of the three *hypostases* of the Godhead. This is because Paul uses three distinct words in his communication of the divine energies. And not only are the various activities or divine energies different, but Paul also explicitly links them with a specific *hypostasis*. It would have been more appropriate, then, for Bezuidenhout to consider the various activities to be "spiritual gifts" from the triune God, rather than gifts from the Spirit.[29] Thus, it is correct to conclude that "the one Spirit distributes a variety of *charismata* according to his will and with a view to what is beneficial."[30]

This latter statement summarizes what Bezuidenhout considers "the criterion of common benefit" found in 1 Corinthians 12:4–11. It has already been argued that Bezuidenhout conflates the hypostatic distinctions

---

28. Bezuidenhout, "Trinitarian Nature," 97.
29. Bezuidenhout, "Trinitarian Nature," 97.
30. Bezuidenhout, "Trinitarian Nature," 97.

(12:4–6) highlighted within the triune God in his proposal of this criterion. It should therefore not be surprising that Bezuidenhout considers 12:7 to be a depiction of 12:4–6, which is also affirmed in 12:11. Bezuidenhout's basic argument is that divine energies such as *charismata*, *diakonia*, and *energēmatōn* are all manifestations of the Spirit for the common good.[31] But is this what Paul is expressing? In 12:7 Paul says, "Now, to each is given the manifestation of the Spirit for the common good." What is the "manifestation of the Spirit" that Paul is talking about? Based on the Trinitarian motif already discussed, and Paul's explicit statement, 12:7–11 is an explanation of the variety of gifts from the Spirit (*charismata*) he mentions in 12:4 and 12:11. Paul is explaining that the manifestations of the Spirit (*charismata*) given to each believer are for the common good.

At least three conclusions can be drawn from Paul's statement in 1 Corinthians 12:7–11. The first is that each believer has been given *charismata* (12:11). Second, as manifestations of the Spirit, *charismata* reveal, communicate, and evidence participation in the triune God. Additionally, they should generally be open to or accountable to the public,[32] who can authenticate them. Finally, *charismata* must be for the common good. Contrary to Thiselton's assertion, this does not mean that one cannot seek individual benefit,[33] for believers are encouraged to seek spiritual gifts (12:31; 14:1, 39). But the gift of tongues has been given by the Spirit for the edification or benefit of the individual, as well as the community—if interpreted (cf. 14:4–5). So, Fee is correct to say that *charismata* are not primarily for the benefit of individuals and are for the edification of the believing community in general.[34] Therefore, any revelatory claim that does not benefit the common good of the people of God should be suspect, for it may not be a genuine *charismata*.

This conclusion was also arrived at in the discussion of OT prophecy (a charism). There it was noted that authentic *charismata* (like prophecy) must be without respect of persons and nations. In other words, it is a requirement for the functioning of the *charismata* that they should be for the common good. Therefore, in terms of the criterion of common benefit, Bezuidenhout's conclusion is apparently valid. This is so because one may argue that not every act that is deemed for the common good may be led by the Spirit. After all, even murderers, for example, can show love or perform

---

31. Bezuidenhout, "Trinitarian Nature," 98.

32. I say "generally" because, unlike the other gifts, Paul suggests that tongues should be done in private if not being interpreted (1 Cor 14:28).

33. Thiselton, *First Corinthians*, 936.

34. Fee, *First Corinthians*, 589.

some other act that is beneficial to the community. However, there does not seem to be any way of proving that such beneficial acts are not influenced by the Spirit. Thus, the criterion of common benefit cannot be disproven, but should probably be accompanied by some other validating criterion. Moreover, Bezuidenhout's concomitant conflation of various spiritual things such as *diakonia* and *energēmata* as depicting *charismata* or gifts from the Spirit is inappropriate.

In 1 Corinthians 12:8–10, Paul particularizes various *charismata* that are given for the edification of the community. He mentions a word of wisdom, a word of knowledge, faith, gifts of healing, works of power, prophecy, discernment of spirits, kinds of tongues, and interpretation of tongues. It is beyond the scope of this work to fully analyze each of these *charismata*, so it will suffice here to define them individually, and to give special emphasis to tongues and prophecy in our later discussions, since the culturally influenced misuse of these two gifts seem to be a major factor influencing Paul to offer revelatory criteria to the Corinthians.

Each of these *charismata* is discussed at length by various commentators.[35] Based on Paul's discussion of wisdom (*sophía*) in 1 Corinthians, especially chapters 1 and 2, it seems reasonable to state that a word of wisdom (*logos sophias*) relates to an inspired utterance concerning "the deep things of God" (2:10), or the power of God, that is consistent with the gospel concerning Jesus Christ.[36] So, any claim of a word of wisdom that is contrary to the revelation of Jesus Christ found in the gospel should not be considered an authentic revelatory experience. This includes a divisive and self-exalting ethos of some of the Corinthians, whose arrogance and pride undermine the power of God which the Holy Spirit teaches (1:17—2:15).

While all the Corinthian believers have been given knowledge by God (1 Cor 1:5; 8:1), a word of knowledge (*logos gnōseōs*) is utterance related to God the Father and the Lord Jesus Christ (1 Cor 8:6–7). It is "charismatic insight into the real nature of things, into the structure of the cosmos and the relationship of divine and human, spiritual and material within the cosmos."[37] Therefore, authentic claims to a word of knowledge should be consistent with the realities of existence. This means claims of a word of knowledge should represent ontological and phenomenological truths, and not be limited to mere human rationale. In other words, a genuine word of

---

35. For example, Fee, *First Corinthians*, 590–99; Thiselton, *First Corinthians*, 938–88; and Schatzmann, *Pauline Theology*, 35–43.

36. Cf. 1 Cor 1:18, 24; 2:4, 5; 4:19–20. See also, Schatzmann, *Pauline Theology*, 36

37. Dunn, *Jesus and the Spirit*, 217–18. Cf. 1 Cor 13:2, 8.

knowledge is open to all sources of truth, for such sources are complimentary and not antithetical to each other.

Some commentators agree that faith (*pistis*) connotes a mysterious surge of confidence,[38] and even suggest that the *charismata* of faith is "a gift alongside others,"[39] for faith does not manifest independently of other *charismata*, and precedes both the gifts of healing and works of power. The former assertion seems to be speculative since Paul does not mention any "surge of confidence" in his discussion of the gift of faith. Further, a mysterious "surge of confidence" would not necessarily preclude non-divine sources of that surge. But the gift of faith, like other *charismata*, has its source in the divine Spirit (1 Cor 12:4, 11). The latter suggestion of a non-independent nature of the gift of faith limits the same charism to situations where other gifts are in operation. Paul's particularization of the gifts, however, suggests that they are all distinct—after all, "there are varieties of gifts" (12:4), and Paul does not seem to infer any dependence of one gift upon another.

The case of interpretation of tongues (*hermēneia glossōn*) seems to be an exception to this latter statement because it is to accompany *genē glossōn* (kinds of tongues) if the community is to be edified (1 Cor 14:5–6, 9–13, 27–28). Accordingly, Schatzmann asserts, "tongues represent the only charism which is not capable of upbuilding the church on its own."[40] But when one considers that tongues is for the edification of the individual (1 Cor 14:4) as they speak to God in the Spirit (14:2), it seems appropriate to conclude that the gift of tongues also does not need to be accompanied by any other *charismata* to be appropriately operated. Further, as discussed above, this edifying of the individual does not violate the fact that *charismata* are given for the common good. Otherwise Paul would be contradicting himself, for he lists tongues as one of the *charismata*. Indeed, when one is edified, all are edified (12:26). The common good is served because individuals cannot be separated from the community they are a part of, just as individual members cannot be separated from the body of Christ (12:12). As part of the church, when an individual believer is edified, the upbuilding of the church is contributed to. So, relative to the gift of faith, based on the 1 Corinthians text, it seems appropriate to conclude that it involves a belief in the power of God (2:5)—who is omnipotent and sovereign relative to the world. And any disbelief or limiting the power and sovereignty of God should not be considered genuine *charismata*.

---

38. Cf. Schatzmann, *Pauline Theology*, 37; Dunn, *Jesus and the Spirit*, 211; Thiselton, *First Corinthians*, 945–46.

39. Cf. Conzelmann, *1 Corinthians*, 209; Schatzmann, *Pauline Theology*, 37.

40. Schatzmann, *Pauline Theology*, 4.

The plural form of the *charismata* that Paul lists as gifts of healing (*charismata iamatōn*) is generally considered to be indicative of a variety of ways and individuals that the Spirit uses to address various ailments.[41] If this is true, there is not a method by which all ailments are healed. And, authentic *charismata iamatōn* can be based on either "spiritual" or "natural" means. The use of medicine, for example, could be considered as part of the gift of healing just as the laying on of hands could also be instrumental for the same purpose. And since the Spirit distributes *charismata iamatōn* as the Spirit wills (1 Cor 12:11), no one individual should claim to be able to heal whenever they want to. Indeed, *charismata iamatōn* can occur "through whatever instrument or human agent, and whatever time God may choose, as one of many specific gifts."[42]

Charismata iamatōn seems like it is a subcategory of works of power (*energēmata dunameōn*), since elsewhere healing is a powerful work done in a human being (Luke 5:17). But the fact that Paul lists *energēmata dunameōn* separately suggests that he was talking about a different *charismata*. Contrary to the gifts of healing, *energēmata dunameōn* refers to the use of God's power to overcome spiritual forces—rather than providing physical healing. The overcoming of spiritual forces can occur, for example, in an exorcism, as well as conquering some earthly forces of opposition that have their source in the human spirit. To be sure, the Spirit is revealed as being able to overcome all opposition as the Spirit wills. Correspondingly, one who claims to be operating in *energēmata dunameōn* should be consistent with the gospel concerning Jesus Christ, who gave his followers power over unclean spirits, as well as to heal sicknesses (Mark 3:15), and perhaps to shake the powers in the heavens in advance of the *Parousia* (Mark 13:24–25).

The gift of prophecy (*prophēteia*) will be discussed in greater detail below. Here, I will simply note that prophecy is inspired and understandable utterance (revelation) for edifying, comforting, and encouraging the people of God (1 Cor 14:2–4).

The gift of discernment of spirits (*diakriseis pneumatōn*) is the Spirit-inspired "ability to discern what is truly of the Spirit of God and what comes from other Spirits."[43] Being one of the *charismata*, it is obvious that *diakriseis pneumatōn* is from the Spirit—who alone knows and reveals the things of God (1 Cor 2:10–11). Thus, mere human rationale is not enough

---

41. Cf. Godet, *Commentary on First Corinthians*, 197; Meyer, *Critical and Exegetical Handbook*, 364; Robertson and Plummer, *Critical and Exegetical Commentary*, 266; Goudge, *First Corinthians*, 110; Carson, *Showing the Spirit*, 39; Schatzmann, *Pauline Theology*, 37.

42. Thiselton, *First Corinthians*, 950.

43. Fee, *First Corinthians*, 596.

to discern the spirits, at least not what relates to the Spirit of God (2:14). The gift of discernment of spirits seems to be an accompanying gift to prophecy, which precedes it in Paul's listing, and is called for when the act of prophesying is mentioned by Paul in his exhortations to the people of God (cf. 1 Cor 14:29; 1 Thess 5:20–21). Certainly, one needs to discern whether their utterances are truly from the Spirit (1 Cor 14:29). But it is equally true that all the *charismata* listed by Paul should be accompanied by the gift of *diakriseis pneumatōn*. For spiritual manifestation, though revelatory (if it is authentically from divine source), is subjective because of the involvement of human beings, and it is virtually impossible to discern whether a claim of *charismata*, in and of itself, is authentic.

As will be the case for the gift of prophecy, the gift of kinds of tongues (*genē glossōn*) will be discussed in greater detail below. For now, what can be said is that *genē glossōn* is Spirit-inspired utterance directed toward God (14:2) that edifies the individual (14:4), is under their control (14:27–28, 32), and is unintelligible to both the individual (14:14) and the hearers (14:16).

Finally, the gift of interpretation of tongues (*hermēneia glossōn*) is the Spirit-inspired "intelligible communication of glossolalic utterance addressed to God,"[44] and is given either to the tongues speaker (14:13) or a hearer of the tongues (14:27), as the Spirit wills (12:11). This communication should be considered an interpretation, or explanation, instead of a translation. So, for example, there does not need to be word-to-word correspondence between the tongues and its interpretation. This gift appears to be restricted in usage in that it is only used to interpret tongues, so that the community—obviously including, but not limited to, the individual—can be edified by the explanation of the tongues. And though Paul would prefer that the Corinthians prophesy in the congregation instead of speaking in tongues—because, being intelligible utterance, prophecy edifies the hearers—when the tongues is interpreted, it holds the same value to the congregation as prophetic speech does (14:5). Both prophecy and interpreted tongues are edifying to the community. Thus, as is the case for prophetic utterances, the interpretation of tongues should be edifying to the community if it is to be considered genuinely revelatory.

Before listing the various *charismata*, Paul made it clear that they are given to individuals for the common good. After listing the various *charismata*, Paul continues his emphasis on unity in diversity by immediately reiterating that the various *charismata* are from the same Spirit and according to the will of the Spirit (1 Cor 12:11). Thus, any claim to charismatic or revelatory experiences should not be based in the exaltation of one's self,

---

44. Schatzmann, *Pauline Theology*, 43.

neither should it be contradictory to the will of the Spirit. This will of the Spirit is not the same as the will of natural humanity, the will of the world (2:12), or human wisdom (12:13).

This biblical truth seemingly contradicts Walter Hollenweger's claim that gifts are natural phenomenon.[45] In his article entitled "Gifts of the Spirit: Natural and Supernatural," the Swiss theologian argues that there is no biblical and scientific basis for suggesting that *glossolalia* is a supernatural phenomenon. There is no biblical basis, he asserts, because the *charismata* listed in the Bible include both "extra-ordinary" gifts like prophecy, healing, and *glossolalia*, as well as "ordinary gifts" like teaching and being married or unmarried.[46] Hollenweger also adds that Paul's criterion for the *charismata* is not phenomenological, but functional (what it does to a person or community). Thus, *charismata* are natural gifts given for the common good. Unfortunately, in the first place, Hollenweger has reduced spiritual gifts to *charismata* (his "extra-ordinary gifts") and concomitantly considers, for example, the spiritual gift, or *diakonia*, of teaching—a service (gift) from Christ—to be among the *charismata*, and also be an "ordinary gift."[47] Second, Hollenweger does not define what he means by "natural gifts"—though it appears that he is thinking of human abilities.[48] But the fact that Paul defines *charismata* as gifts from the Spirit for the common good (12:4, 7–11) makes it explicit that the *charismata* function to benefit a person or community, and are ontologically gifts from the Spirit.

Thomas Aquinas agreed with such an interpretation of Paul, for he affirmed that the charism of prophecy "surpass all human knowledge and . . . are revealed from God [and] cannot find confirmation in that human reasoning which they transcend, but only in the working of divine power."[49] In light of Aquinas's evaluation of prophecy, it becomes even clearer why charismatic experiences by themselves cannot be considered criteria for authenticating what is truly spiritual.

Concerning Hollenweger, however, it is also worth critiquing his statement that "Paul's criterion for a charism is not phenomenological but functional."[50] Essentially, the *charismata* are ontological, phenomenological, as well as functional. This is because *charismata* are essentially observable

---

45. Hollenweger, "Gifts of the Spirit," 667–68.
46. Hollenweger, "Gifts of the Spirit," 667.
47. Cf. 1 Cor 12:5; Eph 4:11.
48. Cf. 1 Cor 12:5; Eph 4:11.
49. Aquinas, *Summa Theologiae Vol. 45 (2a2ae 171–178) Prophecy and Other Charisms*, 7.
50. Hollenweger, "Gifts of the Spirit," 667.

manifestations of the Spirit that function to reveal God and edify whomever God wills. Additionally, if Hollenweger considers a "natural gift" to be an ability that has its source in humans—instead of God—he has misinterpreted Paul, who makes it clear that the *charismata* are supernatural gifts—from the Spirit. Moreover, if the *charismata* were "natural gifts," then individuals would have justifiable cause to boast in their abilities and be able to use them whenever they wanted to. But Paul's use of *charismata* suggests the Spirit gives the gifts as the Spirit wills (1 Cor 12:11), so charismatic activity is only manifested when the Spirit sovereignly chooses it to be manifested. Therefore, there is no cause for human boasting (1:26–31; 3:21; 4:7). Hollenweger, as is common in much of modern studies relative to the 1 Corinthians 12–14 pericope, fails to identify the phenomenological and spiritual aspect of Paul's "criterion of common benefit."

In terms of there being no scientific basis that the *charismata* are supernatural, Hollenweger argues that science has determined the *charismata* to be human abilities.[51] This might be true because one could speak in different tongues by mere human abilities, but this truth, and scientific methodology, in general, tends to rule out the supernatural aspect of life. For example, Hollenweger's distinction of "extra-ordinary" and "ordinary" gifts does not consider that though there may be "ordinary gifts," the charismatic or divinely inspired use of such gifts may be quite different, as the Spirit and/or the triune God sovereignly activates them. For example, one may be able to naturally speak in various tongues to others, but the *charismata* of tongues, while it may be phenomenologically like natural tongues, is speech directed to God, and not humanity (1 Cor 14:2). Therefore, lack of scientific rationale should not preclude that the Spirit graciously activates charismatic activity for the common good, as the Spirit wills.

In brief, the claim that there is no biblical and scientific basis to suggest that the *charismata* are supernatural is without merit since the Bible considers *charismata* to be sourced in the Spirit. Scientific rationale, while it can quantify natural phenomenon, is not able to prove the supernatural, and dismisses non-quantifiable knowledge, which is ontologically inseparable. In his well-intentioned zeal to show that the Spirit operates in the lives of all people, whether they are Christians or not—which I believe is correct—Hollenweger asserts that God, as creator of everything, is gracious to all, and has given everyone abilities, which may or may not be revelatory of God, or used in an authentically "spiritual" manner. Additionally, such God given abilities should not necessarily be considered *charismata*. Again, as Thomas Aquinas has said, the Spirit can sovereignly activate *charismata* in

---

51. Hollenweger, "Gifts of the Spirit," 667.

non-Christians;[52] but whether abilities that appear to be *charismata* should rightly be considered so is another issue. When one's abilities are not directed by the Spirit, they are purely natural, but supernatural abilities such as the *charismata* are activated by and are according to the will of the Spirit. Hollenweger's conclusions offer further justification of the need for criteria for authentic spirituality.

4.4 The Criterion of Service (12:12–30)

According to Bezuidenhout, 1 Corinthians 12:12–30 concerns the criterion of service to the body of Christ.[53] This assertion is based primarily on the implications of Paul's explaining, by way of comparative language, how the Spirit sovereignly distributes *charismata* to individuals. Paul says, "For just as the body is one and it has many members, and all the members of the body, being many, is one body, thus, also the [body of] Christ" (12:12). Paul's analogy is between members of the body of Christ through whom various *charismata* operate and parts of the human body with their various functions. There are many parts (members) of the human body with a variety of functions, all of which serve to keep the body operating optimally. Likewise, in the body of Christ, there are many members with a variety of *charismata*, all of which has the purpose of keeping the body of Christ operating at its best.

For Bezuidenhout, there is a clear Trinitarian aspect of this "criterion of service,"[54] for in 1 Corinthians 12:12 it is made clear that the unity of the various members is grounded in Christ. Further, it is in the Spirit that all the members have their identity (12:13). Furthermore, God places the members of the body (12:18) so that they would have the same care for one another (12:25). Indeed, God places members of the body to perform various services, affiliated, for example, with being an apostle, a prophet, and a teacher (12:28).

It is still yet to be determined if his criterion of service is valid, but Bezuidenhout is right that there is a Trinitarian motif throughout this pericope. In fact, there is another way in which this hermeneutic can be expressed, which Bezuidenhout has not suggested. This approach has already been alluded to briefly in the previous discussion of Paul's Trinitarian theology. But now this Trinitarian theme will be specifically explained in terms

---

52. Aquinas, *Prophecy and Other Charisms*, 41.
53. Bezuidenhout, "Trinitarian Nature," 99.
54. Bezuidenhout, "Trinitarian Nature," 100.

of the "criterion of service." This approach is an unpacking of the Trinitarian hermeneutic evident in 1 Corinthians 12:4–6.

Having explained that there are various *charismata* that are distributed by the Spirit (1 Cor 12:4, 7–11),[55] in 12:12–17 Paul is now explaining what he means when he says, "there are varieties of services, and the same Lord" (12:5). Paul's use of the logical connective *gar* (for) makes clear that he is starting an explanation. His explicit comparison of the physical body—which has many members, or parts, that are all one and same body—to the body of Christ (12:12) makes clear that Christ is now the subject of discussion. The repeated metaphoric use of the term *sōma* (body) for the church, or the body of Christ, also leads one to the same conclusion. More specifically, however, the literary context of 12:12–17 suggests that Paul is explaining how the body of Christ is administered or works. So, one can agree with Bezuidenhout that this pericope deals with the notion of service. However, it still is not yet clear if a "criterion of service" is valid.

Regarding Paul's use of the term "body," Ernst Käsemann suggests that the body of Christ is "the means whereby Christ reveals himself on earth and becomes incarnate in the world through his Spirit."[56] This is because the manifestation of the divine energy in charismatic activity through members of the body of Christ is a sovereign act of the Spirit in service of humanity.

Paul makes it clear that the "body" has many members united in Christ (1 Cor 12:12). Their manifestation of *charismata*, then, evidences a unity in diversity, because despite the diversity of members in terms of varieties of gifts received (12:4, 11), cultural backgrounds, or socioeconomic status (12:13), every member has it in common that they have been baptized by, or received the same Spirit. In fact, even though the members of the body are different, and have different roles or ways in which they serve the body, all these services are vital and complimentary for the optimal operation of the body (12:14–17). So, instead of using their differences for self-exalting purposes, the Corinthians should use their gifts from God to serve others and strengthen the body of Christ.

The final aspect of the Trinitarian motif is found in 1 Corinthians 12:18–26. Just as there are varieties of gifts (1 Cor 12:4), and services (12:5), 12:18–26 explains how there are varieties of works, but the same God works them all in the members of the body (12:6). Paul's use of the phrase *nunì dè* ("but now") in 12:18 suggests that he is now moving on from his discussion of the body of Christ to explaining the third statement of his triadic

---

55. In these verses, the Spirit is the focus.
56. Käsemann, "Motif of the Body of Christ," 110 and 117.

formulation (12:4–6). Verse 18 also makes it clear that God is now the subject, and though the term *sōma* ("body") is also repeated in these verses, the literary context and the repeated use of the term *melē* ("members")—whom God has placed—affirms that God the Father is now the subject.

Paul says it is God who sovereignly places the members of the body (1 Cor 12:18). And just as these members have various services or administrations, they also have different operations that are vital for the body regardless of how big or small, strong or weak, honorable or dishonorable they appear (12:19–24). God has placed the members to care for each other, avoid schisms, as well as share in each other's sufferings and joys (12:25–26).

With this Trinitarian motif in 1 Corinthians 12 now established, it is time to directly address the idea of the "criterion of service." Undeniably, there is great value in members of the body of Christ offering of themselves to others. In fact, as has already been shown, such service would be contrary to the self-serving ethos of the Corinthian context and would be a great indicator that instead of being a pagan, one is a Christian. The question at hand, however, is: can such service rightly be called a criterion for authentic spirituality? In other words, are all who serve being led by the Spirit? Based on what has already been gleaned regarding outer experiences—and one's service is an outer experience—contrary to Bezuidenhout, it must be concluded that one's service—at least not by itself—cannot be a criterion for authentic spirituality. For though the Spirit sovereignly distributes *charismata* to individuals so that they can serve others, one can also be performing acts of service such as teaching, or even prophesying, for example, without being led by the Spirit of God.

In a similar way, it seems like another criterion for authentic spirituality can be inferred from Paul's explanation of how the body works (12:12–17). That is, authentic spirituality is not unique to one community, people, or socioeconomic class. And if authentically spiritual claims are not inclusive of or representative of the diverse body of Christ, they are likely inauthentic. For, regardless of one's gender, racial, and socioeconomic status—indeed, regardless of what makes one diverse—one's service is essential to the body, and authentically spiritual claims should affirm this truth. But by itself, this principle of authentic Christian living also cannot be considered a criterion for authenticating spirituality, because one that is not operating by the Spirit can also participate in activity that is not out of respect of individuals or nations.

4.5 Conclusion

Paul concludes his remarks in 1 Corinthians 12 by commanding the Corinthians to seek *charismata* (12:31). This makes sense since the *charismata* evidence the presence of or a manifestation of God the Spirit. This study thus far, however, has made it clear that such revelation may not be so easily discerned. Bezuidenhout's "confessional criterion," for example, should not be appropriately considered a criterion in this regard—at least not by itself—since the confession of Jesus as Lord can be made regardless of whether one is doing so by the Spirit. This confession is made by all who consider themselves Christians and should more appropriately be considered in terms of discerning who is a Christian.

In a similar way, the "criterion of service" should not be rightfully considered a criterion for the functioning of the *charismata*, because acts of service, like other observable outer experiences, can be done by individuals whether they are doing them according to the will of the Spirit or not. On the other hand, the "criterion of common benefit" is to be accepted since OT precedent affirms that authentic revelatory experiences are always without respect of persons or nations, in that they apply to all people. Moreover, inauthentic claims of revelation usually violate such a principle.

Whether Bezuidenhout's criteria are to be accepted is therefore debatable. At least two things about these criteria, however, are clear. The first is that all the proposed criteria are prescriptions that should be normative in authentic Christian living. Hence, all Christians should continually confess Jesus as Lord and exercise their gifts in service that is for the common good.

The other undeniable point regarding Bezuidenhout's list of criteria relative to 1 Corinthians 12 is the absolute requirement of the manifestation of the Holy Spirit. For an authentic Christian confession of Jesus as Lord is only done by the Spirit. Also, it is the Spirit who sovereignly distributes *charismata* so that recipients can optimally serve towards the common benefit.

It is one thing to agree on certain Christian principles, but it is also challenging to communicate them in a pluralistic culture that is resistant to them. That was the case for Paul, as he wrote to the Corinthians, who were being influenced by the broader Graeco-Roman culture. To effectively make his point of encouraging the Corinthians to stand fast in the things of Christ, however, we have seen that Paul had at least one hermeneutical consideration: he employed a Trinitarian theology. Paul conveyed to a pluralistic and self-exalting culture the reality of one God who is manifested in three different *hypostases*, revealing a unity in diversity as an example of how the church ought to relate to each other. For, even though the Corinthians possessed a variety of the *charismata*, rather than exercising their gifts in a self-exalting way, their charismatic activity should be according to the will of the Spirit and for the common benefit.

Thus, in terms of criteria for authentic spirituality, the lesson from 1 Corinthians 12—and the OT background—for the contemporary church is that talk about revelatory experiences should be sensitively Trinitarian to effectively speak to a pluralistic culture. Additionally, charismatic activity, and the one who is genuinely spiritual, must evidence the manifestation of the Spirit (*charismata*). However, for Paul, there is still a more excellent way (12:31). For while *charismata* are requisite in authentic spirituality, the *charismata* by themselves cannot authenticate revelatory claims, since there are often ambiguously similar "natural" activities. Thus, there needs to be a more excellent way to authenticate revelatory claims. It is this more excellent way, discussed in 1 Corinthians 13, that we will now focus on.

Chapter 5

The Criterion of Love (1 Cor 13:1–13)

5.1 The Criterion of Love (1 Cor 13:1–13)

Before discussing the "criterion of love" (1 Cor 13:1–13), it is important to note that some commentators—though the authenticity of 1 Corinthians is generally acknowledged—question the authenticity or originality of the present composition of the epistle. For example, Conzelmann asserts that a different situation other than what is found in chapter 13 must be presupposed between chapters 12 and 14. In other words, chapter 13 is an interpolation that interrupts the continuity of the pericope.[1] If Conzelmann's assertion is correct, it stands to reason that the criterion already discussed and that to be discussed below may also be inauthentic, since they would be derived apart from their original context.

Contrary to Conzelmann, Fee and Thiselton agree that there is genuine coherence in the 1 Corinthians epistle, in general, and 1 Corinthians 12–14, in particular.[2] According to Thiselton, this coherence can be clearly shown with patient exegesis.[3] For two further reasons, this work agrees with the latter commentators, and presupposes that the 1 Corinthians 12–14 pericope, as it stands, is an original and coherent expression of Pauline thought from which criteria for authentic spirituality can be appropriately gleaned.

In the first place, those who deny the continuity of 1 Corinthians 12–14 have not noted the "Trinitarian" scheme already discussed, which Paul employs throughout the pericope, particularly as it relates to the structure of the three chapters. This Trinitarian scheme suggests that Paul, having discussed the manifestations of the Spirit (ch. 12), will now present the inseparability of

---

1. Conzelmann, *1 Corinthians*, 3.
2. Cf. Fee, *First Corinthians*, 626; and Thiselton, *First Corinthians*, 39.
3. Thiselton, *First Corinthians*, 39, 1027.

the love that is exemplified in Christ (ch. 13); then the requisite edification of the members of the body, whom God has placed (ch. 14).

The other reason, which will be expounded below, is that the entire chapter is an explanation of Paul's exhortation in 1 Corinthians 12:31 to "passionately seek the greatest gifts! And yet I show to you a way to excellence."[4] For these reasons, "chapter 13 is not to be regarded as interrupting the discourse concerning the *charismata*. Rather, it is a necessary link in the argument which has as its purpose to assign *glossolalia* its rightful place."[5] Indeed, *charismata* such as tongues and prophecy, which are temporal, will fail, but love is eternal (13:8).

This understanding, then, is the fundamental presupposition undergirding the following analysis of what Bezuidenhout considers the "criterion of love." Regardless of the outcome of the investigation, the hermeneutical consideration behind Paul's emphasis, and the reason for such a hermeneutic, will be dealt with through the lens of the 1 Corinthians 12–14 context, as well as the broader 1 Corinthians epistolary context before making conclusive comments.

5.2 Analyzing Bezuidenhout's "Criterion of Love"

For Bezuidenhout, "the unequivocal message of 1 Corinthians 13" is that of love as criterion for the functioning of the *charismata*. This is because, "in 1 Corinthians 13 we do not have a discussion of love per se, but of love as criterion for the practice of the *charismata*."[6] A casual reading of Paul's continuous referencing of love in the entire chapter, and especially his identification of love in 13:4, for example, seems to contradict this claim distinguishing between love and the idea of love as a criterion. The idea of love as a criterion also needs to be confirmed. Therefore, it behooves us to now conduct extensive exegesis to find out if Bezuidenhout is correct in saying that love is a criterion for the functioning of the *charismata*. To be sure, major scholarship on this subject overwhelmingly agrees that love is a criterion for the functioning of the *charismata*.[7] But, because this was also the case for the so-called christological criterion, which this work has

---

4. Schrage, *Erste Brief an die Korinther*, 276–77.

5. Grosheide, *First Corinthians*, 303.

6. Bezuidenhout "Trinitarian Nature," 100–101.

7. Cf. for example, Dunn, *Christ and the Spirit*, 71, 159, 280; Schatzmann, *Pauline Theology*, 48; and Thiselton, *First Corinthians*, 1026.

revised, extensive analysis of 1 Corinthians 13 needs to be conducted before accepting such a conclusion.

5.2.1 Authentic revelatory claims must evidence love (1 Cor 13:1–3)

Through the continuous use of conditional cause-effect statements, Paul makes it clear that authentic revelatory claims—particularly, for example, those based in the *charismata* of tongues (1 Cor 13:1), prophecy (13:2), word of knowledge (13:2), and faith (13:2)—must include love. Here it appears that Paul is positing love as a criterion for the functioning of the *charismata*, in particular, and authentic spirituality, in general. And it would make sense because just as God is the Spirit, or God is Spirit (John 4:24), and manifestations of the Spirit such as the *charismata* reveal, communicate, and evidence participation in the things of God; God is also love (1 John 4:8, 16), and manifestations of this love should be revelatory of God. Still, a thorough exegesis of this chapter has just begun. Indeed, in 1 Corinthians 13:1–3 Paul concludes that one may speak in human or angelic tongues, but if there is no love involved, such speech amounts to mere noise. Likewise, one may prophesy, and be full of knowledge and faith, but without love such a person can be considered insignificant. One may even give away all their possessions, including their body, but without love nothing is gained. Summarily, human manifestations, without love, do not authentically reveal God, for they originate in the human spirit.

For Paul, love is a "more excellent way" than mere manifestations of "spiritual gifts" (1 Cor 12:31). But exactly what is this love Paul speaks of? And why is it a more excellent way than spiritual gifts? Does love render the *charismata* useless? In 1 Corinthians 13:4–7, Paul identifies love by offering both positive and negative expressions of the authentic nature or character of love. He says, "Love is patient, love is kind, not envious, love does not boast itself, or get puffed up. It does not act improperly, seek itself, provoke, nor does it think about what is evil. [Love] does not rejoice in unrighteousness but rejoices with the truth. It bears all, believes all, hopes all, and endures all."

Two positive expressions of the nature of love are identified as being patient and kind (1 Cor 13:4a). These expressions convey the necessary passive and active responses of love towards others, as well as the divine attitude toward humanity. On the one hand, God passively and patiently holds back his wrath towards rebellious humanity (Rom 5:9). But on the other hand, God actively shows kindness to all (Eph 2:7), including rebellious humanity.

Since love is patient and kind, expressions that do not evidence patience and kindness towards others should not be considered loving. Additional positive expressions of the nature of love include rejoicing with the truth, bearing all, believing all, hoping for all, and enduring all (1 Cor 13:6b–7).

Paul also identifies negative expressions that do not represent the nature of love. Among them are being boastful or puffed up, acting improperly, being self-seeking, provoking, thinking about evil, and rejoicing in unrighteousness (1 Cor 13:4b–6a). These negative expressions are not characteristic of love, or divine revelation, and are therefore not authentically "spiritual." But as our discussion of the 1 Corinthians context has made clear, these negative expressions were ongoing issues in the Corinthian church that motivated Paul's letter and his discussion of criteria for authentic spirituality—including defining the authentic nature of love.

Elsewhere, Paul considers love to be a summary of the whole Law of God in those who live by the Spirit (Gal 5:13–14) and not by the works of the flesh, human or natural inclinations (Gal 5:16–21). The works of the flesh are to be destroyed or discontinued (1 Cor 5:5). They include, but are not limited to, such things as fornication, drunkenness, licentiousness, idolatry, quarrels, and factions—all which Paul is also addressing in the 1 Corinthians epistle.[8] Contrary to the works of the flesh, Paul considers love a supernatural grace of God, for love is a fruit of the Spirit (Gal 5:22) evident in those who, like Christ, live and are guided by the Spirit (Gal 5:24–26).

Paul's identification of love as a fruit of the Spirit makes it clear that love is not among the *charismata*, and therefore should not be considered as the greatest of gifts of the Spirit. "Love is not set over against the gifts precisely because it belongs in a different category altogether . . . love is the way in which the gifts are to function."[9] For this same reason, love does not render the *charismata* useless. The *charismata* are to be sought out (1 Cor 12:31; 14:1), but they must be practiced in or evidence love (13:1–3; 14:1). In the context of Paul speaking primarily about spiritual gifts (1 Cor 12), then, it appears that love is to be considered a criterion for their functioning, because without love the *charismata*, and other "spiritual things" such as the giving of one's possessions and body (13:3), are inauthentic and spiritually bankrupt (13:1–3). It is in this sense of being a criterion for the *charismata* that love is a more excellent way than *charismata*, or gifts

---

8. The works of the flesh are not marks of authentic spirituality; thus, they are like the various spiritual issues Paul is addressing in 1 Corinthians and providing criteria for in chs. 12–14. For example, factions, jealousy, and quarrels are addressed in 1:10—4:21, while unrighteous acts such as idolatry, fornication and drunkenness are addressed in 5:1—6:20.

9. Fee, *First Corinthians*, 628.

of the Spirit. Moreover, this fruit of love is exemplified in the perfect life of Christ (2 Cor 5:21), who died for all so that humanity may also live selfless lives (2 Cor 5:14–15).

Christ's perfect love may cause one to wonder if they must be perfect to truly love. The writings of John Wesley speak to this issue. In his *A Plain Account of Christian Perfection*, Wesley writes to explain whether Christians are perfect or not. On the one hand, the Methodist founder says, "there is no perfection in this life as implies an entire deliverance, either from ignorance or mistake, in things not essential to salvation, or from manifold temptations, or from numberless infirmities, wherewith the corruptible body more or less presses down the soul."[10] There is also no "sinless perfection,"[11] for a person filled with the love of God is still liable to involuntarily transgress.[12] In other words, one can be filled with pure love and still be liable to mistakes.[13]

On the other hand, because of the grace of God, one does not have to commit sin. Therefore, it is important to note that, for Wesley, one "cannot infer . . . that all Christians do, and must commit sin, as long as they live."[14] Thus, Christians are "perfect," or relatively mature, in that they love God with their entire being and their "thoughts, words and actions are governed by pure love."[15]

Like the apostle Paul (1 Cor 12:31), Wesley considers love to be a "more excellent way" by which the *charismata* must function. For Wesley, love concerns being diligent to attain the whole mind of Christ, "a continuous course of self-denial," a striving for holiness of life, "leaving the first principles of the doctrine of Christ to go on to perfection," laboring in every way to be as Christ.[16]

Wesley's account of Christian perfection, then, makes clear that one does not have to be "perfect" or without sin to love. Rather, the one who loves does not continuously live by the flesh (Gal 5:16–23). Instead they continuously seek to live and be guided by the Spirit. A more nuanced, interpretation of Wesley, however, could also suggest that one must be "perfect" to truly love. Such perfection, however, obviously does not mean one

10. Wesley, *Plain Account*, 41. Cf. also pages 21–22.
11. Wesley, *Plain Account*, 66.
12. Wesley, *Plain Account*, 67.
13. Wesley, *Plain Account*, 67.
14. Wesley, *Plain Account*, 24.
15. Wesley, *Plain Account*, 62.
16. Taken from John Wesley's 1872 sermon 89, entitled "The More Excellent Way." Here Wesley is describing the love by which the gifts of God can be optimally manifested in the life of a Christian.

has never sinned or is presently sinless. Instead, those who are in Christ are considered perfect because of the substitutionary atoning work of Christ, who died to take away the sins of the world, rendering believers positionally holy or perfect (Rom 5:11–15, 18).

Out of this perfection, one can truly love. Thus, while *charismata* reveal God, fruit of the Spirit, such as love, reveals God as well as one's authentic spirituality. After all, it is by their fruit that one can tell who is authentically spiritual (Matt 7:15–20). And fruit of the Spirit such as love are only evident in authentic revelatory claims. Hence, a false prophet, for example, does not evidence the love that Paul is describing. It therefore stands to reason that those who claim revelatory experiences should also manifest the fruit of the Spirit, and love in particular.

This love that Paul describes in 1 Corinthians 13:4–7 is also considered to be personified in Christ by various commentators. For example, Nils Johansson says love equals Christ.[17] For Fee, love has been given concrete expression in the life, ministry, and death of Christ. Thus, one could substitute the name of Jesus for the noun "love."[18] Moreover, Thiselton appropriately notes that while it is inappropriate to read the Johannine notion that God is love (1 John 4:8, 16) onto Paul, the same notion is already there. This is because love, for Paul, is "profoundly christological" in that love denotes an attitude of "regard, respect, and concern for the welfare of the other," which is the essence of the cross.[19] Accepting that Paul's description of love is personified in Christ, and the notion that such love is a criterion for the functioning of the *charismata*, it should therefore be clear why 1 Corinthians 13, rather than 1 Corinthians 12:3, should be more appropriately considered the "christological criterion" for authentic spirituality.

To be sure, Paul's comments in 1 Corinthians 13:4–7, along with those of the contemporary scholars just cited, suggest that love is personified in Christ.[20] This is because Jesus is patient (Rev 1:9) and kind (Tit 3:4–6). And because he was sinless (2 Cor 5:21), Jesus was also not envious, boastful, selfish, or easily provoked, nor did he rejoice in unrighteousness. Instead, Jesus died on the cross, bearing all, believing all, hoping all, enduring all, so that whomever would believe in him could have eternal life (John 3:16). So, there is no greater example of love than Jesus' laying down his life for all (John 15:13).

---

17. Johansson, "1 Cor xiii and 1 Cor xiv."
18. Fee, *First Corinthians*, 628, 640.
19. Thiselton, *First Corinthians*, 1035.
20. Spicq, *Agape in the New Testament*, 150.

Another testament to love as being personified in Christ is implicit in Paul's saying that "love never fails" (1 Cor 13:8). By saying this, Paul is suggesting that love, like Christ, is eternal (1 John 5:20). The eternality of love is made clear because love is contrasted with the spiritual gifts of prophecy and tongues, which are temporal and will be discontinued (13:8–10). Love, however, which is personified in Christ, is the "end goal," and is eternal. Paul says, "love never fails. But as for prophecies, they will be discontinued, as for tongues, they will cease. As for knowledge, it will be discontinued, for we know in part, and we prophesy in part. But whenever the end goal comes, that which is in part will be discontinued." Despite an interpretation of "the end goal" to be Scripture by some who claim the *charismata* has ceased with the close of the canon of Scripture,[21] the context of 1 Corinthians suggests that Paul is referring to the *Parousia*, or second coming of Jesus Christ. Paul's reference to "the end goal" is also further affirmation of his Trinitarian hermeneutic—already described—in which he is now focusing on the love of Christ in 1 Corinthians 13.

5.2.2 Authentic revelation, lovingly, does not claim to know everything (13:8–12)

Paul's contrasting of the eternality of love with the temporality of the *charismata* (1 Cor 13:8) is elaborated upon in 13:9–12. Therein, Paul gives another principle for authentic revelatory claims. He explains, "we know in part and we prophesy in part" (13:9). This verifies that the temporal manifestation of gifts is only partially revelatory of the things of God, for gifts reveal the energies of God and not God's essence. When Jesus returns, temporal things such as the *charismata* will be discontinued (13:10). This *Parousia* signals the end of the temporal realm and the ushering in of the reign of Christ (1 Cor 15:22–25), when only the things that are eternal will last (1 Cor 15:50–55). It is only at the *Parousia* that Jesus Christ—indeed, the things of God—will be fully known. Implicit in these comments, then, is the principle that authentic revelation, lovingly, should not claim to know everything. For now we know only in part, and while the fruit of love is a more excellent way, in that love must accompany the practice of *charismata*, in the present dispensation—prior to the *Parousia*—gifts of the Spirit, being divine energies, are still not complete revelations of God.

Having now exegeted 1 Corinthians 13 to assess Bezuidenhout's "criterion of love," it can now be concluded that Bezuidenhout's distinction of Paul's message as being not about love per se, but of love as a criterion,

---

21. Cf. Unger, *New Testament Teaching on Tongues*, 96.

seems to be an unnecessary distinction since Paul talks about love, and love as a criterion that must be included with the proper functioning of the *charismata*. In fact, this may have been a false dichotomy, for it may be impossible to appropriately discuss the criterion of love without focusing on the specific topic of love and the *charismata*. Thus far, we have determined that the love Paul describes is a criterion for the functioning of the *charismata*. There is a caveat, however, for it is impossible to live up to such a standard of love without the work of the Spirit. Such a love can be manifested in whomever the Spirit wills (1 Cor 12:11), but is especially available to those who have accepted the substitutionary atoning work of Christ, and therefore are indwelt by the Spirit.

But even if this love of Christ is being manifested in one's life, can such a work of the Spirit be clearly discerned from other types of seemingly selfless acts that are not representative of the love of Christ? For example, when one seemingly loves something or someone, but purely out of selfish motives that are not easily discerned. Moreover, since one does not have to be sinless to love, and is positionally righteous, one could be functioning in love, but because of human infallibility, the love of God is not always easily discerned, and it may appear that one is not functioning in love. The point here is that the love of Christ is a principle for what is truly spiritual, but this love, at least by itself, like the *charismata*, is subjective and therefore should not be considered the criterion for the functioning of the *charismata*. Therefore, Paul inextricably links the *charismata* and love.

Therefore, we have derived at least two principles of authentic Christian living from 1 Corinthians 13. Indeed, for Paul, authentic revelatory claims must evidence love (13:1–3) and should not claim to know everything (13:8–12). These principles will now be analyzed to discover the major hermeneutical consideration that Paul has in putting forth his argument. Then, the entire pericope will be considered to see if this hermeneutical theme can be affirmed. Regardless of the outcome of this investigation, the hermeneutical consideration will be filtered through the lens of Paul's context to determine why he communicates the way he does.

5.3 Excursion 2: Paul's Contextual Theology

What is the hermeneutical consideration behind Paul's discussion of love? Answering this question demands a closer look at the principles that Paul has given for authentic spirituality. In 1 Corinthians 13:1–3 Paul makes it clear that revelatory experience, including the *charismata*, must evidence love. He says, for example, that one could speak in human or angelic tongues, but such speech, without love, is as noise (13:1). From this statement, it is observable that Paul acknowledges both human or natural, and divine or supernatural, ways of discussing charismatic activity. This is also indicated in 13:2 when Paul mentions mysteries and faith, which requires tacit and supernatural discernment (cf. 14:2).

To the contrary, a prophetic word, revelation, and the communication of knowledge are understandable with the natural senses (14:3, 6). These charismatic manifestations can be discerned either naturally or supernaturally, but they must evidence love to be truly revelatory of God. As already alluded to, this truth is also expressed in 1 Corinthians 14:1–3 and 6, where Paul expresses that spiritual gifts can be either edifying (e.g. prophecy)—in that they can be understood by natural means—or only discernible by supernatural means (e. g. tongues, mysteries), but they require love. Paul's allowing for both natural and supernatural ways of discerning authentic spirituality is also made explicit in 14:14–16, where he suggests that both the spirit (supernatural) and the mind (natural) should be productive, in terms of discerning *charismata*. Paul says, "I will pray with the spirit, but I will pray with the mind also; I will sing with the spirit, but I will sing praise with the mind also."

The second principle relative to love that Paul gives is that authentic *charismata*, lovingly, does not claim to know everything (1 Cor 13:8–12). For, while love is eternal (13:8), the *charismata* are temporal and partial expressions of the divine nature (13:9–10), and based on one's physical and/or spiritual development, they are likely to express and discern the *charismata* in different ways. Moreover, it is only at the *Parousia* that one will be truly able to claim absolute understanding of who God is (13:11–12). Therefore, charismatic practice and understanding should be grounded in the eternal principle of love (13:13). Accordingly, authentic *charismata* should not cause one to boast or pridefully insist on the authenticity of their revelatory claim (13:4–5). Instead, the one who is involved with the *charismata* rejoices only with what is true (13:6).

This principle that authentic *charismata*, lovingly, does not claim to know everything is also found in 1 Corinthians 12 and 14, where it is inferred that no one has absolute knowledge of what is truly spiritual. For example, in 12:12–13 Paul implies that all people impacted by the Spirit—whether Jew or Gentile, slaves or free (12:13, 15–17, 21–22)—can participate in the *charismata* and contribute to charismatic understanding. This also suggests that in terms of understanding the *charismata*, one ought to be open and accountable to feedback from all who are impacted by the Spirit. In fact, prophets should judge each other's charismatic expressions (14:29). And even those whom the culture deems to be less honorable should be treated with great respect (12:23). One does not have to be ordained, or even be a Christian, to offer valuable feedback concerning authentic spirituality (14:24–25).

The Pauline principle that the one who claims charismatic experience should not presume to have complete understanding of the things of God is also evidenced by Paul's continuous usage of questions in his communicating. For instance, in discussing the charismatic unity and diversity among believers, in 1 Corinthians 12:17, Paul asks, "if the whole body is an eye, where is the hearing?" In 12:19 and 29, respectively, referring to the various gifted members of the church, the questions are posed: "if all these were one member, where is the body?" "Are all apostles? Are all prophets? Are all teachers? Are all miracle workers?" Then in 14:36 the disruptive Corinthian women are asked, "did the word of God come out from you, or come upon you only?" These various questions make it clear that Paul is engaged in a dialogue with the cosmopolitan Corinthian church regarding criteria for authentic spirituality. And because of the recognition of the variety of individuals activated by the Spirit, it is implicit that Paul wants the Corinthians to be open and accountable to feedback from all such dialogue partners.

Paul's further questioning in 1 Corinthians 14 suggests that he wants the Corinthians to be open to both natural and supernatural ways of discerning the *charismata*. This is evident, for example, in 14:6–9, where Paul rhetorically encourages both tongues—which require supernatural discernment—as well as revelation, knowledge, prophecy, and teaching—which are understandable by natural means. In 14:15 and 16, Paul encourages rational praying and singing with the mind, as well as supernatural praying and singing with the spirit. In 14:23 Paul's question suggests that the supernaturally understood speaking in tongues, alone in the congregation, is not edifying and in the fullest spirit of love, because unbelievers and outsiders cannot understand it. Instead, it is more loving to prophesy because the natural mind of those hearing can hold the word to account and discern or authenticate its usefulness (14:24). Finally, in 14:26 Paul's question-and-answer complement implies that charismatic activity involves both natural and supernatural elements which are requisite for the edification of the hearers.

Therefore, Paul's principles regarding love suggest that authentic spirituality must evidence love and not claim to communicate knowledge of the absolute essence of God. For that reason, Paul communicates to the pluralistic church of Corinth in at least three ways. First, he employs a continuous series of questions and answers. Second, he is open to rational or philosophical ways of knowing things as well as tacit and supernatural knowledge such as that derived from faith. Finally, Paul is welcoming of truth from various sources, for example, regardless of race, gender, ethnicity, or even religious background. Considering this, it can be said that Paul adopts a contextual approach in his communication.[22] In fact, the occasional nature of the 1 Corinthians epistle suggest that it is contextual, for out of love Paul is communicating with the Corinthians to address their specific spiritual issues, or contextual needs. His hermeneutic takes into consideration the particularity of their context and adapts to the occasion.

Thus, Paul proclaims his message in a variety of ways to effectively speak to those in his context (1 Cor 9:22; 10:33). This contextual hermeneutic is apparently like the "global theology" discussed by Amos Yong and Peter Heltzel. In this way of thinking, "theological issues and questions [can] be broached from as many vantage points and perspectives as possible. Each approach will shed light on the issue at hand and will correct other viewpoints, even as it is itself corrected and supplemented by other approaches."[23] Paul does not change his Christian message, but he lovingly and consciously makes it relevant for the Corinthians.

5.4 What Is the Reason for Paul's Contextual Theology?

Perhaps Paul's being contextual was unavoidable because of the pluralistic nature of the Corinthian church. Regardless of whether this statement is true, in the first place, it is fair to say that Paul had to strike the right balance between his message and a pastoral sensitivity to his Gentile converts. For, despite the fact that his Gentile converts were accustomed to Hellenistic religion (1 Cor 12:2)—which assumed that a criterion for revelation is a suspension of the rational for the ecstatic or supernatural—Paul's gospel included the supernatural as well as the natural, or rational (14:15). Correspondingly, Paul wants the Corinthians to know that truly spiritual things cannot be separated from the historic Jesus (12:1–3), and while he prescribes that one seeks spiritual gifts, he is careful to explain that the manifestation of such gifts should be inseparably linked with the evidence of love (12:31).

Second, Paul considers all Christians—whether they are Jews, Greeks, male, females, slaves, or free persons, that is, regardless of their socioeconomic status, gender, and nationality—because the same Spirit of God indwells them—to be valid and valuable sources of knowledge concerning God. Therefore, what God has revealed to any Christian is of some significance (12:13, 21–22). And revelatory claims are accountable to, and should be in dialogue with, what God has revealed to other believers, irrespective of their

22. cf. Beker, *Paul the Apostle*, 38.
23. Yong, Heltzel, *Theology in Global Context*, 38.

backgrounds, and especially in light of human fallibility and the communication process—in which language is incapable of completely conveying ones thought, leaving one's hearer with only an approximation of one's thought. Such "'epistemic humility' . . . recognizes the fallibility of human cognition without denying the import of religious truth,"[24] and implies that everyone impacted by the Spirit is potentially an equal dialogue partner.

But what does it mean to be impacted by the Spirit? Does being impacted by the Spirit mean that one must be a Christian? Are Christians to be the only dialog partners concerning the truth of God? Apparently not, for the love of Christ demands that there be dialogue with any source of truth (1 Cor 13:6b–7). Moreover, if all truth is God's truth, then one should be open to truth from whomever, and in whatever way God chooses to reveal it. Thus, the Protestant Reformer John Calvin remarks, "if we regard the Spirit of God as the sole fountain of truth, we shall neither reject the truth itself, nor despise it wherever it shall appear, unless we wish to dishonor the Spirit of God."[25] Paul apparently understood such a principle, for he dialogued with Corinthians from the East (e.g. Jews), West (e.g. Graeco-Romans), and South (Africa/Egypt), and acknowledged both natural and supernatural ways of knowing things. He did not separate religion from philosophy or culture.

Regardless of who is being dialogued with and the source of the truth, dialogue should be conducted in such a way as to be edifying to the people of God (1 Cor 14:1–6),[26] as well as unbelievers (14:23–25). Thus, Paul highlights that unbelievers have access to and are present in the gathering of the Corinthian church. These unbelievers can discern if a revelatory claim is authentic (14:25). But their discernment is only possible because Paul and the Corinthians are open to the presence and participation of unbelievers—when they practice their spiritual gifts in a loving and edifying manner. Then, the unbeliever can comprehend divine revelation and become affected by it to the end that they might become repentant towards God (14:25). Considering this, it appears that, for Paul, practicing the *charismata* and love are inextricably linked with each other, being Trinitarian and contextual. If this is true, it is also reasonable to say that being contextual is a principle for communicating the revelation of God.

A final reason why Paul employs a contextual hermeneutic is that he expects authentic spirituality to be accountable to feedback. This is made clear when he suggests that revelatory dialogue is to be judged by those

---

24. Yong, *Theology in Global Context*, 39.

25. Calvin, *Institutes of Christian Religion*, 1.2.11.15.

26. This concept of edification will be discussed extensively in the next chapter, on the criterion of edification.

who hear it (1 Cor 14:29). This judgment is part of the process by which all may be able to learn and be encouraged from charismatic activity (14:31)—believers and unbelievers alike (14:23–25). This begs the question, what is acceptable feedback? For Paul, such feedback is revealed by the Spirit (2:13), and must be proper and according to order, so that all may be edified (14:26, 40). It is accountable to the charismatic community of believers (14:23–25) and consistent with the word of God (14:21, 34). Acceptable feedback, then, requires the same criteria as authentic spirituality.

5.5 Conclusion

Bezuidenhout is right that 1 Corinthians 13 focuses on love as a criterion for the functioning of the *charismata*. In fact, for Paul, authentic spirituality must evidence love and not claim absolute knowledge of God. The evidence of love is required because charismatic activity, without the fruit of love, does not authentically reveal the character of God. And while the *charismata* are temporal, like the Godhead, in general, and Christ, in particular, love is eternal. In fact, the love that Paul describes in 1 Corinthians 13 is personified in Christ, who is "the exact imprint of God's very being" (Heb 1:3). Therefore, 1 Corinthians 13 should be properly considered the christological criterion. But because of the subjectivity involved in determining what truly represents the love of Christ, love, at least not by itself, should not be considered the criterion for authentic spirituality. This love, however, is clearly among the principles of genuine Christian living, including the proper functioning of the *charismata*.

The principle that authentic revelatory claims, lovingly, do not claim absolute knowledge relative to the things of God is true for at least two reasons. The first is because human beings and the communication process are fallible. The other reason concerns the nature of the *charismata*. Being divine energies, gifts of the Spirit are not complete revelations of God. Thus, out of love for others, authentic claims to revelation should not suggest their manifestation is absolute truth representative of the essence of God. Instead of claiming absolute knowledge, the one who practices and/or seek to discern authentic spirituality will seek and rejoice only in what is truth and allow the Spirit of God to bear witness to the hearts and minds of individuals.

This study has also shown that Paul communicates his criterion for authentic spirituality in his pluralistic context in a contextual way. This is demonstrated in at least three ways. First, Paul repeatedly allows for both natural and supernatural ways of discerning *charismata*. Second, Paul encourages openness and accountability to feedback from a variety of sources of truth. Finally, Paul continuously asks questions and provides answers as he discusses spiritual things so that his audience is aware that he is in dialogue with them.

Paul adapts this contextual mode of communicating for a variety of reasons. For example, he wants to counterbalance the pagan background of the Corinthians from which they generally shunned rational ways of knowing things in favor of what is supernatural. The latter pursuit could provide for things they desire in this life such as healing and a means of self-exaltation. Instead, Paul presents a balanced and ontological epistemology that considers both the natural and supernatural ways of knowing things.

Another reason why Paul is contextual in his communication is that he wants to express that everyone impacted by the Spirit is potentially an equal dialog partner from whom much of the revelation of God can be gleaned. Third, Paul is emphatic that everything must be done for the edification of all. And this requires that the *charismata* be practiced in a way that believers and unbelievers alike can understand and benefit from the revelation of God. Finally, for Paul authentic spirituality occurs when there is accountability to feedback from all who are impacted by the Spirit.

With this principle of love and Paul's contextual hermeneutic in mind, and considering the discussion on 1 Corinthians 12, as well as the previous chapter on revelatory criteria in the OT, it can now be posited that a manifestation of the Spirit is required in authentic revelatory claims, but such manifestation must also be inseparably linked to the love of Christ. Additionally, theological communication, especially considering a pluralistic setting, must be Trinitarian as well as contextual in nature. Stated differently, authentic spiritual claims exhibit both the gifts and the fruit of the Spirit—love, in particular. And such claims are accountable to feedback from an authenticating community. In this way, authentic revelatory claims allow the Spirit to be revealed as the Spirit wills. To further elucidate this concept, the text of 1 Corinthians 14 and Bezuidenhout's criterion of edification will now be considered.

Chapter 6

The Criterion of Edification (1 Cor 14:1–40)

6.1 Introduction

According to Bezuidenhout, "the criterion of the edification of the assembly is the normative basis from which the practice of the *charismata* is judged in 1 Corinthians 14."[1] This conclusion is reached primarily because of the repeated use of the root *oikodomē* ("edification"), which appears seven times throughout the chapter.[2] These appearances will be elaborated on below, for it is the task of this chapter to assess, in dialogue with Bezuidenhout and others, this "criterion of edification" relative to the functioning of the *charismata*. This study will also try to determine if there are other such criteria and/or principles for authentic spirituality in 1 Corinthians 14. Because of their repeated use throughout this work, it is important to formally note here a subtle distinction between the terms "criterion" and "principle." I am using the term criterion to mean a "fixed norm," while a principle reflects "broad trajectories."[3] If there are criteria or principles, they will be identified and discussed to find out the major hermeneutical consideration Paul has in writing 1 Corinthians 14. This hermeneutic will then be analyzed considering the overall 1 Corinthians context to understand more clearly how, and why, Paul communicates the things he does to the pluralistic church. Subsequently, conclusive comments will be given.

---

1. Bezuidenhout, "Trinitarian Nature," 102.
2. Cf. 14:3, 4 (2x), 5, 12, 17, 26.
3. Van der Watt, *Identity, Ethics, and Ethos*, vii.

6.2 Authentic Revelation through Tongues Is Not Spoken to People, but to God (1 Cor 14:2)

In 1 Corinthians 14:1, Paul brings to climax his arguments from the previous two chapters. He exhorts, "pursue love, and passionately seek spiritual things [*pneumatika*], and even more that you may prophesy." The use of two present active imperatival verbs (*diōkete*—"pursue," and *zēloute*—"passionately seek") makes clear that Paul wants the Corinthian believers to continue pursuing or seeking spiritual things—including the *charismata*—and love collectively, and even more that they may prophesy (14:1). In his effort to offer criteria or a criterion for what is authentically spiritual, Paul seems to have arrived at a triadic formula. That is, for one to be truly considered "spiritual," or for a revelatory claim to be considered authentic, there must be a manifestation of spiritual gifts, the presence of love, and "prophesying." While spiritual gifts and love have been discussed at length, the third part of this formula, relative to prophesying, is yet to be discussed in detail, so we will turn to that now.

Paul's use of the conjunction "for" (*gar*) in 1 Corinthians 14:2 makes it explicit that vv. 2–4, and as will become clear, the entire chapter, is an explanation of why one should pursue spiritual things—including the *charismata*—and love, and even more that they may prophesy (14:1). Having already explicated the requisite and inseparable principles of the manifestation of spiritual gifts and love for authentic revelatory claims, Paul is about to explain why it is even more essential that one prophesy by particularly contrasting the gift of tongues with prophecy.

For Paul, the spiritual gift of tongues is used mysteriously to speak with God in the spirit (1 Cor 14:2). When this occurs, one's mind is unfruitful or does not understand the communication (14:14). It has even been considered a criterion that authentic revelation through tongues should not be spoken to people, but to God (1 Cor 14:2).[4] Perhaps this is because it is usually understandable if one is claiming to speak in tongues to God or humans. However, because speaking to God is a personal and subjective experience, this statement of Paul, relative to speaking in tongues, should not be considered a criterion. Rather, it is a principle for communicating authentic spirituality, since it can only convincingly determine inauthentic tongues speech (spoken to humans).

In view of this, if one claims to have a revelation from God, in tongues, but communicates it to a fellow human being (without interpretation), such a claim should be considered inauthentic. Likewise, as will be discussed at

---

4. Fee, *Paul, the Spirit*, 148.

length in discussing implications of criteria for authentic spirituality on the contemporary worship service, it seems that any notion that everyone should have the gift of tongues—as is often believed, for example, among many Pentecostals—is to be discredited since it is not a requirement for all to speak in tongues (12:30). *Charismata* are allotted to individuals as the Spirit wills (12:11). But what is the relationship between speaking in tongues and Paul's command to pursue and passionately seek to prophesy?

6.3 Authentic Revelation through Prophecy Should Be for Edification, Encouragement, and Comfort (14:3-4)

In 1 Corinthians 14:3-4, Paul contrasts the one who speak in tongues with the one who prophesies. The one who speak in uninterpreted tongues does not speak to people but speaks mysteries in the Spirit to God (14:2), thereby directly edifying only themselves (14:4a). This will be further expounded below. However, for Paul, the one who prophesies receives a revelation (14:30) that "speaks edification, encouragement, and comfort" (14:3) to the church (14:4b). That is, authentic prophecy accomplishes these three things in others (14:3), and in the Corinthian context prophecy builds up the church (14:4). In still other words, if a prophetic claim is not edifying, encouraging, and comforting to those hearing it, such a claim should not be considered authentically spiritual. It is not revelatory of God. To determine if this principle regarding prophecy should be considered a criterion for authentic spirituality, it is now important to more clearly understand what Paul means by the terms "edifying," "encouraging," and "comforting."

"Edification" (*oikodomē*) is a spiritual strengthening,[5] or a "building up in mutuality for the benefit of the whole."[6] It has already been suggested that edification is a repeated theme in 1 Corinthians 14, but in her book *Paul and the Rhetoric of Reconciliation*, Margaret Mitchell shows that edification is also a theme throughout the entire 1 Corinthians epistle.[7] This makes sense since Paul is addressing various spiritual things for the purpose of spiritually strengthening the Corinthians, especially in terms of their discarding of the self-exalting ethos of their pagan background and becoming considerate of others. Edification, then, is exclusive of things that are detrimental to the community. To the contrary, it involves things that help and mutually support the community.[8] Edification, however, is also an ambiguous notion, for it is

---

5. BAGD, 696.
6. Thiselton, *First Corinthians*, 901. See also Gillespie, *First Theologians*, 129–64.
7. Mitchell, *Paul and the Rhetoric of Reconciliation*, 241, 248, 256, 258–83.
8. Vielhauer, *Oikodome*, 91–98.

not always apparent when one is being spiritually strengthened. And even when one appears to be edified, they may not have been.

Having now defined what it means to edify, Paul's message in that regard can be put in greater perspective. For Paul, those who are authentically spiritual should seek to spiritually strengthen the church (1 Cor 14:12). For, while knowledge makes one prideful, love, in contrast, spiritually strengthens (8:1). As it is with love, authentic prophecy spiritually strengthens the hearer (14:3), both those who are part of the church (14:4) as well as unbelievers (14:24–25). Also, uninterpreted tongues do not spiritually strengthen others (14:17). But interpreted tongues can spiritually strengthen the church (14:5). In brief, when the church meets, all things are to be for edification, or spiritual strengthening (14:26). Even if something is lawful, if it is not spiritually strengthening, one should not do it (10:23).

The second requirement for authentic prophecy is *paraklēsin* or "encouragement" (1 Cor 14:3). This is an act that emboldens one in their belief or course of action.[9] In fact, all those who devote themselves to serve the believers should be emboldened in their faith and course of action (16:15–16). Unfortunately, however, one can be emboldened by what is not necessarily of God. For example, prophets can embolden the people of God with their dreams, even though the Lord did not send them (Jer 23:32). Regardless, for Paul, as an apostle, even when others are slanderous and abusive, he is to encourage them on in the faith (4:13). Such encouragement is to be imitated by the Corinthians (4:16).

The third feature of authentic prophecy in 1 Corinthians 14 is that it "comforts" (*paramuthian*). This signifies a consoling or encouraging of one who is depressed or in grief.[10] Elsewhere, Paul uses the word "comfort" in describing his actions toward Thessalonian believers who are not "living a life worthy of God" (1 Thess 2:11). Paul recognizes that when one is not living worthy of God, they can be depressed and in grief. But authentic prophecy can console and comfort such people, whether they are believers or not (1 Cor 14:24–25).

One can therefore conclude that in 1 Corinthians 14:3–4 Paul is saying that authentic claims to prophecy should spiritually strengthen, embolden the church in their belief or course of action, and console or encourage the depressed and grieving individual. But because of the ambiguities and subjectivity involved with determining if one is spiritually strengthened, emboldened, and encouraged, Paul's statement concerning prophecy is to be considered a principle for authentic revelatory claims instead of a criterion.

9. BAGD, 766.
10. BAGD, 769.

In 1 Corinthians 14:5–14 Paul continues to explain that speaking in tongues is important and worthy of one being zealous for, but it is even more significant when one prophesies—unless the tongue is interpreted so that the church can have understanding and be edified or spiritually strengthened by it (14:5). So, it is not that the gift of prophecy is essentially greater than the gift of tongues. For Paul, what is significant is the edification of the church (14:12). Intelligible speech like prophecy, as well as a revelation, knowledge, and teaching, can edify, but unintelligible speech like an uninterpreted tongue, though it has value for the individual, will not spiritually strengthen the community when it is spoken to them (14:6). Even the Law suggests that the people of God will not listen to unintelligible tongues (14:21).

Because of the inherent value of both the gift of tongues and the gift of prophecy, however, Paul will practice both (1 Cor 14:15). The gift of tongues is valuable because it is used to give thanks to God, and the gift of prophecy is valuable because it edifies the community—the church (14:12, 17, and 19). When the community gathers together, they should not publicly speak in uninterpreted tongues, for even laypeople and unbelievers might consider such an act insane (14:23). To the contrary, when the community gathers together and everyone prophesies, even the layperson and unbeliever can affirm if the prophecy is a revelation from God (14:24–25). Implicit in this observation is the principle that prophecy, along with the requirement that it be edifying to the church, should also be accountable to an authenticating community. Prophecy that is both edifying and accountable is a mark of authentic spirituality.

6.4 All Revelatory Claims Should Be for Edification (1 Cor 14:26–36)

In 1 Corinthians 14:26–36, Paul explains that authentically spiritual things, or all authentic revelatory claims, including those involving gifts of the Spirit like tongues and prophecy, whether intelligible or not, when done in the assembly, should be for edification. This premise is expressed in 14:26 and expounded in 14:27–36. There Paul provides two principles regarding the gifts of tongues and prophecy: tongues should be silenced in public if there is no interpreter (14:28), and a prophet's spirit should be subject to the prophet (14:32).

6.4.1 Authentic revelation through tongues should be silent if there is no interpreter (14:28)

Relative to the notion of tongues being silent in public if there is no interpreter, in 1 Corinthians 14:27–28 Paul makes clear that speaking in tongues should be done in an orderly manner with speakers taking turns, and there must be an interpretation of such tongues so that the church may be edified. If there is no interpreter, the spiritual person should not share their tongues with the church, but quietly speak to themselves and to God (v.28). This is because the church does not understand what is being communicated and therefore cannot be edified—though the individual's spirit is edified (14:4).

6.4.2 In an authentic revelation, a prophet's spirit should be subject to the prophet (14:32)

The principle that a prophet's spirit should be subject to the prophet is explained in 1 Corinthians 14:29–33. Two or three prophets can speak—one at a time—and others should judge the prophecy so that all may learn and be encouraged as order and peace is maintained in the church (vv. 29–33). Fee appropriately notes that "prophecies did not have independent authority in the church, but must always be the province of the corporate body."[11] So, just as tongues need to be interpreted in the public, prophecy needs to be judged or authenticated by the community. This is because the one who is truly spiritual has not lost control of their prophetic spirit (14:32), and prophecy, like all spiritual things, should be done in an orderly manner, for the edification of the church (14:12, 26, 40). Thus, it would be inauthentic for a believer to claim a prophetic revelation when they are not in control of themselves or what they were saying. For Paul, even the Law makes this clear (14:34).

It is noteworthy that to communicate the last two principles for authentic spirituality, instead of relying solely on his "eloquent wisdom" (1:17; 2:1–7), Paul dialogues with, and resorts to, the authority of the Law to make his case (cf. 1 Cor 14:21, 34). The Law that Paul refers to consists of teachings of the OT, or Hebrew Bible, relative to the revelation of God and God's purposes for humanity. This Law was handed down through Jewish tradition, and includes teachings that were either recorded by, or chronicled the

---

11. Fee, *First Corinthians*, 694.

lives of, various Hebrew authority figures, including kings,[12] prophets,[13] and priests.[14] Paul's referencing the Law is consistent with what has already been said in our discussion of revelatory criteria in the OT, for Paul's understanding of the revelation of God is in direct continuity with the OT. Thus, he continuously cites these religious authorities throughout the 1 Corinthians epistle.[15] In light of this, and because the Law is used to directly defend the "criterion of edification," Paul's third major hermeneutical consideration will now be considered before addressing two other principles relative to the "criterion of edification." As was the case for the previous two hermeneutical considerations, it will first be determined what is behind the principles that Paul gives by examining the immediate context (ch. 14), then that of the 1 Corinthians 12–14 pericope, before also discussing why Paul deemed such a hermeneutic to be necessary.

6.5 Excursion 3: Paul's Traditional Theology

Paul's reliance on the authority of the Law is evident throughout 1 Corinthians 14. One evidence of this is in 14:3, where he says, "the one who prophesies to men speaks edification, encouragement, and comfort." This principle is reflective of the OT tradition of prophecy being a word from God reflecting God's fatherly concerns for his people.[16] Indeed, David Aune has shown that the Pauline understanding of prophecy—as an edifying word of God—is based on the OT prophetic role.[17] In other words, as already alluded to, the prophesying that Paul speaks of in 14:3 can be correctly related to OT tradition.

Second, in 1 Corinthians 14:5, Paul's wishing that all the Corinthians could prophesy is rooted in the biblical text of Numbers 11:29, where Moses corrected Joshua's implicit suggestion that only Moses should prophesy to the people of God. Joshua asked Moses to forbid the prophesying of the elders Eldad and Medad among the people of Israel. But Moses replied, "would God that all the Lord's people were prophets, and that the Lord would put his Spirit upon them!" Just as Moses wanted the people of God to

12. For example, 1 and 2 Kings and Chronicles, as well as some psalms written by King David and perhaps Proverbs and the Songs of King Solomon.
13. For example, 1 and 2 Samuel, Isaiah–Malachi.
14. For example, Ezra.
15. Cf. 1 Cor 1:19; 2:9; 6:1–7; 9:9; 10:1–14; 15:1–4, 45, 54, 56.
16. Thiselton, *First Corinthians*, 1089. Cf. Jer 1:10; 11:1–8; 29:10–15; Isa 11:1–5; 48:16–20; 59:21; 61:1; 2 Sam 23:2–4.
17. Aune, *Prophecy in Early Christianity*, 195.

prophesy, Paul wants the Corinthian believers to practice the *charismata* so that the people of God will be edified.

Third, Paul's citation of the "Law" in 1 Corinthians 14:21 is a reference to Isaiah 28:11–12 and is an attempt to express that uninterpreted tongues are not comprehensible to the people of God, and are therefore not edifying, for they cannot lead to their obeying God. This citation, however, is not precise since it does not completely agree with either the Greek Septuagint—which is the Greek translation of the OT—or the Hebrew Masoretic Texts (MT)—which is the authoritative Hebrew text of the OT.[18] Even though 14:21 is not in complete agreement with either the Greek or Hebrew texts of the OT, its citation shows that the OT remained authoritative for Paul, who is combining exegesis and application of the text to make his point.

Such joining of exegesis and application is consistent with the thought of Gadamer, who, in the more contemporary context, explains that these two components of the hermeneutical process cannot be separated because the understanding one derives from exegesis, for example, is determined by the application they make.[19] Moreover, understanding is participating in an event of tradition,[20] for it cannot be separated from one's historical situation and their historically effected consciousness.[21] In other words, tradition is an unavoidable partner in dialogue.[22] For Gadamer, however, this affirmation of tradition does not mean that one has blind obedience to it.[23] Rather, the authority of tradition is earned when it has constantly proven itself by allowing something true to come into being. The acceptance of tradition is therefore "reasonable and is based on knowledge that the other is superior in judgment and insight."[24] From this perspective, tradition is to be considered the ground of validity. Paul's repeated use of tradition evidences his validation of it.

A fourth evidence of Paul's validation of OT tradition is found in 1 Corinthians 14:23–25, where Paul rationalizes that prophecy should be both convicting of and accountable to the ones who hear it. Additionally, the one who is truly spiritual should discern what the Spirit is revealing. This reasoning is consistent with the OT view of prophecy as an inspired word that exposes one

---

18. Cf. Aune, *Prophecy in Early Christianity*, 679–80; Thiselton, *First Corinthians*, 1120–22; or Garland, *1 Corinthians*, 646–47, for a discussion of the various points of disagreement.

19. Gadamer, *Truth and Method*, 321 and 336.

20. Gadamer, *Truth and Method*, 291.

21. Gadamer, *Truth and Method*, 299–300.

22. Gadamer, *Truth and Method*, 352.

23. Gadamer, *Truth and Method*, 281.

24. Gadamer, *Truth and Method*, 281.

to their need for repentance before God. But Fee is only partially correct when he suggests that Paul's saying, "falling upon his face he will worship God while announcing that 'God is really in you'" (14:25)—concerning the unbeliever who hears the prophetic word—signifies conversion.[25]

On the one hand, Fee is correct in saying the statement is "a conscious reflection of Isaiah 45:14," where it is prophesied that unbelieving Egypt, and Ethiopia, as well as the Sabeans, will convert and bow down before believing Israel acknowledging God as Savior (45:15). On the other hand, however, repentance, in the 1 Corinthians 14:25 context, for example, could be either the conversion of an unbeliever or the changing of heart of a believing layperson (*idiōtēs*). Though the word *idiōtēs* is interpreted as "unbeliever" by commentators such as Fee,[26] Keener,[27] and Garland,[28] based on 14:16—where the context is edification of the church, or believers (c.f., 14:12)—Paul uses the same word, *idiōtēs*, to discuss a member of the church. This is one reason why, herein, *idiōtēs* is interpreted as "layperson," who, for whatever reason, does not perceive what is going on when one exercise tongues without its interpretation (14:16).

Further, in the same verse, Paul does not use the word *apistos* (unbelievers) alongside *idiōtēs* as he does in verses 23–24. In the latter verses, Paul is discussing both the layperson as well as unbelievers. This is because when Paul mentions the *idiōtēs* (vv. 23–24) he is carefully considering a situation where unbelievers could "enter" (*eiselthē*) the church. For example, in verse 23 Paul asks, "therefore, if the whole church should come together and everyone should speak in tongues, and a layman or unbelievers should enter, will they not say you are insane?" Then, in verse 24 he says, "but if all should prophesy, and someone who does not believe, or a layman should come in, he is reproved by all, and examined by all." In other words, the *idiōtēs* are outsiders and unbelievers who do not belong to the congregation and need to enter the church. This was not the case for the *idiōtēs* in 14:16 (who, again, based on the context, is a non-perceiving member of the church).

Finally, Paul's use of the conjunction *ḗ* ("or"), as in *apistos ḗ idiōtēs* ("unbeliever or layman") is a "marker of an alternative" among two mutually exclusive items.[29] Therefore, contrary to the assertion of the scholars just mentioned, *apistos ḗ idiōtēs* does not refer to the same thing (unbeliever). And, for Paul, then, repentance before God is proper for believers

---

25. Fee, *First Corinthians*, 687.
26. Fee, *First Corinthians*, 684.
27. Keener, *1–2 Corinthians*, 114.
28. Garland, *1 Corinthians*, 651.
29. BAGD, 432.

and unbelievers alike. Both sets of people are prone to sin and need God's grace. Indeed, Spirit-led "prophecy both edifies God's people and leads to the conversion of others."[30]

Paul's final referencing of the Law in 1 Corinthians 14 is found in verses 34–36 and seems to affirm the subordination of women in the churches. Paul says, "let the women be silent in the churches" (v. 34). In regard to these verses, two major views will be mentioned here and this subject will be dealt with in detail when the implications of Paul's criteria for authentic spirituality in the contemporary worship service are discussed.

On the one hand, commentators such as Barrett, Conzelmann, Fee, and Andreas Lindemann consider these verses an interpolation by a non-Pauline author.[31] For Lindemann, this interruption occurred in a "very early copy."[32] Conzelmann says, "this self-contained section upsets the context: it interrupts the theme of prophecy and spoils the flow of thought."[33] Fee considers the verses to be an interpolation because they do not meet the text-critical criteria of being intrinsically probable.[34] For Fee, the content of the verses does not fit in with the present argument regarding manifestations of the Spirit in the worshipping community.[35] Furthermore, for Fee, the author is restricting women from joining in the worship, 1 Corinthians 14:34 is a rule for all the churches, and the Law affirms the restriction on women.[36]

But these assertions do not seem to correlate with the context of the verses in which Paul is talking about the need for edification in the manifestation of all gifts of the Spirit (1 Cor 14:26). Neither is there any exegetical support for claiming Paul is restricting women from joining in the worship. To be sure, Paul is focusing on the need for edification and order, thus he commands that authentic manifestations of the Spirit, in tongues, should be communicated in turn (14:27), and if there is no interpreter, the one who speaks in tongues should be silent in the church (14:28). Likewise, prophecy should be spoken in turn, others should judge it, and if another has a manifestation of the Spirit, they should first be silent and wait their turn to speak so that all may benefit from the prophecy (14:29–31). Stated differently, the one who is truly spiritual, unless

30. Fee, *First Corinthians*, 687.

31. Fee, *First Corinthians*, 707–8; Barrett, *First Corinthians*, 332–33; Conzelmann, *1 Corinthians*, 246; and Lindemann, *Erste Korintherbrief*, 316–21.

32. Lindemann, *Erste Korintherbrief*, 320–21.

33. Conzelmann, *1 Corinthians*, 246.

34. Fee, *First Corinthians*, 699. Barrett, *First Corinthians*, 332–33; and Conzelmann, *1 Corinthians*, 246, also share this view.

35. Fee, *First Corinthians*, 701–2.

36. Fee, *First Corinthians*, 707–8.

their speech is edifying, should remain silent and exercise their gift in an orderly manner in the church, for they should be in control of their spirit (14:32). This principle of all things in the church being done in order and for edification is applicable to all the churches (14:33).

So, when Paul commands the women to be silent in the churches, and be subject according to the Law (1 Cor 14:34), he is not absolutely restricting women from speaking in the church. It is not a criterion of authentic spirituality that women should be silent in church—unless they are being disruptive. If absolute silence on the part of women was a criterion for authentic spirituality, Paul would be contradicting himself, for he has already allowed for women to pray[37] and prophesy in the church (11:5)— although in the Corinthian context, such women should be veiled or they risk signaling a lack of respectability and sexual availability, since cultic prostitutes wore unveiled hair. Nonetheless, Paul is using an example of disorder (14:33) that should be controlled to make his point for all things in the church being done for edification. Again, he is not prescribing that all women should be silent in the church. Rather, he is further expanding the topic of order in the churches and citing the universal principle that manifestation of the Spirit in the church should be in order and for edification, even as the Law affirms (14:34).

These Corinthian women need to be in order because they seem to have been involved in some form of disruptive speech.[38] They were speaking, and not being silent or orderly, and asking questions (14:35), rightly exercising their need to judge or discern prophetic speech (cf. 14:29). But even such speech needs to be in order, or done in turn. The women need to be silent, subject to the principle of edification and order that the Law affirms, even as men are required to be.[39] Otherwise, they should speak at home (14:35), just as uninterpreted tongues should not be exercised in the congregation, but in privacy (14:5–6). Therefore, the issue in 14:34 is not gender, or "speech," but the "abuse of speech."[40] It is people who speak out of turn that should be silent, and not women in general. This conclusion is consistent with the socially inclusive Christian ethos that allows for all to be represented in Christ. Graeco-Roman social stratification, on

---

37. The use of "pray" here could be a metonymy for tongues, because uninterpreted tongues, according to Paul, are spoken to God (14:2), and edify the individual (14:4), just as prayer does.

38. Sevenster, *Paul and Seneca*, 198 (see Fee, *First Corinthians*, 703); Bruce, *1 & 2 Corinthians*, 135; and Barrett, *First Corinthians*, 332.

39. Kistemaker, *First Corinthians*, 512; and Witherington, *Women in the Earliest Churches*, 102–3.

40. Witherington, *Women in the Earliest Churches*, 104.

the other hand, suggested that only males have authority in the public sphere,[41] while females could exercise authority—on behalf of male head of households—only in private domain (including the right to publicly function in the *charismata*). This, of course, would preclude women from prophesying in the worship service.

The other major view regarding 1 Corinthians 14:34–36, and the one that this study affirms, disagrees with the above-mentioned theory of interpolation. This alternative view considers the verses a part of "pre-Pauline tradition which Paul accepts and adapts."[42] Proponents of this view argue that the objections of interpolation theorists such as Fee are cleared up with patient exegesis.[43] Such exegesis has shown that in these verses Paul is simply encouraging controlled speech, including manifestations of the gifts of the Spirit, that is edifying for the church. This kind of "controlled speech reflects the traditions of the Bible, the synagogue, and the early churches."[44]

Paul's referencing the authority of such traditions is also evident in 1 Corinthians 12 and 13. This is seen, for example, in 1 Corinthians 12:2–3, where Paul, to inform the Corinthians about authentic spirituality, reminds the Corinthians of their idol-worshipping past as Gentiles when they did not consider Jesus to be their Lord. It was only after the work of the Spirit in their lives that they could say that Jesus is Lord. Paul's hearkening back to the Corinthians' "non-spiritual" idolatrous ways is consistent with his Jewish heritage in terms of the scorning of idols. Paul, in effect, has "played the traditional Jewish idolatry card" to encourage the Corinthians in what is authentically Christian.

Likewise, in 12:12–17 Paul depends on typical biblical and Jewish tradition, which suggests that all people are equally significant to God (Joel 2:28–29). Even as Joel prophesied of a day when all people—regardless of their age and sex—would be potential recipients of the Spirit of the Lord and be involved in the exercise of the *charismata*, Paul explains that because of the Spirit, all people, regardless of their race, gender, or socioeconomic status (12:13) and abilities (12:14–27), can participate in the exercise of the *charismata* and play a vital role in the body of Christ. This point of view affirms the notion that Paul's commanding of women to be silent in the churches, and be subject according to the Law (1 Cor 14:34), is not absolutely restricting women from speaking in the church. To be sure, for Paul,

---

41. For example, in politics, rhetoric, and philosophy.

42. Thiselton, *First Corinthians*, 1147; Barton, "Paul's Sense of Place," 229–30; Eriksson, *Traditions as Rhetorical Proof*, 214–16.

43. Thiselton, *First Corinthians*, 1150. Cf. Collins, *First Corinthians*, 515–17 and 520–21.

44. Thiselton, *First Corinthians*, 1157.

it is not a criterion of authentic spirituality that women be silent in church—unless they are being disruptive.

Paul's use of love in 1 Corinthians 13 also evidences his reliance on his tradition. Indeed, 13:2 is an allusion to the mountain-moving faith that Jesus spoke of (Mark 11:23) in applying Zechariah's prophecy concerning what the Spirit would accomplish through Zerubbabel (Zech 4:7). This was a typical Jewish hyperbole for being able to do something that is practically impossible.[45] Paul's point in 13:2, then, is that even if one is so gifted by the Spirit that they can virtually do what seems to be impossible, without love they are not benefited and they are as insignificant individuals (13:2–3).

6.6 Why Does Paul Employ a Traditional Theology?

It should now be clear that in 1 Corinthians 12–14 Paul has employed a hermeneutic that values and embraces the history of effects of his tradition. In fact, Paul uses his tradition as part of his rhetoric in making his case for what is authentically spiritual. And this should not be surprising, for Paul was zealous for the traditions of his fathers (Gal 1:14), and he commends their maintenance and handing down to others. He regards his tradition as being foundational for the church, but he also interprets this tradition mindful of the revelation of Jesus Christ. In fact, at times Paul directly quotes (1:19) and other times he freely varies such traditional sources (14:21). This traditional emphasis for Paul seems to be unavoidable, and consistent with Gadamer's insight that one cannot be separated from their tradition and context—and understanding occurs when one applies accepted traditional meanings to their context.[46] If this assertion is right, analyzing Paul's traditional theology through the lens of his first-century context to find out why he employed such a hermeneutic should provide further clues on how to communicate what is authentically spiritual in a pluralistic setting.

Indeed, the 1 Corinthians epistolary context gives various clues as to why Paul appeals to traditional and religious authorities. Among these clues is Paul's belief that the one who is spiritual ought to live their lives in obedience to the commandments of God (1 Cor 7:19) and the law of Christ (9:21). Second, for Paul, it is advisable that one learns and grows because of knowing their tradition (12:2–3). Thus, Paul reminds the Corinthians of their pagan background so that they can learn from it, gain a broader perspective of what is authentically Christian, and not revert to idolatrous behavior. Instead of being led astray, the Corinthians should affirm that

---

45. Keener, *1–2 Corinthians*, 108.
46. Recall, for example, Paul's applying the Law to his context in 1 Cor 14:21.

Jesus is Lord. This line of thought is also similar to that of Gadamer, who suggests that temporal distance, or the time between individuals and the past, instead of being an hindrance to understanding, is actually a positive product that enables true meaning to fully emerge as things that distort understanding are set aside and new traces of understanding are considered.[47] For Gadamer, one is inextricably linked with their tradition, and should therefore apply the lessons of tradition to their context in developing meaning.[48] This is exactly what Paul has done (14:21).

Paul's traditional hermeneutic was also influenced by the broader Graeco-Roman context, for he was primarily seeking to reconcile the competing claims of philosophy and religion, and particularly to deter the self-exalting ethos of the Graeco-Roman culture. The Corinthians were being influenced by the secular Graeco-Roman culture, which, though they were fascinated with human knowledge (1 Cor 8:1–3), devalued tradition and truth. Essentially, the Corinthians were modifying the gospel of Jesus Christ towards Hellenism. Consequently, for example, Paul explains to the Corinthians that "the one who speaks in tongues does not speak to humans, but to God" (14:2). The Corinthians were abusing the gift of tongues to speak to, and impress each other with supernatural abilities. But because such speech is unfruitful to the natural mind, Paul reminds the Corinthians of prophecy (14:3), which, in the OT, reflects God's fatherly concern for his people.[49] In other words, contrary to the self-exalting use of tongues, Paul wants the Corinthians to practice the *charismata* as it was traditionally exercised. Instead of being used for self-exalting purposes, the proper functioning of the *charismata* is for serving God. Indeed, authentic spirituality is of benefit to others (14:26–36).

This understanding is important for Paul because he considers his tradition to be of great value. In fact, based on this tradition—particularly, the OT scripture—Paul considers revelatory experiences to be of transformative value to all who participate in them (14:23–25). And this is quite unlike the pluralistic Graeco-Roman culture, which participated in religion and sought charismatic experiences to be assimilated in their lifestyle and to be of present benefit to their lives, instead of being of service to God and others.

For first-century Graeco-Romans, *charismata* affirmed pluralism because the apparent exercise of spiritual gifts was inclusive of various pagan cults. Furthermore, such supernatural manifestations could lead

---

47. Gadamer, *Truth and Method*, 298.
48. Gadamer, *Truth and Method*, 293, 300.
49. Thiselton, *First Corinthians*, 1089.

to immediate acclaim in a culture that valued boasting, self-display, the manifestation of power, and the benefits of healing. Belief in Jesus as Lord and Savior, however, is an exclusively Christian claim. Ironically, however, the unity and diversity evident in the Godhead, as well as the Christians tolerance/love of all—despite their background—is in stark contrast with the Graeco-Roman social stratification and intolerance of Christians. This truth suggests that authentic inclusivity and "tolerance" is represented by Christianity, which, based on the loving example of Christ, accepts individuals regardless of their beliefs.

In brief, the argument being made here, through a consideration of 1 Corinthians 12–14, is that traditional and religious authoritative sources were valuable and inseparably linked to Paul's communicating of authentic spirituality to the Corinthians. Having stated this case, it is time to discuss two other principles that Paul discusses in 1 Corinthians 12–14.

6.7 In an Authentic Revelatory Claim, the Word of God Is Affirmed (14:37)

In 1 Corinthians 14:37 Paul says, "if someone seems to be a prophet or spiritual, let him acknowledge that what I write to you is a command of the Lord." This conditional cause-effect statement can also be considered a command from Paul. The apostle is declaring that the one who considers himself to be a prophet or authentically spiritual person must affirm the word of God. As an apostle and prophet, Paul considers himself a bearer of the word of God. And because of that, the truly spiritual person must acknowledge and affirm his words. Is Paul saying that one should have blind allegiance to what he says, or writes? The answer to this question is an emphatic no! This is because Paul suggests that prophecy should be judged by the hearers (14:29–30). Therefore, for one to acknowledge Paul's word as being from God, Paul is suggesting that his word should be judged and reasoned with to earn authority. And since tradition consists of what is authoritative, Paul—consistent with his traditional theology—is suggesting that one should conduct rational dialogue to make sure that what he says is consistent with what is known about God in tradition. If someone does not conduct this due diligence in acknowledging what he says, they should not be considered a true prophet or spiritual person (14:38).

6.8 Truly Spiritual Things Should Be Proper and According to Order (14:40)

Subsequently, Paul presents conclusive comments concerning spiritual things (1 Cor 14:39-40). He advocates that one should passionately seek to prophesy, but also not forbid speaking in tongues (14:39). As already noted, both gifts of the Spirit have their purposes in building up the church (prophecy) and individuals (tongues), respectively. Finally, in 14:40 Paul adds one last principle that concludes his argument in 1 Corinthians 14, and even summarizes the thrust of his message regarding criteria for what is authentically spiritual. For Paul, all things, indeed, all that is truly spiritual, should "be proper and according to order" (14:40). Since he also says all things should be for edification (14:26), being proper and according to order, for Paul, is like being edifying, and both are requisite for authentic spirituality.

6.9 Conclusion

1 Corinthians 14 offers various principles for authentic spirituality. For example, an uninterpreted tongue is not to be spoken to people, for it is incomprehensible and therefore not edifying. Rather, such communication should be made to God (14:2). Likewise, the charism of prophecy should be for edification, encouragement, and comfort (14:3). In fact, all revelatory claims should be for edification (14:26-36), affirming the word of God (14:37), and be conducted properly and according to order (14:40). These principles can be coalesced into a unifying theme that authentic revelatory claims must be edifying to the church. Based on this understanding, the question being discussed becomes, is edification rightly to be considered a criterion for authentic spirituality?

On the one hand, edification appears to be a criterion for authentic spirituality since it is usually discernible if others are benefited by an action. Even one's spiritual strengthening can be acknowledged as well as recognized by others. On the other hand, one can be spiritually strengthened, and the community on a whole may even benefit from an act, but that act may not necessarily be led by the Spirit. For example, in Israel's history, those who prophesied weal, or the well-being of the nation, may have "strengthened" the spirits of the community at that time, yet it was often the prophets of woe—who did not appear to edify the people—who were the true prophets of God. Because one can be edified whether or not a revelatory claim is authentic, edification—at least not by itself—cannot rightly be considered

THE CRITERION OF EDIFICATION (1 COR 14:1–40)

a criterion for authentic spirituality. Edification, however, is undoubtedly a key principle for authentic Christian living.

Because of the significance of edification to Paul, Bezuidenhout has well stated, "the edification of the assembly is the normative basis from which the practice of the *charismata* is judged in 1 Corinthians 14."[50] And Paul has relied heavily on the authority of his Jewish tradition, as found in the teachings of the Law, in order to effectively communicate the various principles of edification by which authentic spirituality depends. Considering all the principles, and the invalidating of the various supposed criteria for authentic spirituality, by this work, however, the obvious question now is, has Paul really given criteria or a criterion for authentic spirituality, or has he just given principles in that regard for individuals to live by?

Based on the evidence gathered, again, it does not appear that there is one criterion for authentic spirituality. But, in the culmination of his argument, Paul has combined three essential principles that, as has been shown, by themselves are not criteria. Taken together, however, this triadic formula appears to be a criterion for authentic spirituality. These principles are given in 1 Corinthians 14:1 and appear to be the thesis for the entire 1 Corinthians 12–14 pericope. Paul commands the Corinthians to "Pursue love, and passionately seek spiritual things, and even more that you may prophesy." The principle of love in this triad is unambiguous,[51] but the other two principles need to be clarified. The first of these principles relate to "spiritual things" (*pneūmatiká*). It is important to remember that *pneūmatiká* concern things that are characteristic of the triune God (Father, Son, and Spirit), and therefore are inclusive of, but not limited to, the *charismata*. But since the primary focus of 1 Corinthians 12 seems to be gifts from the Spirit (*charismata*), and because God is Spirit (John 4:24), this second triadic principle can be considered "the Spirit," or manifestations of the Spirit.

The other principle to be clarified concerns Paul's saying, ". . . and even more that you may prophesy." Though Paul is specifically referring to the charism of prophecy, he is doing so to emphasize his main point of the need for edification. To be sure, Paul explains that uninterpreted tongues are not understandable to people, but prophecy is edifying to others (14:2–3). Thus, the third part of Paul's triad of principles concerning the criteria for authentic spirituality is edification. The triad can therefore be summed up as love, the Spirit, and edification. Or, placed in order of their emphasis: the Spirit (ch. 12), love (ch. 13), and edification (ch. 14).

---

50. Bezuidenhout, "Trinitarian Nature," 102.

51. No further clarification other than what has already been given regarding love (1 Cor 13) is suggested here.

Paul's imperatival language concerning the pursuit of these principles as well as their articulated inseparability suggests that this triadic combination is a criterion for authentic spirituality.

Having now considered the entire 1 Corinthians 12–14 pericope, it can be concluded that, for Paul, authentic spirituality includes a combination of the Spirit's manifestation, love, and edification of the church. Additionally, Paul conveys the notion that theological communication should be sensitively Trinitarian, contextual, and traditional to speak effectively to a pluralistic context. In other words, the criterion for an authentic revelatory claim includes a manifestation of gifts of the Spirit, or spiritual phenomenon—which by itself is not a criterion for being authentically spiritual, since there are "nothing distinctly Christian in charismatic phenomena[on] themselves."[52] However, "the ambiguity of the manifestation of the divine does not make that manifestation any less essential to spiritual and community life."[53] Thus, charismatic phenomena must be accompanied by love, and be for the edification of the church, in order to be considered truly revelatory of God. Additionally, authentic spirituality concerns the triune God, all sources of truth, and is affirmed by tradition. Having reached this conclusion, the following chapters will now address contemporary implications of Paul's criteria for authentic spirituality, especially as they relate to the church and its worship service. Thereafter, a perspective on discerning the authenticity of divine revelatory claims will be posited.

---

52. Dunn, *Jesus and the Spirit*, 307.
53. Dunn, *Jesus and the Spirit*, 307.

Part III

Contemporary Implications of Authentic Spirituality in Pluralistic Contexts

This study is investigating the issue of having criteria for authentic spirituality from the perspective of the OT and the context of 1 Corinthians—including the text of 1 Corinthians 12-14. Additionally, this study is exploring how to effectively communicate such experiences in a pluralistic context. The following chapters continue the discussion and seek to appropriate the insights gained thus far by including the ethical implications for the contemporary church and the communication that takes place within the worship service.[1] After all, the church and its worship service are among the major *pneumatika* or "spiritual things" (12:1) that Paul addresses.[2] Indeed, various insights have been uncovered from the OT and the early church. However, it is now time to also discuss the issue of contemporary relevance. Are there lessons to be learned from the OT and Pauline instructions concerning authentic spirituality that are applicable to the con-

---

1. This works focus is on authentic spirituality, especially through the *charismata*, and presupposes that as manifestations of the Spirit, each charism (spiritual gift) is revelatory of God. Thus, in order to sharpen the argument herein, the *charismata* of prophecy and tongues (along with the complementary interpretation of tongues) will be focused upon since it is generally agreed that these gifts were the primary concern of Paul in 1 Cor 12-14 (cf., for example, Ewert, "Glossolalia in the Church Today," 175; Best, "Interpretation of Tongues," 45; and Fee, "Tongues—Least of the Gifts?," 6-7, who says speaking in tongues in the congregation is the major issue that Paul is dealing with).

2. In regards to the church, Ackerman, "Fighting Fire with Fire," 347, notes that "1 Corinthians offer valuable lessons for developing the church as community." Additionally, Schweizer, " Service of Worship," 400, concludes that "1 Cor 14 is the clearest NT passage on Christian worship". Likewise, Rowe, "1 Corinthians 12-14," 119, says, "Paul's comments in 1 Corinthians 14 is primary evidence for understanding principles of early Christian worship."

temporary context? In what ways can this study deepen our understanding about what is authentically spiritual in the church and its worship service? These chapters seek to derive meaning from the previous chapters by first determining some major similarities between the ancient and contemporary contexts that can serve as a validation or a platform from which contemporary implications of Paul's criteria for authentic spirituality can then be addressed. Subsequently, conclusive comments relative to discerning the authenticity in claims of revelatory experiences will be offered.

Chapter 7

The Basis, Acceptability, and the Appropriation of Paul's Criterion for Authentic Spirituality

7.1 Introduction

Can the lessons of the OT and NT period regarding authentic spirituality be applied to the contemporary context? It has been said, for example, that "OT abuses of prophecy are just as relevant to our contemporary situation as they are in the OT context and in the early church."[1] The immediate task of this chapter is to determine if and why such a statement might be true by briefly evaluating the contemporary context.

7.2 Major Similarities between the Ancient and Contemporary Contexts

Like the ancient contexts described above, the contemporary American context, for example, is pluralistic and would therefore stand to benefit from a knowledge of what is authentically spiritual. America is "host to numerous world religions, sects, cults, ancient and new age spiritualities, occult practices, beliefs, and philosophies, not to mention the virtually countless Christian denominations."[2]

According to Diana Eck, the director of the Pluralism Project at Harvard University, this is because forces such as global communication and immigration have led to at least five types of religious pluralism. In the spring

---

1. Hildebrandt, *Old Testament Theology*, 182.

2. Hildebrandt, *Old Testament Theology*, 210. This does not mean that Christianity is less popular or has lost its influence, for Christianity is still the most popular religion in the world. And even in places that have become increasingly pluralistic, through immigration, for example, Christianity has often gained adherents, as individuals from non-Christian cultures are often converted to Christianity.

2009 Gifford Lecture series at the University of Edinburgh, Eck presented a lecture entitled "Globalization and Religious Pluralism."[3] Therein, she identified five types of pluralism. First, there is a global pluralism in which the world is without border because of technologies such as the Internet as well as increasing urbanization in which people from various cultures are living in the same place and are therefore in constant engagement which each other. Second, there is national pluralism, or the existence of multi-religious societies within the same nation. Third, there is local pluralism evidenced by the interaction of diverse groups in cities and towns. Fourth, there is pluralism within various communities; for example, within Christianity there is diversity among the adherents. Amos Yong has documented an example of pluralism within a (global) community in his book entitled *The Spirit Poured Out on All Flesh: Pentecostalism and the Possibility of Global Theology*.[4] He makes the case that the (global) Pentecostal community is multifarious and dynamic, as evidenced by the fact that: Pentecostalism(s) in Latin America tends to be existential, political, egalitarian, and ecumenical-liberation theological. Pentecostalism(s) in Asia involves indigenous and syncretistic worship. Pentecostalism(s) in India is also indigenous, and includes other phenomena like tongues, dreams, and visions. Finally, while there has been a neglect of black theological reflection in the development of Pentecostal theology, Africa and its diaspora's Pentecostalism(s) tend to be pneumatocentric, indigenous, involving the whole range of manifestations previously mentioned.[5] Despite the phenomenological pluralism, pneumatocentricity is the common thread throughout all these different types of Pentecostalism.[6] The final type of pluralism, for Eck, is found within individuals, when, as a consequence of being exposed to various cultures and religions, one has an internal conflict or tension in terms of the acceptance of the various religions.

The existence of such pluralism worldwide has led Yong to conclude that a major challenge for contemporary Christian theology is figuring out how to effectively communicate Christian principles in a pluralistic and post-Christendom context where Christianity is not the overriding religious influence. This work is addressing the communication of Christian principles as well as what is authentic Christian living. In her work, however, Diana Eck claims there is a weakening influence of Christianity

---

3. Eck, "Globalization & Religious Pluralism." Cf. www.pluralism.org.
4. Yong, *Spirit Poured Out*.
5. Yong, *Spirit Poured Out*, 60–61, 63–64, 69–71, 74–75, 78.
6. Yong, "Between the Local and the Global."

compared to other religions and considers tolerance a criterion for what is authentically spiritual.

In her book entitled *A New Religious America: How a Christian Country Has Now Become the World's Most Religiously Diverse Nation*, though she admits it is most visible in America's cosmopolitan cities,[7] Eck argues that America "has become the most religiously diverse nation on earth."[8] If this assumption is true, does it mean that "tolerance" should therefore be a criterion for what is authentically spiritual? One's experience of various religious groups in major US cities and some universities would seem to authenticate the claim that America is the world's most religiously diverse nation. But the professor of comparative religion and Indian studies does not provide specific evidence to substantiate her very significant assertion. Nonetheless, as a result of such pluralism, she declares that the only way for her to live authentically spiritual is as a Christian pluralist, or one who is tolerant, in that she encounters and defines people of different faiths by their roots, and not by their borders.[9] One wonders, however, if this self-identification as a "Christian pluralist" is appropriate, for it is unclear how such a person, in terms of relating to others, differs from one who lives and communicates what is authentically spiritual, or, in this case, aims to become like Christ. In other words, being a Christian does not need an accompanying modifier like "pluralist" to convey one's love and respect for all people. Love and contextuality are requisite in authentic Christian living (cf. 1 Cor 9:19–27 and 1 Cor 13). Indeed, this work has already shown that the unity that comes from possessing the Spirit of Jesus renders social stratification obsolete, for there is to be a unity in diversity among Christians where all are accepted in Christ regardless of their ethnicity, gender, or socioeconomic background. This is because Jesus Christ exhibited his love for all, regardless of faiths, roots, or borders, through his charismatic lifestyle and his dying on the cross (cf. Luke 2:10–11, 28–32; John 3:16). Moreover, Christ's resurrection has affirmed his saying, "I am the way, and the truth, and the life. No one comes to the Father except through me" (John 14:6). If this is the idea of "tolerance" that Eck has in mind, then tolerance would be at least a principle for authentic spirituality. But if Eck is trying to say that all religious "roots" have equally acceptable criteria for truth, this would be at odds with the teachings of Christ and Christianity. In fact, such a claim would also be at odds with the teachings of other faiths. The Qur'an of Islam, for example, teaches that others have sincerely held religious beliefs that are incompatible

---

7. Yong, "Between the Local and the Global," 20.
8. Eck, *New Religious America*, 4, 30.
9. Eck, *New Religious America*, 23.

to that of Islam,[10] but such differences, says Islamic scholar Rashied Omar, "represent a God-willed, basic factor of human existence."[11]

Again, if tolerance, for Eck, means that one ought to be contextual in their approach to people of different faiths then she would be consistent with the mission of Christ (John 3:16–18) and the teaching of the apostle Paul, as well as Omar's interpretation of Islam's higher vision of pluralism that goes beyond the idea of mere tolerance. For Omar, Muslims—and other faiths—should not be tolerant. Instead, there is a higher calling that is expressed in the notion of Ta'aruf, or an "embracing the other as an extension of yourself," which "obliges Muslims not merely to tolerate but to honor the dignity of all human beings, and to look upon each and every human being—whether he or she is a Jew, an atheist, or an adherent of an extra-scriptural religion—as carrying within her, within him, a part of God."[12] Based on the similar viewpoints of Eck and Omar—who also advocates a pluralistic society, but from an Islamic perspective—Eck seems to be appropriately advocating contextuality as a criterion for being authentically spiritual, or relating with others, in particular.

Embracing the concept of tolerance should not lead us to think religions are all the same or that all religious beliefs are compatible. Indeed, one can have interfaith dialogue, but the evidence from Paul suggests "there is never a dialogue in the sense that both partners are in search for the truth; the apostle is unquestionably convinced that Christ's Gospel is the ultimate truth and unique, without any alternative."[13] Therefore, tolerance should not preclude Christians from humbly and joyfully witnessing to the truth about God revealed to them in Jesus Christ. Christians are called to proclaim this distinct truth, while proclaiming the kind of religious tolerance that arises from their own belief—the kind voiced by the apostle Peter when he said, "God shows no partiality, but in every nation, everyone who fears him and does what is right is acceptable to him" (Acts 10:34b–35).

Because pluralism has influenced Eck to consider tolerance a criterion for what is authentically spiritual, it is important to understand what the term "pluralism" means to her. Eck explains, "pluralism is the dynamic process through which we engage with one another in and through our very deepest differences."[14] Thus, pluralism is not simply diversity. Rather, it involves actively engaging others of different faith. Further, pluralism is not just

10. Cf. *Surah al-Tawbah* 10:99.
11. Omar, "Islam Beyond Tolerance," 17.
12. Omar, "Islam Beyond Tolerance," 19.
13. Lindemann, "Pauline Mission and Religious Pluralism," 285, 288.
14. Eck, *New Religious America*, 70.

tolerance, but it actively and constructively tries to comprehend others. And pluralism is not just relativism that does not acknowledge real differences between religions. Instead, pluralism appropriates one's faith in dialogue with the religiously other for the sake of relationship.[15]

On a surface level, these statements seem to be representative of authentic spirituality, for they acknowledge that there are real differences between different faith traditions while seeking out relationship with the religious other. But Eck's understanding of pluralism does not speak to the essential issue of whether conflicting truth claims can be acceptable or equally valid. Are there specific criteria for what is authentically revealed by God? Does the truth of God depend on one's opinion? Is Jesus the way, the truth, and the life (John 14:6)? These questions are important because, as Neuhaus indicates, "different faiths come with different rituals and customs, and therefore assume and assert different truth claims, which, if excluded, effectively stifles the reality of pluralism."[16] Additionally, accepting the existence of the pluralism Eck describes does not mean that America "has now become the world's most religiously diverse nation," as Eck argues.[17] This is the case made by Philip Jenkins in his article entitled "A New Religious America." For Jenkins, Eck "is flat wrong,"[18] for while there may be a diversity of cultures in the United States, America is not to be considered "the world's most religiously diverse nation, and the idea of American religious diversity is a myth."[19] Non-Christian religious groups comprise only about 5 percent of the population, whereas religious minorities often make up 10–20 percent of the population of some countries.[20] Thus, Eck's assertion that the relative number of religious minorities does not matter since enough of them are around to impact American society is puzzling,[21] for numbers do matter, given that they can be misrepresented to serve particular agendas.

David Barrett's *World Christian Encyclopedia* confirms Jenkins's argument, for even though at the start of the twentieth century America had a virtual Christendom situation, with at least 96 percent of its population being adherents to Christianity, and at the end of the century this number dropped to 85.7 percent, other religions have increased only at an average

---

15. Eck, *New Religious America*, 70–72.
16. Neuhaus, "One Nation under Many Gods," 74.
17. Eck, *New Religious America*, 4.
18. Jenkins, "New Religious America," 26.
19. Jenkins, "New Religious America," 27.
20. Jenkins, "New Religious America," 27.
21. Cf. Eck, *New Religious America*, 383.

of 0.65 percent of the population.[22] The decline in Christian adherents is a result of more people considering themselves "non-religious."

United States: Religious Adherents as a Percentage of the Population[23]

Year	1900	Mid–1970	Mid–1975	1980	2000
Christians	96.4	90.8	89.4	88.0	85.7
Non-Religious	1.3	4.8	5.8	6.7	8.4
Jews	2.0	3.3	3.3	3.2	3.1
Muslims	0.0	0.4	0.6	0.8	1.2
Buddhism	0.0	0.1	0.1	0.1	0.0
Hinduism	0.0	0.0	0.1	0.2	0.3

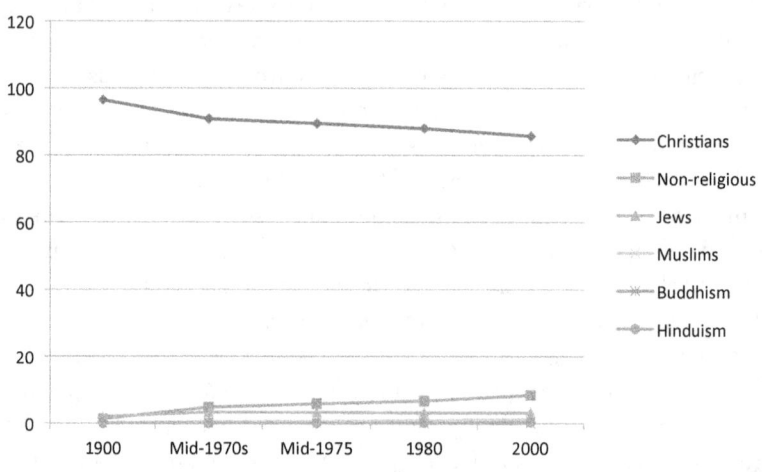

Line Graph of Religious Adherents in the US as a Percentage of the Population from 1900 to 2000

Nations like India, and Kenya, for example, evidence far greater religious pluralism. In the year 2000, 76.1 percent of Indians were Hindus, 12 percent Muslims, 4.7 percent Christians, 2.2 percent Sikhs, 2 percent non-religious,

---

22. This figure is based on the average percentage increase among Jews, Muslims, Buddhists, and Hindus over the one-hundred-year period.

23. Barrett, *World Christian Encyclopedia*, 711.

and 1 percent Buddhists.[24] In the same year, in Kenya, there were 82 percent Christians, 10.5 percent tribal religionists, 5.5 percent Muslims, and 1.4 percent Baha'is.[25]

Thus, Eck is right to argue that America is pluralistic in that there exists a diversity of religious traditions, but it is an overstatement to conclude that there is a new religious America that is the most religiously diverse nation in the world. A more accurate argument would defend "how America has managed to become both a Christian country and a multi-religious society at the same time."[26] Perhaps a more appropriate description of America—and the contemporary church—can be found by comparing America to the four major defining features of first-century Graeco-Roman society and the Corinthian church. If both contexts are comparable, then it is justifiable to apply the lessons learned from the ancient context, regarding criteria for authentic spirituality, to the contemporary context. Since the ancient contexts have already been discussed, the following will focus on its comparison to the contemporary American context.

The presence of various cultural and socioeconomic backgrounds among its citizens, along with a capitalistic ethos, where hard work and one's creativity and/or gifting usually provide substantial reward, makes it fair to consider Americans upwardly mobile. As a nation of immigrants and former slaves (African Americans), Americans believe they have been endowed by God with the unalienable rights of life, liberty, and the pursuit of happiness. This ethos has led to a competitive spirit which has produced unparalleled success in the world and in virtually all aspects of society. And this competitiveness has both its benefits and drawbacks. Benefits include an increasingly productive society in which individuals usually work and produce based on their gifting or abilities, since only those who can perform a function are generally selected to do it. Further, financial and substantive rewards are given to those who are successful, making it possible for American resources to be used in helping others in times of national and/or global tragedies.

Drawbacks of an upwardly mobile and competitive American ethos, however, include an often apathetic and aloof attitude towards one's neighbor, who is often seen as a competitor to be outdone, or at least kept up with. Often, there is also an unhealthy pride in accomplishments. For example, when a sports player flaunts their success in front of their rivals, or when sports fans brag about their cities and hold other cities in

---

24. Barrett, *World Christian Encyclopedia*, 370.
25. Barrett, *World Christian Encyclopedia*, 432.
26. Neuhaus, "One Nation under Many Gods," 78.

derision. An additional drawback is evident when individuals pursue fame and wealth, no matter what the cost to others. Examples of such behavior include the drug dealers, pornographers, false prophets, preachers, and politicians who exalt themselves, and abuse their abilities and fellow citizens, in pursuit of filthy lucre.

The second major characteristic of first-century Graeco-Roman society—rejection of rationalism—is also present in contemporary American society and is usually associated with postmodernism and its rejection of the modern mindset with its claim to "objectivity." Modern reasoning is based on the Enlightenment and its scientific exclusion of non-rational ways of knowing things—such as faith and the supernatural. In other words, the Enlightenment's criterion for truth is human reasoning. In contrast to modernism, the relativistic outlook of postmodernism allows for non-rational and supernatural ways of knowing, but it rejects authoritative traditions such as that of the Bible. The postmodern criterion for truth seems to be consensus, or what a given community tolerates. However, as has already been noted, this is not a true criterion for authentic spirituality, for such relativism does not provide an effective means of evaluating truth from falsehood. Postmodernism, as stated here, then, is contrary to Paul's way of thinking. Pauline epistemology is inclusive of traditional means of knowing things and encourages a balance of the spiritual and rational (1 Cor 1:22–24),[27] as well as a combination of spiritual activity, in love, for the edification of all (1 Cor 12–14).

The third major characteristic of the first-century Graeco-Roman context relates to the concept of *sōtēria*, or a salvific yearning. Graeco-Romans understood *sōtēria* in terms of having their needs provided for in the present world by the Roman emperor. A comparable notion of salvation is also prevalent in the contemporary context, for example, when citizens expect their government to provide for their health care and general well-being through various social services. Whether or not it is intended, or admitted, such an entitlement attitude effectively elevates the government to the place of God, for only deity is able to meet all of our needs. This is not to say that one's government has no role in providing for its citizens. After all, government—including that of the church—is ordained by God (1 Cor 12:28; Rom 13:1) and should not be despised (2 Pet 2:10). Government, however, is not meant to replace God as Savior of the world, and prevent individuals from using their gifts to glorify God and build each other up, both in the present and in the future.

---

27. Cf. Dunn, *Jesus and the Spirit*, 217. Thiselton, *Living Paul*, 150.

The final Graeco-Roman characteristic being considered is tolerance. Despite the religious pluralism of the various first-century pagan cults, a religiously tolerant ethos was present among their adherents. However, groups with exclusive claims—such as Christians and their belief that Jesus Christ is the Lord—were often ridiculed. This tolerance of religion, and intolerance of Christianity, is also characteristic of the contemporary context, and is evidenced in a political correctness that, on the one hand, seems to defend and accept others regardless of their behavior. To be sure, all people are to be accepted, for they are made in the image of God. But "tolerance" is not a criterion for authentic spirituality if abhorrent behavior is defended for the sake of "tolerance." John Calvin (1509–64 C.E.), the Protestant Reformer, has rightly said that we must

> make it our aim, that the truth of God may, without contention, maintain its ground; but if the wicked resist, we must set our face against them, and have no fear, lest the blame of the disturbances should be laid to our charge. For accursed is that peace of which revolt from God is the bond, and blessed are those contentions by which it is necessary to maintain the kingdom of Christ.[28]

Thus, while it is commendable to be "tolerant," one should be tolerant only of the things that are of the Spirit, in love, and are edifying for the community.

The absurdity of tolerating abhorrent behavior was made clear, for example, when, commenting on her relationship with her homosexual ex-husband, Fran Drescher, the star of *The Nanny*, said, she believes "in preserving the American dream, which is tolerance of diversity and the separation of church and state."[29] While America encourages and even embodies diversity—being a nation of immigrants—the American dream, which, contrary to *The Nanny*, is probably more appropriately described in terms of the unalienable rights of life, liberty, and the pursuit of happiness, does not encourage diversity for the sake of diversity, or diversity that is immoral or possibly harmful to individuals or society. And becoming divorced because of sexual improprieties—whether heterosexual or homosexual—is not to be defended. Again, one should lovingly affirm the value of individuals, but their unrighteousness should not be tolerated.

Another example of the contemporary misappropriation of tolerance is demonstrated by Monica Garcia, the former Los Angeles school board president, in commenting on the Arizona immigration law SB 1070, which

---

28. Calvin, *Commentary*, 466.

29. Drescher, "Fran Drescher 'Blessed to Have Met Gay Ex-Husband,'" http://www.popeater.com/2010/06/02fran-drescher-gay-ex-husband/?xicid=webmaildl2.

intends "to discourage and deter the unlawful entry and presence of aliens and economic activity by persons unlawfully present in the United States" (section 1). The school administrator says, "America must stand up for tolerance, inclusiveness, and equality . . . by teaching our students to value themselves; to respect others; and to demand fairness and justice for all. . . ."[30] Polls have shown that Americans are tolerant in that they respect others and their beliefs.[31] But tolerance does not mean a putting aside of one's beliefs and laws. Instead, tolerance should mean no partiality—regardless of one's race, culture, or sexual orientation. Miscreant behavior should not be tolerated. Ironically, as it was in Graeco-Roman society, this supposed tolerance in contemporary society does not seem to extend to those who hold to traditional Christian values. To be "tolerant" of minorities, cultures, and faiths, there has been an increasing intolerance of Christianity.[32] But true tolerance, which is authentically spiritual, is consistent with the Christian ethos, where, empowered by the Spirit, one is able to love and edify others, being united despite any diversity.

Having now concluded our comparison of the ancient and contemporary contexts, one can agree with the conclusions of commentators like Thiselton and Fee. For Thiselton, "the pluralism of Corinth brings us nearer to the heart of similarities with some twenty-first century contexts."[33] Corinth's pluralism has much in common with the pluralism characteristic of postmodernity. And "1 Corinthians stands in a distinctive position of relevance to our own times."[34]

It is appropriate to also say that the ancient and contemporary contexts can both be pluralistic and non-Christendom.[35] To Fee,

> the cosmopolitan character of the city and church, the strident individualism that emerges in so many of their behavioral aberrations, the arrogance that attends their understanding of spirituality, the accommodation of the Gospel to the surrounding culture, in so many ways—these and many other features of the

---

30. Romero, "L.A. School District Decries Arizona's Immigration Law,'" *LA Weekly*, June 2, 2010, http://blogs.laweekly.com/informer/city-news/lausd-arizona-un-american/.

31. In an article entitled "Degree of Tolerance" (*Christian Century*, July 2008), the editors cite a survey by the Pew Forum on Religion and Public Life.

32. Pell, "Intolerant Tolerance," 9.

33. Thiselton, *First Corinthians*, 10.

34. Thiselton, *First Corinthians*, 17.

35. The idea that both the ancient and the contemporary context are non-Christendom is suggesting that the ancient contexts were pre-Christendom and the contemporary context is post-Christendom.

Corinthian church are but mirrors held up before the church of today. Likewise, the need for discipleship modeled after the "weakness of Christ" (4:9–13), for love to rule over all (13:1–13), for edification to be the aim of worship (14:1–33), for sexual immorality to be seen for what it is (5:1–13; 6:12–20), . . . these and many others are every bit relevant to us as to those to whom they were first spoken.[36]

In other words, there is much we can glean from how Paul deals with the various "spiritual things" he addresses in 1 Corinthians.

Considering the similarities or relevance between the ancient and the contemporary contexts, it is therefore also reasonable to say that there are lessons relative to authentic spirituality from the ancient contexts that can be applied to the contemporary context. Before addressing such applications and their implications for the contemporary church and the corporate worship service, the basis and acceptability of Paul's spiritual instructions will now be further validated.

7.3 The Basis, Acceptability, and the Appropriation of Paul's Spiritual Instructions

It is evident that in 1 Corinthians 12–14 Paul is imparting knowledge regarding "spiritual things" (*tōn pneumatikōn*) to his pluralistic audience (cf. 12:1). The occasional manner of these teachings to the Corinthians warrants that they be viewed through the lens of the entire Pauline corpus to determine their proper context, consistency, relevance, and whether such impartations can rightly be considered Paul's theology. That is why this study has and will continue to dialogue with contemporary commentators, who have considered the entirety of the Pauline corpus, before coming to conclusions on Paul's thinking. And before accepting, and ultimately appropriating, Paul's theology, it is important to understand its source or roots. Stated differently, what is the basis of Paul's criteria for authentic spirituality? Is the root of Paul's theology epistemologically acceptable? And if it is epistemologically acceptable, what are its implications for contemporary listeners?

7.3.1 The basis of Paul's spiritual instructions

Clues to the basis of Paul's theology can be found throughout his epistles. In 1 Corinthians 2, for example, Paul makes it clear that, in contrast to mere

---

36. Fee, *First Corinthians*, 20.

human wisdom,[37] such as that of his Graeco-Roman context, or his Jewish upbringing—both of which influenced his message, in that he was contextual—the gospel he proclaims, indeed, his theology—including his criteria for authentic spirituality (1 Cor 12–14)—is based on the wisdom of God (2:5–7). This wisdom of God, for Paul, is "Jesus Christ and him crucified" (1:24; 30; 2:2); it is a demonstration of the Spirit and power of God (2:4–5), which is "secret and hidden, which God decreed before the ages for our glory" (1 Cor 2:7; Rom 16:25). The wisdom of God is also revealed to Paul by God, through the Spirit (1 Cor 2:7, 10), who teaches (2:13) and enables Paul to understand it (2:12).

Paul also suggests that the basis of his theology is a revelation, knowledge, prophecy, or teaching (1 Cor 14:6). This is because he was not sent by humans, but by the risen Christ and God the Father (Gal 1:1), who, through his grace, called and set apart Paul before he was born. Indeed, referring to his various and exceptional revelatory experiences (2 Cor 12:1–7), Paul says, "I did not receive it [them] from a human source, nor was I taught it [them], but I received it [them] through a revelation of Jesus Christ," by God (Gal 1:12, 15–16; 2:2; cf. Rom 16:25–26). In fact, Paul even considers his proclamation to be a "command of the Lord" (1 Cor 14:37), which compels him to share his message with conviction. In short, then, the basis for Paul's theology—including criteria for authentic spirituality—is Trinitarian. Paul's theology is centered in the revelation of Jesus Christ, which God gave to him through the Spirit.

7.3.2 The acceptability of Paul's spiritual instructions

Whether the revelatory basis of Paul's theology is acceptable in one's epistemological outlook depends on their ideological or theological viewpoint. If one accepts revealed theology, for example, as found in the Bible, then the source of Paul's theology, being based in the supernaturally triune God, is epistemologically acceptable even if one does not comprehend all that Paul says. If one accepts Paul's theology but does not meditate on it, however, Paul's communication may not be totally fruitful. Similarly, if one subscribes to a natural theological outlook such as that derived from the Enlightenment's rationalism, then Paul's theology will only be partially acceptable. This may be the case because Paul's theology, and revelation in general, can be comprehended both by the mind (rational) and the spirit (supernatural), but rationalism does not allow for what is spiritual as a criterion for

---

37. Cf. 1 Cor 1:17; 2:1, 4, 6, 13; 2 Cor 1:12.

understanding a matter. Paul's theology may be understandable to rationalists, but they reject its source.

7.4 Conclusion: The Appropriation of Paul's Spiritual Instructions

For the contemporary reader of Paul to effectively appropriate his criteria for the functioning of the *charismata*, then, they need to employ a balanced epistemological worldview in order to dialog with Paul, both with their mind and their spirit. This will allow them to be sensitively contextual in that they are open to both what is natural and supernatural. This posture, therefore, will allow for the discernment of how to live and communicate in a manner that is authentically spiritual by grasping and appropriating the revelation of Jesus Christ, which God gave to Paul through the Spirit. Such appropriation of the revelation of the triune God would be tremendously impacting of the church and its worship service. Thus, some of these specific implications will now be considered. And since the 1 Corinthians epistle has been the focus of this work, in the chapters to follow attention will be paid to Paul's exhortations to that church—especially those related to criteria for authenticating spirituality, in general, and the functioning of the *charismata*, in particular.

Chapter 8

Implications of Authentic Spirituality for the Contemporary Church

8.1 Introduction

In 1 Corinthians 12–14, the pluralistic Corinthian church is the addressee for the spiritual criteria that Paul is discussing.[1] It is important to remember, however, that Paul is not only writing his exhortations to the Corinthians, but also to "all those who in every place call on the name of our Lord Jesus Christ" (1:2). Putting it a different way, Paul infers that his remarks will be edifying for all Christians of his time. And, considering the similarities between the ancient and the contemporary context already highlighted, as well as the fact that Paul believes the writings of Scripture can patiently teach, comfort, and provide hope into the future (Rom 15:4), it is reasonable to assume that Paul understands that his proclamation will also be relevant for the contemporary church. Consequently, this chapter, and the next, will focus on the implications of Paul's criteria for authentic spirituality. The latter will deal with implications for the contemporary worship service. But this chapter will deal with implications for the contemporary church and specifically address the following questions that are continually being debated in the contemporary context: 1) What is the church, or what are the essential characteristics of the church when it is authentically functioning in the *charismata*? 2) What is the purpose of the church, and how does it relate to criteria for the functioning of the *charismata*? 3) Is the functioning of the *charismata* limited to the church? 4) If the functioning of the *charismata* is not limited to the church, who, then, can function in the *charismata*?

---

1. Cf. 1 Cor 1:2; 12:1; 14:20, 26, 39.

8.2 What Are the Essential Characteristics of the Church that Is Authentically Functioning in the *Charismata*?

What is the church? And what does the church look like when it authentically functions in the *charismata*? According to Paul, first, the church (*ekklēsia*) consists of "those who are sanctified in Christ Jesus, called to be saints . . . who in every place call on the name of our Lord Jesus Christ" (1 Cor 1:2). The members of the body of Christ, or the *ekklēsia*, are called out of the world to be Christlike, thus, they can be considered countercultural communities for the healing of the world.[2] The church is in the world, but not of or like the world (John 15:19). As people who have been sanctified or set apart from the world, every member of the church can be considered saints, who are holy or sanctified. This sanctification is not because the members of the church are perfect. Rather, the church is positionally sanctified and holy—even as their Lord Jesus Christ is holy (1 Pet 1:13–16)—because of the substitutionary atoning work of Christ, who died for their sins (Rom 5:18).

Second, the church is the "body of Christ" (12:12), through which the ascended Christ himself is present in the world. This body of Christ can therefore be considered a "living organism."[3] Paul's notion of the church as the "body of Christ" is rooted in his Graeco-Roman context, in which the state is the body politic, or a group of people politically organized under one governmental authority.[4] In this way of thinking, for Paul, the church is a group of people organized by God to fulfill his agenda. They are indwelt by the Holy Spirit (12:13; Rom 8:9), who empowers and renders them "dead to sin and alive to God in Christ Jesus" (Rom 6:11). The church is therefore under the lordship of the triune God.

As the body of Christ, the church is also "an "organic community," arranged by God (1 Cor 12:18, 24, 28), with interdependent members (12:12), through whom Christ will fulfill his mission in the contemporary context.[5] Because the members have diverse yet similarly significant gifts from the Spirit (12:12–31), they are not to be divided by race, gender, or socioeconomic status (12:13). And while "inferior" members (12:24) are greatly honored by God, it does not follow that any kind of injustice or marginalization of any member is to be tolerated.[6] Such unrighteousness is contrary to authentic spirituality. The differences between members should

---

2. Hays, "Ecclesiology and Ethics," 31–32.
3. Callan, *Dying and Rising with Christ*, 181.
4. Seneca, *Epistulae Morales* 95.52; cf. Fitzmyer, *According to Paul*, 8.
5. Cf. Bittlinger, "Charismatic Worship Service," 217; and MacGorman, "Glossolalic Error and Its Correction," 392.
6. Troupe, "One Body, Many Parts," 40–41.

be embraced and acknowledged as the body of Christ exemplifies a unity in diversity, where all gifts of the Spirit function in a manner that is sensitively contextual and edifying to the world.[7]

Finally, for Paul, the church is "the spiritual and moral space created by God through Christ's triumph over the powers in the cross . . . creating a new human community to announce, enact, and celebrate through Spirit enabled practices that the rule of rebellious powers have been broken in Christ."[8] The church, then, consists of communities of human beings in whom the Holy Spirit dwells, and serve to empower righteous (Rom 8:9-14) and charismatic living as evidence of their Lord's overcoming of the world (John 16:33). Hence, the church is not to be considered, for example, a building—which, though it may be a symbol of the Christian faith, cannot partake in the personal purposes of God. Instead of being focused solely on physical structures, the church is more about Spirit-empowered loving relationships of believers among themselves and with Christ, all in the context of continuously seeking to edify one another and reaching out to the world. This speaks to the purpose of the church, so a more in depth look at criteria for authentic spirituality as they relate to the purpose of the church will now be considered.

8.3 Implications of Authentic Spirituality upon the Purpose of the Church

What is the purpose of the church? For Paul, the church is "called to be saints . . . who in every place call on the name of our Lord Jesus Christ" (1 Cor 1:2). The church is to be holy and dedicated to the service of its Lord, and this is inseparably linked with their worshipping or calling on the name of the Lord. To be sure, such worshipping of the Lord and edifying each other is perhaps the main reason why the church gathers (cf. 11:18a; 14:23, 26).

Another purpose of the church is to reprove and call unbelievers to account as they communicate in a manner that is edifying or intelligible to all (14:24). When the church succeeds at this purpose, unbelievers will also be able to worship their Lord (14:25). Finally, the church is to judge or discern if the actions or communications of its members are authentically spiritual (14:29). Indeed, "the purpose of the assembly of believers [church] is to engage in a process of discernment about the ongoing shape of the community's faithfulness."[9] This discernment of spirits, as with the functioning of

---

7. Cf. 1 Cor 14:4-5, 12, 19, 26, 28, 40.
8. Harink, *Paul among the Postliberals*, 149.
9. Harink, *Paul among the Postliberals*, 130-31.

all the *charismata*, should be activated by the Spirit to individual members that the Spirit chooses (12:10–11). In that way, the judgment of the church will not be judgmental. Rather, this gift of the Spirit will be exercised in a loving manner, being sensitive to observers, with the aim of communication being intelligible and edifying to others.

This notion of being intelligible and edifying to others is important, for it is not only the church, or believers, who are able to judge the authenticity of an utterance. Even unbelievers should be able to understand and approve of—judge—what is being said (14:16). This is because, while the realm of the Spirit's activity is usually in the church, whom the Spirit indwells (Rom 8:9; 1 Cor 12:12–13), the Spirit sovereignly distributes gifts as the Spirit chooses (12:11). According to Arnold Bittlinger, this includes unbelievers, for though charismatic experiences are significant for the mission of the church, or the people of God, charismatic experiences are not limited to the church.[10]

Thus, while it is a purpose of the church to reflect "the way of Jesus Christ amid other people, bodies, and cities . . . continue(s) to live in the world, not only as a paradigmatic sign of the world's destiny under the lordship of Christ, but also as a witness within and to the world's structures and powers,"[11] the church is also being judged by the world. This notion of the church and its witness to the world speaks to the idea of missions, and in discussing his book *People of the Spirit: Exploring Luke's View of the Church*, NT scholar Graham Twelftree concludes that "the church exists . . . for mission. Not to be on mission would be to forfeit being the church."[12] In other words, for Twelftree, mission is a purpose of the church. And this mission is the same as that which Jesus carried out as part of the divine plan of salvation,[13] when he gave his life so that the entire world could be saved (John 3:16). After his resurrection, he told his disciples to "go into the entire world and preach the gospel to all" (Mark 16:15). This Great Commission was part of Paul's purpose, and the NT evidences that he was an extraordinary and contextual missionary,[14] for he communicated to Jews

---

10. Bittlinger, "Significance of Charismatic Experiences," 121. Cf. Mark 9:38–40.

11. Harink, *Paul among the Post Liberals*, 149.

12. Twelftree, in response to a review of his book entitled *People of the Spirit: Exploring Luke's View of the Church* by David Seal. These specific comments were made in a *Renewal Dynamics* blog, June 28, 2010, http://renewaldynamics.com/2010/06/27/people-of-the-spirit-exploring-luke%e2%80%99s-view-of-the-church-by-graham-h-twelftree/.

13. Twelftree, *People of the Spirit*, 43.

14. Note, for example the missionary journeys of Paul described in the book of Acts (13:4–14, 51; 14:6, 24–25; 15:41–16:12; 17:1, 15; 18:1, 18–23; 19:21; 20:2–6, 13–17;

and Gentiles alike that the gospel of Jesus Christ, which had been revealed to him by the Spirit, is good news for all.

This missionary purpose of the church, considering the criteria(on) for authentic spirituality, then, has tremendous implications for the contemporary context. As disciples of Jesus and the body of Christ, through whom the ascended Christ is active in the world today, the church is to continue the mission of Jesus, who is concerned for the individual, the community, and the world. The church is to share the love of God with individuals, exercise their spiritual gifts for the edification of the community, and contextually proclaim the gospel tradition in and to the whole world.

Additionally, in the pluralistic contemporary context, worship services of the church should seek to become effective missionary outreaches by allowing charismatic or spiritual experiences to be expressed in gatherings. When this occurs, congregants can comfortably express their gifts, allowing the Spirit of God to sovereignly lead the service, ensuring that all are ministered to in a way that is meaningful to them. The church should be involved in what John Wimber calls "power evangelism," by allowing God's presence and power to be demonstrated through charismatic signs and wonders, enabling the gospel message to be communicated more effectively—even supernaturally.[15]

In brief, the church consists of people in whom the Spirit dwells, rendering them sanctified. This body of Christ is sovereignly gifted by God to charismatically continue the mission and purposes of Christ in the world and is therefore to be united towards that end. For this reason, the church is to be holy and dedicated to the worship and service of their Lord to effectively carry out the missionary purpose of Jesus in a world that often needs to be reproved and held to account for their manner of living. Thus,

> dialogue is no substitute for witness and mission. . . . Faced with the religions and religious communities they encounter, the churches cannot give up their knowledge of God in favor of a neutral view of the world . . . this does not mean rejecting dialogue with other religions. On the contrary, in dialogue the attempt is to be made to understand other religions, to eliminate misunderstandings, to do away with prejudices, to discover genuinely common features, to recognize erroneously assumed common features as such and to widen one's own horizon of perception . . . Syncretistic harmonizations or the systematization of aspects of truth from other religions into a

---

21:1–8, 17).

15. Wimber and Springer, *Power Evangelism*, 78.

new super-religion are excluded for Christian faith. The revelation of God in Jesus Christ is for faith a constant reminder of the limits of dialogue between the religions. Christians owe all people, including the representatives of other religions, the clarity of their witness of faith and life.[16]

Indeed, the one who is authentically spiritual judges all things (1 Cor 2:15). But the world is also able to judge and discern when the church is communicating in a way that is authentically spiritual as a faithful witness to Christ. This faithfulness on the part of the church is therefore pivotal towards providing a revelation of who Jesus is to the world. With such high stakes, the missionary endeavors of the church should always be charismatic. Indeed, all activities of each member of the church should be led by the Spirit and done decently, and in order, so that others might be edified and the kingdom of God be optimally advanced.

8.4 Is Authentic Spirituality Limited to the Church?

But, is authentic spirituality limited to the church? Exactly who can function in the *charismata*? Is there a relationship between one's gender, ethnicity, and socioeconomic status to the functioning of the *charismata*? Stated differently, are charismatic activities limited to a gender, ethnicity, or socioeconomic class? It is generally agreed upon that the latter two categories are not factors that affect the functioning of the *charismata*, but, as will be elaborated upon below in our discussion of the implications of criteria for authentic spirituality in the worship service, the category of gender is continuously being debated and of great significance to the church. Regardless of the relationship of these categories to criteria for authentic spirituality, for now, suffice it to say, it is evident that, for Paul, these categories do not determine the presence of the Spirit—and spiritual gifts—in individuals (cf. 1 Cor 12:12–13; Gal 3:27–28). Rather, for believers, their faith in Christ leads to the indwelling of the Holy Spirit and the concomitant spiritual gifts. And apparently, though the Holy Spirit may not indwell unbelievers, the Spirit can sovereignly distribute gifts to them as the Spirit chooses (1 Cor 12:11).

Scholars generally agree on the implications of this teaching by Paul. For example, J. MacGorman suggests that in the church all differences in racial and social status have lost their ability to divide.[17] That is, all categories of people are equal opportunity exercisers of spiritual gifts. To Hays,

---

16. Hüffmeier, ed., *Church of Jesus Christ*, 117–18.
17. MacGorman, "Glossolalic Error and Its Correction," 393.

the church should no longer be divided by former distinctions of gender, ethnicity, or social status,[18] for all believers possess the same Spirit, who has distributed gifts to them.

The question of exactly who can function in the *charismata* concerns the ethical behavior of individuals. This is relevant in view of 1 Corinthians 1:2, where Paul considers the church to be "sanctified in Christ Jesus, [and] called to be saints." Additionally, in 1 Corinthians 12–14 Paul is offering his criteria for what is authentically spiritual (cf. 12:1), because ethical issues were creating conflict in the church. So, does one have to be "holy" and righteous to function in the *charismata*? Are there ethical requirements for functioning in the *charismata*? If there are ethical requirements, what might some of them be?

Examples of Paul's ethical teachings include his declaration that all Christians are given manifestations of the Spirit for the common good (12:7). In other words, the gifts of the Spirit are given so that one can conduct a lifestyle that is beneficial to their community. Possessors of the Spirit, therefore, should not live in a self-exalting manner. Instead, they should care for one another, and seek to use their gifts to provide what may be lacking in the community. Rather than being involved in schisms and other antagonistic behavior, Christians should complement each other's gifting, making sure that the community is whole and well provided for (12:25). Moreover, when individuals suffer, all should be sympathetic. And when one has cause for rejoicing, all should rejoice with and for them (12:26). This will be possible because of the empowering presence of the Spirit.

But the Spirit's power in one's life must be accompanied by a loving lifestyle so that it can be truly beneficial (1 Cor 13:1–3). Hence, fruit of the Spirit such as patience, kindness, gentleness, humility, self-control, truthfulness, faithfulness, goodness, hope, and endurance should be characteristic of the one who is authentically spiritual (1 Cor 13:4–7; cf. Gal 5:22–23). Rather than continuously living in an immature way, one should grow in the grace that God has given them (1 Cor 13:11) through the exemplary life of Christ.

For Paul, certainly, the gifts of the Spirit and the love of Christ are essential for authentic Christian living. But it is also necessary that all things be done in an edifying manner (1 Cor 14:1). This is especially true when gathering in public (vv. 26–33). In such cases, one should be self-controlled, and all communication should be done in a manner that evidences accountability to the community, who should be able to comprehend and judge what is being said, to ensure that all may learn and be encouraged from it.

---

18. Hays, "Ecclesiology and Ethics," 32.

Further, individuals should be submissive to one another (vv. 34–36), and not forbid the gifts of others (v. 39), but "let all things be proper and according to order" (v. 40).

Summarily, to be authentically spiritual, the exercise of the *charismata* should evidence the presence of the Spirit and be inseparably linked with the love of Christ and godly edification. For, although one may be gifted by the Spirit, they may not necessarily be authentically spiritual. The Corinthians validate this claim, because though they "are not lacking in any spiritual gift" (1 Cor 1:7), Paul is writing to inform them of what it means to be authentically spiritual—including the appropriate functioning of the *charismata* (12:1).

It can also be surmised that relative to the functioning of the *charismata*, ethical behavior, or the rules according to which one should act, ought to be Trinitarian. Gordon Fee agrees with this. First, Pauline ethics is Trinitarian because the Spirit transforms the believer into the likeness of Christ to the glory of God.[19] More specifically, authentically Christian living can only be by the Spirit's empowering.[20] Indeed, the Spirit as an experienced and living reality is an essential component of the Christian life for Paul, to whom the entirety of the Christian life is a matter of the Spirit.[21] These sentiments are echoed by Richard Hays, who says, "ethics cannot be sufficiently guided by law or by institutionalized rules, instead, Spirit empowered, Spirit discerned conformity to Christ is required."[22]

Second, the pattern of Christian ethics, for Fee, is Jesus Christ (cf. 1 Cor 4:16–17; 11:1)—another member of the Trinity.[23] Hays, again, agrees with Fee when he says, "the fundamental norm of Pauline ethics is the christomorphic life.[24] Thiselton adds that the cross also provides a theological basis for Paul's ethics.[25] A similar conclusion had already been reached by Callan, who asserts that Paul stresses the cross as the basis on which the ways of God are different from human ways.[26] In other words, Jesus' exemplary life climaxed at the cross as the ultimate example of love (John 15:13). Thus, if the aim of the ethical life is to be more like God, how one conducts themselves in the "body" shows the genuineness of their confession of Jesus

---

19. Fee, *God's Empowering Presence*, 598.
20. Fee, *God's Empowering Presence*, 5878–79.
21. Fee, *God's Empowering Presence*, 5876.
22. Hays, *Moral Vision*, 43.
23. Fee, *God's Empowering Presence*, 879.
24. Hays, *Moral vision*, 43.
25. Thiselton, *Living Paul*, 127.
26. Callan, *Dying and Rising with Christ*, 178.

as Lord (1 Cor 6:13). Selflessness and unconditional love should be characteristic of the Christian ethic.

Such a love, for Fee, is the principle of Christian ethics.[27] This explains why Paul reacts to the selfish and prideful display of charismatic activity in Corinth (1 Cor 12–14) and "ethicizes" the Spirit by declaring love and edification as inseparable criteria for the functioning of the *charismata*.[28] But while Udo Schnelle maintains that in the Pauline ethic, love is the criterion by which to orient all actions,[29] Paul's teachings in 1 Corinthians 12–14, however, suggest that love, by itself, is not the criterion for ethical living (cf. 14:1). Instead, Paul ascribes spiritual manifestations, love, and edification as criteria(on) for authentic Christian living. Moreover, love, by itself cannot be considered the criterion for ethical behavior since, on the one hand, even those who may not be acting ethically may also love others (Matt 5:46–47). On the other hand, love cannot be separated from the works of the Spirit, for it is the Spirit that empowers one to love. Therefore, love is not to be considered the way believers ought to respond to God's grace revealed in Christ. Instead, love is to be viewed as a necessary component of ethical behavior that must be coupled with godly edification and the gracious activity of the Spirit. So, one should not love, or perform any ethical activity, out of compulsion, but in light of the grace of God.

This grace of God changes our perspective, not our accountability or responsibility. Rather than being anthropocentric, because of grace, our perspective becomes Trinitarian. That is, one continues to be accountable to God for what they do in this life (Rom 14:12), but now they live more conscious of a purpose to glorify God, following the loving pattern of the Son, by the power of the Holy Spirit. In doing so, one's ethical acts will meet a higher standard than those of human laws. For grace is an intensification of the law,[30] that God—who holds individuals responsible to such ethical activity—will also enable them to do.

Nevertheless, the more conscious one is of their being accountable to God, the more careful they are likely to be in choosing their ethical behavior.[31] Thus, it is essential that Christian ethic recover the notion of accountability. Accountability is mindful both of what Christ has done on the cross as well as a pending future judgment. If it is true, as Hays asserts,

---

27. Fee, *God's Empowering Presence*, 879.
28. Beker, *Paul the Apostle*, 291; cf. Elias, *Remember the Future*, 383.
29. Schnelle, *Apostle Paul*, 550.
30. Consider the ethical teachings of Jesus in the Sermon on the Mount/Plain (cf. Matt 5:21–22, 27–28, 38–39, 43–44).
31. Keck, "Accountable Self," 10.

that Paul's ethics is more specifically eschatological,[32] then the reality of the future already determines the present. And, relative to the other member of the Trinity, if in the present one is glorifying God in their actions, for Fee, they are accomplishing the purpose of Christian ethics,[33] for according to Paul all things are to be done for the glory of God (1 Cor 10:31) and for edification (14:26).

8.5 Conclusion

In the contemporary church, therefore, ethical behavior should be conscious of, and consistent with, the triune God, who sovereignly and graciously imparts the Spirit so that individuals may act in a way that is beneficial for all (1 Cor 12:7). As it was for Paul, whose theology was filtered through the lens of his revelation of Jesus Christ (Gal 1:12, 15–16), this Trinitarian ethic should be more robustly centered in Christ,[34] who is the motivation behind Paul's thinking (cf. 1 Cor 2:2–5) and way of life (Phil 1:21). Christ is also inseparable from the Spirit, who empowers him to glorify the Father. Moreover, unlike the subjectivity associated with the person of the Spirit and the Father—whom no one has ever seen (John 1:18; 6:46; 1 John 4:12)—Christ has been an objective presence in the world revealing the Father (John 14:9). Consequently, authentic spirituality should be gauged by Christlikeness, as revealed in the Bible.

Considering this, behaviors associated with preferring one group over another, such as racism and sexism, are to be shunned and never tolerated. In this same way of thinking, for example, it is redundant to claim to be such a thing as a "Christian pluralist." Indeed, Christlikeness is the pattern of ethical behavior. And Christ lived and died for all. He was not a respecter of persons. He focused on the good of all, for all people are of equal value in Christ (1 Cor 12:13; Gal 3:26–28). Instead of being racist, sexist, or a Christian pluralist, then, one should simply be Christian, or an authentic follower of Christ who allows the Holy Spirit to first transform them, before impacting all of society for the glory of God.

Because of the sovereign act of God to be involved in our ethical behavior, the church should act boldly and authoritatively, with full confidence that God is able to accomplish the works he intends through them.

---

32. Hays, *Moral Vision*, 18.

33. Fee, *God's Empowering Presence*, 879.

34. This Trinitarianism is different from a theology of the second order, or the Reformed focus on Christ, for it maintains a healthy respect for the continuous work of the Spirit throughout the history of the church, including in the contemporary context.

This work, however, must be consistent with the revelation of God in Scripture and tradition, for there is no dichotomy between the person and works of God. That is, ethical practices should evidence the loving character of Christ, and godly edification that is peaceable and orderly, so that all people may grasp the soteriological implications of what God is graciously doing or revealing to them in their contexts.

In short, the Trinitarian basis for ethical behavior permeates Paul's thinking. Consequently, ethical behavior can be assessed by the following criteria: Are the actions in question led and empowered by the Spirit? Are the actions marked by the love of Christ? Are the actions glorifying to God? And, are the actions edifying? Only when the answer is affirmative for all these questions can the church rightfully claim to be practicing Christian ethics in true worship of their Lord.

Chapter 9

Implications of Authentic Spirituality for the Contemporary Worship Service

9.1 Introduction

Considering the significance of ethical living for the contemporary church, it becomes clear that it is also important to discuss the ethics of communication. After all, in 1 Corinthians 12–14, and especially in chapter 14, it is evident that Paul addresses appropriate communication in the worship service, or public gathering of the church.[1] In his article entitled "Charismatic Worship in the New Testament and Today," Bittlinger explains why the concept of communication is important relative to the worship service. He appropriately notes that 1 Corinthians 14:26 evidences two criteria of the worship service that renders it a conversation between God and his people.[2] In that verse Paul says, "How is it then brothers? Whenever you come together, each one has a psalm, a teaching, a revelation, a tongue, an interpretation? Let all things be for edification!" Bittlinger's first criterion for communication in the worship service is that God is speaking to the gathered church. This takes place through revelatory acts like the prophetic utterance (cf. 14:6, 29–30), interpretation of tongues, and scriptural preaching and teaching.

The other criterion is that the congregation is speaking to God. This occurs through psalms (hymns) and tongues (a form of prayer and praise, cf. 14:2, 16–17). In terms of this latter criterion, Bittlinger is correct that psalms and tongues are ways in which people communicate to God. But he also ascribes such communication to the public worship service. The relegating of psalms and tongues to the worship service is questionable, however, because while psalms can be expressed either in public or private worship, tongues—at least when uninterpreted—belongs to private worship (14:2–5).

---

1. Cf. 1 Cor 14:4–5, 16–17, 19, 23, 25–26, 28, 33, 35.
2. Bittlinger, "Charismatic Worship," 223.

Considering this, what follows is an attempt to gain insights and derive contemporary implications regarding criteria for authentic spirituality in the worship service. While the *charismata* are all revelatory of the God who distributes them,[3] the *charismata* of prophecy, interpretation of tongues, and tongues will be focused upon because they represent the focus of Paul's remarks, as well as being key concerns in the contemporary worship service.

After highlighting ancient and contemporary concerns regarding communicating in the worship service, the views of the Reformed theologian John Calvin with regards to prophecy, and the gift of tongues will be focused upon. The comments of relevant contemporary thinkers on the same issues will also be considered. The focus on Calvin will be relevant because much of the contemporary concerns regarding the *charismata* stems from how he has been interpreted over the years.[4] Subsequently, it will be asked, respectively, are prophecy, tongues, and the *charismata* in general, to be exercised in the contemporary worship service, or were they just for the NT period? If the *charismata* are to be practiced today, are there criteria for when they should be exercised? And, are there gender criteria relative to the functioning of the *charismata* in the worship service?

9.2 Ancient and Contemporary Concerns regarding Communicating in the Worship Service

Certainly, Paul's emphasis in 1 Corinthians 12–14 makes it clear that one of the *pneumatika*, or spiritual things (12:1), that he is addressing concerns what is appropriate communication—relative to utterances of prophecy, tongues, and interpretation of tongues—in the worship service.[5] This is the general conclusion of scholarship on this text, especially 1 Corinthians 14. For example, David Ackerman says, "there is a communication problem at Corinth," and Paul is seeking to position the *charismata* of prophecy and tongues into the context of being edifying to the church;[6] he is condemning their wrong interpretation of what it means to be spiritual. Max Turner concludes that there were too many occurrences and concurrent outbursts of tongues in

---

3. Rowe, "1 Corinthians 12–14," 122; cf. Calvin, *Institutes of Christian Religion*, 2.4.3.2; Ward, "Significance of Tongues," 145; Synan, "Speaking in Tongues," 326.

4. Cf. Randy Colver, "The Baptism in the Holy Spirit, the Charismata, and Cessationism" (2006), 22, http://www.netministry.com/clientfiles/62181/mw_colver-baptismintheholyspirit.pdf.

5. Aune, *Prophecy in Early Christianity*, 220.

6. Ackerman, "Fighting Fire with Fire," 350–51.

the worship service (cf. 1 Cor 14:23, 27), and these tongues were not being interpreted or being exercised in a loving manner.[7] To John Calvin, the communication problem at Corinth involves their preference for tongues over prophecy because tongues "had more of a show connected with it," in that tongues excites the admiration of the hearers.[8] These comments affirm the characteristic Graeco-Roman influence present in the Corinthian church, for they highlight a tolerance, upward mobility, and salvific zeal for the perceived benefits of these visible manifestations of supernatural activity.

Paul also addresses appropriate communication in the worship service when he discusses the cessation of charismatic speech by saying, "Love never fails, but as for prophecies, they will be discontinued, as for tongues, they will cease, as for knowledge, it will be discontinued" (1 Cor 13:8). But the relationship of Paul's statement to criteria for authentic spirituality—as will be discussed below—is variously interpreted by contemporary scholars.

Finally, appropriate communication in the worship service is addressed when Paul says, "let the women be silent in the churches. For it is not permitted for them to speak, but (to) be subject, just as even the law says. And if they wish to learn something, let them ask their own husbands at home, for it is shameful for a woman to speak in church" (14:34–35). Based on these verses, commonly referred to as the *mulier taceat* (let the women be silent), contemporary scholarship has raised the question of whether there are gender criteria relative to the functioning of the *charismata* in the worship service. To more fully understand the implications of criteria for authentic spirituality in the contemporary worship service, it will be instructive to take an in-depth look at the Reformation and contemporary interpreter's criteria for the functioning of prophecy and the gift of tongues in the worship service.

9.3 Reformation and Contemporary Interpretations of Authentic Prophecy and the Gift of Tongues in the Worship Service

Perhaps, even as criteria for the functioning of the *charismata*—particularly prophecy, tongues, and interpretation of tongues—was a major focus of Paul's scriptural exhortations, criteria for the functioning of the same gifts of the Spirit was of concern for Reformed thinkers. Thus, the issue has been widely discussed among them. And—as will become apparent—many of the

---

7. Turner, "Tongues," 235–36.
8. Calvin, *Commentary*, 435.

contemporary issues relative to the functioning of prophecy and tongues in the worship service are based in how Reformed scholars, such as Calvin, have been interpreted. What follows, respectively, is a detailed analysis of Reformation and contemporary interpreters' criteria for the functioning of prophecy and tongues in the worship service.

9.3.1 Reformation and contemporary interpreters' criteria for authentic prophecy in the worship service

For the Reformed theologian Calvin, prophecy is a "peculiar gift" for interpreting and applying scripture wisely in the present.[9] The prophet, or the one who prophesies, is therefore an interpreter and administrator of received revelation.[10] Prophets, however, are not interpreting the direct will of God. Rather, their interpretation particularly concerns what has already been revealed in Scripture.[11] Calvin's view of prophecy is consistent with that of fellow Reformers like Ulrich Zwingli (1484–1531 C.E.), who notes that prophecy is an explaining of Scripture,[12] and Desiderius Erasmus (1466–1536 C.E.), who, relative to 1 Corinthians 14:1, remarks that "prophecy is interpretation of Holy scripture."[13]

While prophets have the gift of interpreting, their interpretation of scriptural revelation is not necessarily what is authentically spiritual. The prophet's interpretation could be a purely anthropocentric understanding of what God has revealed in Scripture. To clarify, Calvin does not seem to be saying that prophecy itself is revelatory—Scripture is. For him, prophets are gifted by God to interpret and apply what has previously been revealed in Scripture. Their interpretation of Scripture, however, is not a direct revelation of God's will. That is why, while Calvin affirms the purpose Paul ascribes to prophecy as being for edification, consoling, and exhorting, he also asserts that such things do not concern foretelling or communication relevant to future events (revelation of the future).[14] Such prognostication would be an entirely supernatural event, attributable only to God. Instead, Calvin relegates prophecy to forthtelling concerning the present, that is based on scriptural revelation. From this perspective, prophecy is just a highly regarded interpretation of Scripture addressing the present needs of the church. And since

---

9. Calvin, *Commentary*, 415.
10. Calvin, *Commentary*, 438.
11. Calvin, *Institutes*, 2.4.3.4.
12. Himmighofer, *Zürcher Bibel*, 180–84.
13. Erasmus, *Novum Instrumentum*, 1516.
14. Calvin, *Commentary*, 436.

prophecy is not the directly revealed will of God, the source of "prophetic" communication can be either natural or supernatural.

Additionally, since, for Calvin, prophecy is human interpretation of what God has already revealed in Scripture, Calvin excludes foretelling from prophecy. But even if prophetic revelation is restricted to the content of Scripture, it does not follow that it should also preclude foretelling. Indeed, though it is historical fact that the canon of Scripture has closed, scriptural revelation of God often speaks into the future and foretells the will of God. For example, because both John the revelator and the apostle Paul foretell a future reign of God (cf. Rev 21:2—22:5; 1 Thess 4:13–18), one can simultaneously be foretelling and scriptural.

Still, contemporary interpretations of Calvin's criteria for the functioning of prophecy in the worship service can be categorized based on whether prophecy is interpreted as being a direct revelation of God's will or an interpretation of scriptural content. On the one hand, Paul Elbert agrees with Calvin that prophecy is forthtelling and not foretelling.[15] It is not a direct revelation of God's will, but it is based on the revelation already found in Scripture. A similar conclusion is reached by J. I. Packer, who says,

> Prophecy is a God prompted application of truth that in general terms had been revealed already rather than a disclosure of divine thoughts and intentions not previously known and not otherwise knowable.... Any verbal enforcement of biblical teaching as it applies to one's present hearers may properly be called prophecy today.[16]

On the other hand, the Lutheran Church of Australia maintains that "to prophesy is to speak God's word to his people on the basis of a special revelation by the inspiration of the Holy Spirit."[17] And Wayne Grudem suggests that prophecy is revelation spontaneously given to individuals,[18] directly from God, and not mediated through Scripture,[19] but is relative to the specific need of the moment.[20] For Grudem, this "direct revelation," though it is not limited to Scripture, when communicated by the NT prophet, is still "human wisdom" or an interpretation of the direct revelation, for it is

---

15. Elbert, "Calvin and the Spiritual Gifts," 244.
16. Packer, *Keep in Step with the Spirit*, 215.
17. Lutheran Church of Australia, "1 Corinthians 14:33b-38 and 1 Timothy 2:11–14 Prohibit," 62. Hereafter "Prohibit."
18. Grudem, *Gift of Prophecy*, 67.
19. Grudem, *Gift of Prophecy*, 162.
20. Grudem, *Gift of Prophecy*, 152.

not the actual words of God, but the general content.²¹ To Grudem, OT prophets and NT apostles communicated with the authority of the actual words of God, but NT prophets only communicate general content. Such a distinction has led Max Turner to criticize Grudem for creating a non-biblical dichotomy between OT and NT prophecy.²²

After surveying the contemporary interpretations of Calvin's views of prophecy, Mark Cartledge concludes that both NT and contemporary (charismatic) prophecy are based on revelation; the appropriate and expected context for their functioning is the worship service; anyone can prophesy; prophecy should be edifying, encouraging, and comforting (1 Cor 14:3); and prophecy has authority of general content, and therefore requires discernment and judgment (14:29)—in light of Scripture—from their hearers. George Mallone adds that prophecy must not contradict scriptural revelation (14:37–38); it must be under the control of the person (14:32); only two or three are to be given at any one meeting (14:29); and the prophet is reluctant and humble, instead of being presumptuous.²³ These views beg the question: what is Calvin's view on the relationship between prophecy and preaching? This understanding should further clarify Calvin's views relative to communicating in the worship service.

9.3.1.1 Calvin's view of the relationship between prophecy and preaching

Contemporary interpreters of Calvin have varying opinions regarding the Reformers' view of the relationship between prophecy and preaching. Perhaps this is because Calvin's views on the subject, rather than being captured in an explicit statement, are scattered throughout his writings, especially those relevant to the offices of the church. For Calvin, the NT office of prophet corresponds to that of the contemporary teacher, and the office of the NT apostles corresponds to the contemporary pastor.²⁴ Teachers and prophets are interpreters of Scripture, but pastors and apostles preach the gospel, discipline,²⁵ and administer the sacraments.²⁶

Considering Calvin's views regarding prophecy in the worship service, it can be concluded that the communication of teachers and prophets, for

21. Grudem, *Gift of Prophecy*, 67.
22. Turner, "Spiritual Gifts Then and Now," 16.
23. Mallone, *Those Controversial Gifts*, 33.
24. Calvin, *Institutes*, 2.4.3.5.
25. Calvin, *Institutes*, 2.4.3.4.
26. Calvin, *Institutes*, 2.4.3.5.

the Reformer, are limited to one's proclamation relative to the present—it is not clearly supernatural, for it is not a direct revelation of God's will. Instead, the prophet and teacher are interpreters of what has already been revealed in Scripture, "to keep doctrine whole and pure among believers."[27] Consequently, such utterances, being an interpretation and an exhortation, can be attributable to either a human or supernatural source.

Likewise, for Calvin, preaching pertains to the communication of scriptural revelation of the gospel of Jesus Christ, "for the salvation of the world."[28] Preaching involves the exhortation of the apostle or pastor to their listeners,[29] and concerns the gospel. Thus, preaching is restricted to Scripture, which, in Calvin's way of thinking, renders it forthtelling and not foretelling. This preaching, then, is not a direct revelation of God's will—which cannot be limited to the present time. Preaching is human exhortation concerning what God has already revealed in the gospel, and, like prophecy, it is effectually an interpretation of scriptural revelation that can be attributable to either a human or supernatural source.

What can be said of Calvin's view of the relationship between prophecy and preaching, then, is that both forms of communication are exhortations and interpretations of scriptural revelation that require listeners to discern whether an utterance is either divine revelation or a manifestation or representation of what is characteristic of the triune God. Therefore, the relationship between prophecy and preaching, for Calvin, is that they are one and the same. If one is to accept Calvin's rationale, then, to be considered revelatory of the direct will of God, prophecy and preaching, like all *charismata*, and forms of communication, respectively, need to be a manifestation of the Spirit, sensitively contextual, and faithful to the tradition of Scripture that has already been revealed.

9.3.1.2 *Contemporary interpretations of the Reformation view of the relationship between prophecy and preaching*

In terms of the relationship between prophecy and preaching, contemporary scholars interpret Calvin as either equating prophecy and preaching or distinguishing between the two forms of communication. Regarding the former, Eduard Schweizer, for example, says, "preaching means prophecy," for both forms of communicating translate the Christian faith, making

27. Calvin, *Institutes*, 2.4.3.4.
28. Calvin, *Institutes*, 2.4.3.4.
29. Calvin, *Institutes*, 2.4.3.4.

it relevant for the hearer.[30] Such "prophetic preaching," however, should not limit the freedom of the Spirit by allowing only ordained preachers to speak. Moreover, overestimated enthusiasm in which a preacher's "utterance of the Spirit" is contradictory to scriptural revelation should be considered inauthentic.[31] "There needs to be a combination of prophetic utterances of members by the Spirit of God with a bold sticking to the unchangeable apostolic truth."[32]

To David Hill, NT prophets are pastoral preachers who give instructions on what it means for the body of Christ to live authentically spiritual.[33] This is based on his interpretation of 1 Corinthians 14:3, where Paul says, "but the one who prophesies to men speaks edification and encouragement, and comfort." For Hill, the terms "encouragement" and "comfort" signify the same thing, and both words describe characteristics of "edification."[34] Thus, "edification," "encouragement," and "comfort" are similar words. Hill chooses to consider prophecy encouraging speech, exhortatory, or pastoral preaching. He asserts, "as pastoral preachers, the New Testament prophets teach and give instruction on what the Christian way requires of individual believers and the community."[35]

Hill's conflating of the terms "edification," "encouragement," and "comfort," however, does not acknowledge that the terms have different meanings, and that Paul explicitly distinguishes between them with the coordinating conjunction καὶ (and), which joins and adds to the overall thought of the sentence. Hill's reductionism, therefore, detracts from the comprehensive thought that Paul is trying to convey, and limits the idea of prophecy to a relatively anthropocentric preaching, which may not effectively communicate the involvement of God. This definition of prophecy as "pastoral preaching" may be "tilted in the direction of moral exhortation that merely presupposes the basic *kerygma* [preaching of the Gospel] of the early church."[36]

By way of contrast, Paul's use of the three mentioned terms is pneumatocentric, for he focuses on conveying that the charism of prophecy is an activity of the Spirit, who spiritually strengthens, emboldens one in their

---

30. Schweizer, "Service of Worship," 406.
31. Schweizer, "Service of Worship," 407.
32. Schweizer, "Service of Worship," 408.
33. Hill, *New Testament Prophecy*, 129. Cf. Hill, "Christian Prophets as Teachers," 114.
34. Hill, *New Testament Prophecy*, 112.
35. Hill, *New Testament Prophecy*, 116–17.
36. Gillespie, *First Theologians*, 28.

course of action, and is a comforter to the one who is grieving. For Hill, however, prophecy is not the interpretation of Scripture, or tongues, and foretelling cannot be excluded from what is prophetic.[37] In contrast to Hill, Packer considers prophecy the preaching and application of biblical truth, and not a revelation of the direct will of God.[38]

Finally, Kenneth Gangel also equates prophecy and preaching. He writes that "the gift of prophecy is congregational preaching which explains and applies God's revelation [in scripture]."[39] Like Calvin, Gangel's equating of prophecy and preaching is based on limiting prophetic activity to Scripture. Gangel does not allow for the continuous functioning of the *charismata* of prophecy outside of Scripture, and therefore also not in the contemporary context. Calvin, on the other hand, is open to the latter, for he acknowledges "traces or shadows of them [prophecy in his time]."[40]

But other contemporary scholars distinguish between prophecy and preaching. One such scholar is Gerhard Dautzenberg. For him, preaching and prophecy are not the same, because preaching has the gospel of Jesus Christ as its content and is directed at the past, but prophecy is future oriented, containing eschatological mysteries (revelation).[41] On the one hand, unlike Hill, Dautzenberg does not conflate the notion of prophecy with "edification" and "exhortation," for he considers the latter two terms to have resulted from prophecy.[42] On the other hand, though it is yet to be conclusive if Dautzenberg is right in not equating prophecy and preaching, his distinction between their contents does not find support in Pauline thought. Paul interrelates his Christology (including the gospel of Jesus Christ) with eschatology—which Dautzenberg says is characteristic of prophecy—as well as soteriology, pneumatology, and ethics.[43] In other words, for Paul, the contents of the gospel being preached and eschatological mysteries are not mutually exclusive, as Dautzenberg implies.

Thomas Gillespie also argues that prophecy and preaching are not the same. For him, instead of preaching, the NT prophets were interpreting the *kerygma*, and should rightly be considered the first theologians of

---

37. Hill, *New Testament Prophecy*, 203–6.
38. Packer, *Keep in Step with the Spirit*, 217.
39. Gangel, *You and Your Spiritual Gifts*, 64. See also his *Unwrap Your Spiritual Gifts*, 38.
40. Calvin, *Commentary*, 416.
41. Dautzenberg, *Urchristliche Prophetie*, 302, 304.
42. Dautzenberg, *Urchristliche Prophetie*, 298.
43. Cf. Schnelle, *Apostle Paul*, 486.

the church.⁴⁴ Their hermeneutic or interpretation of the *kerygma* was done under the inspiration of the Holy Spirit, and therefore should be considered divine revelation.⁴⁵ It is noteworthy that Gillespie considers prophecy to be revelation, but such divine disclosure is still to be criticized under the criteria of the church's confession, the *kerygma*, and Scripture because of the subjectivity of claiming inspiration by the Spirit. However, he does not make it clear if he also considers preaching to be revelation.

John Leith says that prophecy is not preaching, but "it is better to relate it [prophecy] to revelation: the prophet discloses God's will for man now and in relation to the future; the element of prediction cannot be excluded."⁴⁶ Despite his equating of prophecy and preaching, David Hill also asserts that "a prophet's utterances cannot and should not be dissociated from the impartation of knowledge not already available and which does not come to him by the application of rational thought, but only by revelation."⁴⁷

To Max Turner, preaching is revelation mediated through Scripture and it may be inspired, but it is not the same as prophecy, which is direct revelation mediated to the person.⁴⁸ For Charles Talbert, prophecy is not just preaching and teaching; it is a supernatural gift.⁴⁹ And according to the joint statement of the Fountain Trust (England) and the Evangelical Anglican Council, "immediacy in receiving and declaring God's present message to men is the hallmark of New Testament prophecy, as of its Old Testament counterpart. Preaching may at times approximate more to prophecy, although its basic character is one of teaching and exhortation."⁵⁰ Likewise, the Lutheran Church of Australia's Commission on Theology and Inter-Church Relations concludes that prophecy is a different genre of communication than preaching, for prophecy is direct revelation from God, and preaching is proclamation of the gospel in light of Scripture.⁵¹

In short, the relationship between prophecy and preaching is that both acts are ways in which the message of God for his people can be communicated. Instead of prophecy being focused either on revelation, and the supernatural activity of God—whether in or out of Scripture

---

44. Gillespie, *First Theologians*, 32.
45. Gillespie, *First Theologians* 199, 262.
46. Leith, "Calvin's Doctrine of the Proclamation," 46.
47. Hill, *New Testament Prophecy*, 129.
48. Turner, *Spiritual Gifts Then and Now*, 14.
49. Talbert, "Paul's Understanding of the Holy Spirit," 103.
50. Fountain Trust (England) and the Evangelical Anglican Council, *Theological Renewal Occasional Paper*, 10.
51. Lutheran Church of Australia, "Prohibit," 62.

(Dautzenberg)—or preaching being limited to the content of Scripture (Hill, Gangel), dialogue on this subject needs to be more balanced and representative of a biblical perspective.

This balanced view of preaching and prophecy suggest that prophecy is revelation from God (1 Cor 14:6) and, as such, can either be foretelling or forthtelling. In terms of preaching, it can be equated to prophecy, if it is based on revelation and is not limited to Scripture, or an anthropocentric hermeneutic. While preaching should not be limited to Scripture, it should also not be contradictory of Scripture. Instead, preaching should be led by the Holy Spirit—who "not only once inspired those who wrote it [scripture], but continually inspires, supernaturally assists, those that read it [scripture] with earnest prayer"[52]—and sensitively prepared by the preacher.

The relationship between preaching and prophecy, then, is that prophecy can be inclusive of preaching, and preaching may not be prophetic. Stated differently, prophecy receives its content through revelation—whether direct or indirect[53]—but the content of preaching may not be from revelation (1 Cor 2:4). If the objective of all communication is to be authentically spiritual, today's preacher—and the church—should be eager to prophesy (14:1, 39) and allow the Holy Spirit to illuminate their mind concerning the gospel of Jesus Christ and its eschatological implications for all people.

Other contemporary commentators, though they have not explicitly commented on the relationship between prophecy and preaching, agree with this perspective that contemporary preaching should strive to be prophetic, in terms of being revelatory of God. John Wimber, for example, suggests that preaching should be done charismatically, for it should accompany a demonstration of the gospel.[54] To Harink, preaching should focus on Christ's redemptive act on the cross, demonstrating God's soteriological purposes for all people.[55] Contrary to the tendency in modernity to preach about one religion versus another, preaching should emphasize the person and gospel of Christ, who is Lord of all people and circumstances. Unlike preaching on religion, christocentric preaching focuses on God's calling out of a people so that they can be transformed as they glorify God by the power of the Holy Spirit.[56] Recognizing this transforming mandate for preaching, Teresa Fry Brown emphasizes that preaching must

---

52. Wesley, *Explanatory Notes*, 794. See also, Pinnock, "Work of the Holy Spirit," 7; and Thorsen, *Wesleyan Quadrilateral*, 77–78.
53. Reisling, "Prophecy, the Spirit and the Church," 70.
54. Wimber, *Power Evangelism*, 79.
55. Harink, *Paul among the Postliberals*, 256.
56. Harink, *Paul among the Postliberals*, 244.

be suitable for all people, and it is therefore essential that preachers work at the delivery and reception of their sermon so that it will be appealing to as many people as possible.[57] This issue of communicating in a way that is broadly appealing is also at the center of the contemporary discussion regarding tongues in the worship service.

9.3.2 Reformation and contemporary interpreters' criteria for authentic tongues in the worship service

Before discussing the issues relevant to the Reformation view of authentic tongues in the worship service, it is important to make clear what Calvin means by "tongues." For the Reformed scholar, the gift of tongues refers to "knowledge of languages—specifically the diversity of human foreign languages—and the gift of interpretation."[58] A tongue, for Calvin, then, is a sign for unbelievers[59] given by the Holy Spirit "merely for the publication of the Gospel among all nations."[60] Despite ascribing such an evangelistic purpose for tongues, Calvin insists that tongues are a "gift of inferior importance."[61] That is, by the gift of the Spirit, the tongue speaker speaks a foreign language to God, and not unto men—who do not hear and understand the particular language, except if there is an interpretation.

Because of such unintelligibility of tongues, there is need for the gift of interpretation of tongues, "for the church can, without any inconvenience, dispense with tongues, except in so far as they are helps to prophecy."[62] Indeed, with the gift of interpretation of tongues, tongues can be exercised in the worship service and, like prophecy, intelligibly communicate to others. Uninterpreted tongues, however, are for private prayers.[63]

Calvin's interpretation of Paul in terms of what he calls "tongues" has fueled contemporary debates in a variety of ways. Some of the questions being debated include: What are the criteria for the functioning of tongues in the worship service? Can the *charismata* function without the Spirit's involvement? Or, is tongues mere human language? Are the gifts of tongues and interpretation of tongues to be grouped together as kinds of tongues, or human foreign languages? Is there a significance in speaking a foreign

57. Fry-Brown, *Delivering the Sermon*, 86.
58. Cf. Calvin, *Commentary*, 417, 419, 435.
59. Calvin, *Commentary*, 454.
60. Calvin, *Commentary*, 437.
61. Calvin, *Commentary*, 459.
62. Calvin, *Commentary*, 459.
63. Calvin, *Commentary*, 460.

language to God? If tongues refer to human foreign language spoken to God, is it authentic if a foreigner hears and understands it? Is tongues a sign or a gift, public or private? Do all who exercise the *charismata* speak in tongues? In other words, is speaking in tongues the initial evidence of baptism in the Spirit? Is there a criterion that a gift is to be preferred over another? Is the functioning of the *charismata* relevant, or authentic, in the contemporary context, or did cease in the NT period? And, are there gender criteria relative to the functioning of the *charismata* in the worship service? Contemporary scholars have much to say regarding these questions.

In terms of defining the concept of tongues, contemporary scholars are divided as to whether tongues are human or supernatural languages. For instance, Charles Talbert suggests that Paul identifies two different phenomena called "tongues."[64] Based on 1 Corinthians 13:1, he identifies "tongues of men" and "tongues of angels." The "tongues of men" refers to *xenolalia*, or human foreign languages, and was evident on the day of Pentecost (Acts 2:1–11), where the crowd of various nationalities could hear in their own languages the tongues that the Spirit gave them the ability to speak. "Tongues of angels" refers to *glossolalia*, which is unintelligible language for humans, but is a way of speaking mysteries to God in the Spirit (1 Cor 14:2–5).

J. W. MacGorman notes that those who consider "tongues" to be human languages maintain that they are foreign languages that one has never learned.[65] This *xenolalia* was and always will be for the spreading of the gospel,[66] for God has strategically chosen to use such tongues throughout church history to expand and renew the church.[67]

But the sense of tongues as human foreign languages does not find support in the biblical text, where tongues are considered supernatural (1 Cor 12:7–11). Indeed, tongues are visible and audible evidence that God is there.[68] And tongues are probably best regarded as special "languages'" not having ordinary human characteristics, inspired by the Holy Spirit for worship, for a sign to unbelievers, and when interpreted, for the edification of the believers. *Glossolalia* can also be a form of prayer, for they are the voice of the unconscious or non-rational, directed towards God, as the Spirit intercedes for us with words too deep for human understanding (Rom 8:26–27). This unconscious or non-rational expression of tongues is

64. Talbert, "Paul's Understanding of the Holy Spirit," 103.
65. MacGorman, "Glossolalic Error and Its Correction," 390.
66. Synan, "Speaking in Tongues," 328.
67. Hynson, "Speaking the Word," 34.
68. Ward, "Significance of Tongues," 145.

like other non-rational expressions, such as dreams and visions, laughing and weeping, painting and dancing—all of which the Holy Spirit can use to communicate.[69]

Whether one believes the source of tongues is human or supernatural, it is observable that for Paul, tongues are given by the Spirit (1 Cor 12:4, 11); are a manifestation of the Spirit to benefit the one practicing it (14:4), as well as those hearing it (12:7); have mystical value (14:2); can be used in prayer (14:14–15), worship (14:15), and evangelism (14:22); and should not be forbidden (14:39). Ernest Best is therefore right to conclude that the report of a special committee of the United Presbyterian Church in the USA to their General Assembly of 1970, regarding the functioning of tongues, is carefully balanced in saying that

> on the basis of scripture, the practice of glossolalia should be neither despised nor forbidden; on the other hand, it should not be emphasized nor made normative for the Christian experience. Generally, the experience should be private, and those who have experienced a genuine renewal of their faith in this way should be on their guard against divisiveness within the congregation. At the same time those who have received no unusual experiences of the Holy Spirit should be alert to the possibility of a deeper understanding of the Gospel and a fuller participation in the gifts of the Spirit.[70]

The notion of the normativity of the practice of tongues will be addressed below, and the idea that tongues should generally be practiced in private probably derives from Paul's thinking that to be exercised in the worship service, tongues should be interpreted so that the congregation will be edified by it (14:27–28).

9.3.2.1 Contemporary understanding of the gift of tongues

What, then, is the contemporary understanding of this gift of interpretation of tongues, as it relates to the criteria for its functioning? It is generally agreed that "interpretation of tongues is an attendant gift to tongues."[71] For the use of tongues in communicating to the gathering of believers requires the complementary gift of interpretation, and "interpretation [of tongues] is a complementary gift which makes possible and meaningful the use of

---

69. Ward, "Significance of Tongues," 145.
70. Cf. Best, "Interpretation of Tongues," 48.
71. MacGorman, "Glossolalic Error and Its Correction," 389.

tongues in the meeting for worship."[72] That interpretation of tongues is complementary to, or in tandem with, the gift of tongues suggests that interpretation of tongues should not be claimed unless there is a public exercise of tongues. Such a claim of interpretation of tongues would be tantamount to a prophetic word that is revelatory of the will of God.

But there is disagreement among scholars as to whether interpretation of tongues can be considered prophecy. On the one hand, for Bittlinger, an interpretation of tongues is an interpretation of speech that is received directly from God, in order to build up the church, and is therefore equal to prophecy.[73] Likewise, Ackerman says, "tongues speaking can become useful to the community only if it is interpreted, which then makes it equivalent to prophecy."[74] On the other hand, David Hill asserts that interpretation of tongues—or one's interpretation or perception of the will of God from Scripture or some other indirect "revelation" from God—does not correspond to prophecy, which is direct revelation of the will of God.[75] This interpretation of tongues may have been a part of the prophet's function, but, rather than being prophecy, it is more analogous to the role of a teacher.[76]

9.3.2.2 Can the charismata function without the Spirit's involvement (is tongues mere human language)?

In the thinking of Calvin and his interpreters, relative to tongues—and interpretation of tongues—there is, therefore, a subtly suggested difference between the direct revelation of God's will and what one interprets as the will of God. This tension begs at least one question relevant to the contemporary context: Can the charismata, in general, and tongues and interpretation of tongues, in particular, authentically function without the Spirit's involvement? This is an important question since Calvin and some of his interpreters consider tongues—and their interpretation—to be gifts given by the Spirit, but define them in anthropocentric categories, seemingly rejecting the role of the Spirit in their functioning. This is evidenced, for example, when Calvin suggests that tongues are human foreign languages, and interpretation of tongues is equivalent to prophecy and preaching of the gospel among the nations. In other words, interpretation of tongues, rather than being a direct revelation of the will of God, is simply a human being's interpretation

72. Bitlinger, *Gifts and Graces*, 51.
73. Bitlinger, *Gifts and Graces*, 51–52.
74. Ackerman, "Fighting Fire with Fire," 351.
75. Hill, *New Testament Prophecy*, 205–6.
76. Hill, *New Testament Prophecy*, 206.

of some foreign language (tongues) that was spoken. The supernatural aspect of the *charismata* seems to be exempted.

Contrary to Calvin, for example, W. G. Putnam says tongues should not be regarded as having ordinary human characteristics; rather, they are special "languages" inspired by the Holy Spirit.[77] William Samarin notes, "in spite of superficial similarities, *glossolalia* (tongues) is fundamentally not language. All specimen of *glossolalia* that has ever been studied have produced no features that would even suggest that they reflect some kind of communicative system."[78] This is because tongues can be considered a form of precognitive speech without specific vocabulary, form, or syntax.[79]

The concepts of exercising the *charismata* without the Spirit's involvement and tongues being mere human languages, however, cannot be substantiated in Pauline thought. This is because the *charismata* are allotted to individuals by the Spirit, who also sovereignly activates them (1 Cor 12:11). And the one who speaks in tongues speaks mysteries to God, in the Spirit, in a manner that nobody understands (1 Cor 14:2).

9.3.2.3 Are the gifts of tongues and interpretation of tongues to be grouped together as kinds of tongues, or human foreign languages?

Why, then, does Calvin categorize tongues and interpretations of tongues together as kinds of tongues, or human foreign languages?[80] If Calvin is suggesting that the two gifts are in tandem, such an interpretation would be consistent with Pauline thought, where interpretation of tongues is to always accompany the exercise of tongues in the worship service (cf. 1 Cor 14:5, 13, 27–28). But if the Reformed theologian is asserting that tongues and interpretation of tongues are to be considered one gift, such an assertion would be devoid of biblical justification. Indeed, Paul itemizes both gifts in 1 Corinthians 12:10. Furthermore, conflating the two gifts as tongues does not seem to consider that tongues do not always need to be interpreted, but are edifying to the individual when exercised in private to God (14:2, 4a).

---

77. Putman, "Tongues, Gift of," 1286–87.
78. Samarin, "Sacred and Profane," 4.
79. Mallone, *Those Controversial Gifts*, 84.
80. Cf. Calvin, *Commentary*, 417, 419, 435.

9.3.2.4 Is there a significance of speaking a foreign language to God?

For Paul, such private use of tongues is "speaking mysteries in the Spirit" to God (1 Cor 14:2). But, as already noted, Calvin considers tongues speech as "human foreign language . . . merely for the publication of the Gospel among all nations."[81] Seemingly paradoxically, however, Calvin also maintains that tongues speech is a foreign language directed to God and not people. Is Calvin contradicting himself? Or is he implying that there are two ways in which tongues is used? One way of exercising a tongue would be to privately direct it to God, and the other would be to publicly direct tongues to all nations. Before answering the latter question, it should be informative to find out the significance Calvin ascribes to speaking a foreign language to God—and not unto people? For Calvin, "the reason why he [the tongues speaker] does not speak to men (people) is because no one heareth, that is, as an articulate voice. For all hear a sound, but they do not understand what is said." Additionally, for Calvin, "speaking in tongues to God" is another way of saying the tongues speaker sings and/or preaches to themselves—thus, a private use of tongues.

It is noteworthy, here, that while Paul describes a tongue that is directed to God (14:2), Calvin interprets such tongues as being directed to oneself—an interpretation that lends itself to various questions that Calvin does not address. One of these questions is: If people are not able to understand tongues, why is it being spoken to oneself? Second, why should tongues be considered "human foreign languages" for spreading the gospel? And even if tongues are human foreign languages, considering Calvin's assessment of why the Corinthians used tongues,[82] is God a respecter of languages? Fourth, is Calvin implying that God is impressed by a foreign language because they have "more of a show connected with it"? Finally, is God's admiration of a person excited when he hears them speak in a foreign language? The answers to these questions are beyond the scope of this work, but since tongues are a gift from God the Spirit, and God is love (1 John 4:8, 16), and not a respecter of persons (Rom 2:11)—or languages, which cannot be foreign to God since he hears all who communicates with him—there does not seem to be a need to speak in a "human foreign language" to God.

---

81. Calvin, *Commentary*, 437.

82. Calvin, *Commentary*, 435. For Calvin, the Corinthians exercised the gift of tongues because it had more of a show connected with it; and people become excited when they hear tongues speech.

9.3.2.5 *If tongues refer to speaking human foreign languages to God, are they authentic if a foreigner hears and understands?*

But even if tongues speech did refer to human foreign languages spoken to God, would the exercise of such tongues be inauthentic if a foreigner heard and understood? The answer to this question would appear to be no, since Calvin seems to describe two usages for tongues and does not suggest that tongues speech is directed to God and not to people—as Paul does (1 Cor 14:2). While Paul also describes two uses of tongues: one that is privately directed to God and does not need to be interpreted but is edifying to the individual, and another that is publicly communicated and must be interpreted for the edification of gathering worshippers.

By contrast, the tongues that Calvin describes as human foreign language to God—despite also having a private and a public use—are never directed to God, but to people. The private use is directed to and edifies the individual; the public use is directed to and edifies the nations. With this understanding, then, it becomes clear that for Calvin, one can authentically be exercising the gift of tongues if a foreigner hears and understands.

9.3.2.6 *Is tongues a sign or a gift, public or private?*

Because of the dual uses ascribed to tongues, both by Paul and Calvin, it is important to address this theme in greater detail because of the further questions that have stemmed from this observation for the contemporary context. The work of Max Turner will be very helpful in this regard, for in his article entitled "Tongues: An Experience for All in the Churches," he examines whether Paul distinguishes between two types of tongues.[83] Turner frames the issue by noting how some Pentecostals, and other scholars, suggest that 1 Corinthians 12:30 deals only with the public manifestation of tongues in the worship service, and 14:5 suggests that all should speak in tongues.[84] In the former verse, when Paul asks the rhetorical questions ". . . Do all speak in tongues? Do all interpret?" he intends an emphatic no. And in the latter verse Paul exhorts, "Now, I wish you all to speak in tongues, but more that you may prophesy. And the one who prophesies is greater than the one who speaks in tongues, unless he should interpret in order that the church may receive edification."

In regards to these verses, even a non-Pentecostal such as Ernest Best concludes that there is a private type of tongue that does not require

---

83. Turner, "Tongues," 234.
84. Turner, "Tongues," 231.

interpretation, and a public tongue communicated in the worship service that requires interpretation.[85] Among Pentecostals, the Assemblies of God scholar Fee, for example, maintains that in 12:30 Paul is discussing the type of tongues that is used in the public worship service—which should not be exercised by all, and must be accompanied by interpretation. To the contrary, however, for Fee, the tongues of 14:5, which is also being referred to in 14:2 and 15–16, is for private devotion, prayer, or doxology, and should be exercised by all.[86]

Pentecostal historian Vinson Synan notes that, on the one hand, the tongues of 14:5 are a "sign . . . that God is at work here," in this, the age of the Holy Spirit.[87] Further, it can be argued, based on scriptural data, that this sign, which is universally given and does not need to be interpreted, is the initial evidence or "the normative sign of the reception of the Spirit."[88] On the other hand, the tongues of 12:30 can be considered a gift that occurs subsequent to the sign, and may or may not be given to individuals, but must be interpreted in order to address people for their edification.

From this perspective, then, tongues can be considered both a sign and a gift of the Spirit. And such a conclusion seems appropriate since Paul did not rule out either option. To be clear, Paul speaks of the gift of "kinds of tongues" (1 Cor 12:4, 10), and even though everyone may not be functioning in the gift of tongues (12:30), it appears that it is possible for all to do so (14:5). Indeed, it is perhaps because of such a possibility that Paul continuously stress the seeking of the gifts (cf. 12:31; 14:1), which the Spirit can sovereignly activate in anyone (12:11). Furthermore, while it is clear from the biblical evidence that the authentic gift of tongues is a supernatural phenomenon, and there are two spheres—public and private—in which it functions, it is also unclear if Paul speaks of the same type of tongues. The "kinds of tongues" Paul refers to could be a variety of supernatural languages, and not merely foreign languages as Calvin interprets.

---

85. Cf. Best, "Interpretation of Tongues," 47.
86. Cf. Fee, "Toward a Pauline Theology of Glossolalia," 33.
87. Synan, "Speaking in Tongues," 326.
88. Synan, "Speaking in Tongues," 328. Synan also notes that the doctrine of initial evidence is not conclusively taught in Scripture, for the same data can be used either for or against the Pentecostal doctrine.

9.3.2.7 Is speaking in tongues the initial evidence of baptism in the Spirit?

But considering this conclusion, and the evidence already presented, is the presence or exercise of the charism of tongues to be considered the initial evidence, or the criterion, that one is functioning in the *charismata*, or is baptized in the Spirit? Is it, as George Mallone has concluded, that "one of the greatest theological tragedies to befall the church is the suggestion that the gift of tongues is a visible sign of having been baptized or filled with the Spirit? This suggestion finds no warrant in scripture."[89] This Pentecostal doctrinal distinctive was formulated by Charles Parham (1873–1929) in 1901. It conveys the idea that tongues usher in and restore the various gifts of the Spirit that were active with the apostles, and are normative in a Christian's life. These tongues are also necessary for the operation of the gifts of the Spirit, who empowers believers to evangelize the world for Christ.[90] Additionally, "the baptism with the Holy Spirit is an operation of the Holy Spirit distinct from, and subsequent from his regenerating work, an impartation of power for service."[91]

The doctrine of tongues as the initial criterion that one can function in the *charismata* has been challenged by both those who hold a sacramental view and those who hold a non-sacramental view of what it means to be baptized in the Holy Spirit or function in the *charismata*. Indeed, sacramentalists such as the Eastern Orthodox, Lutheran, Anglican, and Roman Catholic Churches maintain that baptism in the Holy Spirit equals Christian initiation, and is inseparable from the sacrament of water baptism, in which the Holy Spirit—including charisms, or the gifts of the Spirit—is imparted. Though the gifts of the Spirit are imparted when one becomes a Christian, they are not necessarily actualized, but may grow and increase, for example, as they are sought in prayer.[92] Other sacraments, like the Eucharist, confirmation, reconciliation, marriage, holy orders, and anointing of the sick, are considered occasions in which charisms—including tongues—are imparted.

There are also non-sacramental views of baptism in the Holy Spirit that challenge the notion that speaking in tongues is the initial evidence or criterion by which it is possible to function in the *charismata*. Such views are represented by mainline Protestants, but also by some Pentecostals. Among the former group, James Dunn asserts that baptism with the Holy

---

89. Mallone, *Those Controversial Gifts*, 90.

90. Cf. Goff, *Fields White unto Harvest*, 67; Synan, *Century of the Holy Spirit*, 42–43.

91. Torrey, *Person and Work*, 176–210.

92. Cf. McDonnell, *Christian Initiation*, 339–40.

AUTHENTIC SPIRITUALITY FOR THE CONTEMPORARY WORSHIP SERVICE   153

Spirit—evidenced by tongues—subsequent to one's conversion is not biblical. For him, in the Bible, baptism in the Holy Spirit is soteriological, or salvific, and is inseparable from the conversion-initiation process.[93]

Pentecostal detractors from the doctrine of tongues as the initial evidence of being baptized with the Holy Spirit, or functioning in the *charismata*, include Gordon Fee. The Assemblies of God scholar articulates that being baptized with the Holy Spirit and speaking in tongues were normative for the early church, but the doctrines of initial evidence and subsequence—the idea that BHS, including the ability to function in the *charismata*, is separate and subsequent to one being saved—were not normative in the early church.[94]

Pentecostal theologian Frank Macchia suggests that Spirit baptism is to be defined more broadly by Pentecostals if it is to continue as a valid distinctive and contribute to a broader ecumenical pneumatology.[95] The Assemblies of God theologian considers that the theologies of scholars such as Roger Stronstad[96] and Menzies[97] concerning baptism with the Holy Spirit rightly emphasize a charismatic empowerment of the Spirit, but they also exclude the inseparable soteriological and eschatological dimension.[98] While this may be true, Macchia, does not note that other Pentecostals—Parham, for example— emphasize tongues and BHS as a means of evangelizing the world—a soteriological and eschatological dimension. So, a soteriological and eschatological dimension is not completely missing among those who ascribe to the initial evidence theory. Nevertheless, based on Romans 5:5, which says, "God's love has been poured into our hearts through the Holy Spirit that has been given to us," Macchia concludes that baptism in the Spirit—and functioning in the *charismata*—relates to all aspects of the spiritual life, for it is a "release of the Spirit in life for concrete experiences of consecration and charismatic enrichment. It is both sanctifying and empowering, arising from the Spirit of God as love."[99]

Not only does Macchia follow the typical fourfold distinctive of the baptistic branch of Pentecostalism, which the Assemblies of God belongs to,[100] and which maintains that justification, salvation, and sanctification are

---

93. Dunn, *Baptism in the Holy Spirit*, 38–54.
94. Fee, *Gospel and Spirit*, 94, 98, 109–17.
95. Macchia, *Baptized in the Spirit*, 17.
96. Cf. Stronstad, *Charismatic Theology of St. Luke*, 12.
97. Cf. Menzies, *Spirit and Power*, 89.
98. Macchia, *Baptized in the Spirit*, 23.
99. Macchia, *Baptized in the Spirit*, 23.
100. Cf. Dayton, *Theological Roots of Pentecostalism*, 19–22.

inseparable, Macchia constructively suggests that BHS and sanctification are also inseparable. In terms of separability, then, Macchia agrees with the sacramentalists. But he disagrees with them in that he does not necessarily deny the doctrine of tongues as initial evidence of BHS. Whether or not one agrees with the initial evidence doctrine, it is evident that the doctrine provides a place of prominence for tongues that is not given to other *charismata*, so the validity of such an honor will now be dealt with it.

9.3.2.8 Is there a criterion that the gift of tongues is to be preferred over other gifts?

Are tongues to be preferred or exalted over other *charismata*? More broadly, is it authentically spiritual that any charism is to be preferred over another? Not surprisingly, throughout church history there have been arguments on either side of the issue. Among those who thought it was necessary to exalt a gift over another, one can include, for example, those who inauthentically considered themselves to be spiritual in Corinth. These zealous and upwardly mobile individuals thought their elitism was reinforced by tongues since it was associated with Paul, and suggested participation in divine mysteries. Christopher Forbes agrees with this assessment when he notes that the Corinthians had a more Hellenistic appraisal of tongues, as both direct communion with God and as speaking divine mysteries with knowledge and wisdom.[101] Additionally, those who exalt tongues over other gifts in the contemporary context include individuals who consider tongues to be a sign of maturity. This latter consideration, however, is foreign to the thinking of Paul, who, instead of the *charismata*—by themselves—considers fruit of the Spirit (1 Cor 13; Gal 5:22–26) and edification to be inseparably linked to authentic spirituality or Christian maturity (cf. 1 Cor 14:1, 12, 39–40).

But there are also those who consider tongues to be inferior to other gifts. For W. Harold Mare,[102] this is the case because Paul lists it last in the gift lists, which conveys that the Corinthian tongues speech is problematic, and contrasts it with the "greater gift/fruit" of love as well as prophecy.[103] Furthermore, contemporary commentators often consider the gift of tongues to be peripheral and inferior when it is not interpreted. This is evident by the continuous assertion that prophecy is to be preferred over

---

101. Forbes, *Prophecy and Inspired Speech*, 14–16, 182–87.
102. Mare, "1 Corinthians," 261–81.
103. Cf. 1 Cor 12:8–10, 28–30; 13:1–3; 14:1–6, 26.

tongues that are not interpreted, because Paul stresses the need for intelligibility in the church.[104]

There are also some commentators who do not consider tongues to be either superior or inferior to other *charismata*. For example, Best notes that each gift is necessary and none takes precedent over another, otherwise the body of Christ will not be in unity.[105] To Fee, the conclusion that tongues is an inferior gift because it is listed last in the gift lists is due to inadequate exegesis of 1 Corinthians 12–14.[106] Fee explains that such an exegesis has failed to grasp an appropriate understanding of the nature of the problem that Paul is addressing, as well as the function of the gift lists. For Fee, Paul lists tongues last on his list, not because it is inferior, but because the abuse of tongues is the major public worship communication problem in Corinth that is being addressed. Paul wants to "expand their horizons to see how much more diverse the ministry of the Spirit is than their singular enthusiasm about tongues had allowed . . . he also tries to replace their false spirituality with a genuine one."[107] Concerning the gift lists, Fee considers them to be "*ad hoc*, not definitive nor exhaustive."[108]

Additionally, the meaning of the term "greater gifts," as used by Paul in 12:31, is misinterpreted as contrasting with 12:4–30 where the gifts are discussed as being equally necessary. Fee, however, maintains that 12:31 is a command, not in contrast to Paul's previous statements, but one that is looking ahead to his further argument for intelligibility and edification in the community.[109] Therefore, the gifts of the Spirit, including tongues, are equally necessary for the edification of the body of Christ, that is, when exercised in a loving and edifying manner.

9.4 Is the Functioning of the *Charismata* Relevant, or Authentic, in the Contemporary Context, or Did They Cease in the NT Period?

One of the major issues concerning authentic spirituality in the contemporary church is whether the *charismata*—or at least some of the gifts—should be exercised at all. Put another way, is the functioning of the *charismata* relevant, or authentic, in the contemporary context, or did they cease in the

104. Cf. Mallone, *Those Controversial Gifts*, 84–87; Hynson, "Speaking the Word," 35.
105. Best, "Interpretation of Tongues," 45.
106. Fee, "Tongues—Least of the Gifts?," 4.
107. Fee, "Tongues—Least of the Gifts?," 6–8.
108. Fee, "Tongues—Least of the Gifts?," 10.
109. Fee, "Tongues—Least of the Gifts?," 13.

NT period? As with most of the other issues already discussed, the contemporary problem stems both from Calvin's interpretation of the biblical text as well as the interpretations of Calvin by those after him.[110] Before laying out the thoughts of Calvin and his interpreters, the concept of "cessationism" needs to be defined.

9.4.1 The concept of cessationism

In his *On the Cessation of the Charismata: The Protestant Polemic on Post-biblical Miracles*, Jon Ruthven explains that cessationism is the idea that the *charismata*—especially "miraculous" ones like tongues and prophecy—were only for the foundation of the church and have since ceased functioning.[111] This notion first appeared in the writings of Augustine (354–430 C.E.), who declared,

> in the earliest times, "the Holy Ghost fell upon them that believed: and they spoke with tongues," which they had not learned, "as the Spirit gave them utterance." These were signs adapted to the time. For there behooved to be that betokening of the Holy Spirit in all tongues, to shew that the Gospel of God was to run through all tongues over the whole earth. That thing was done for a betokening, and it passed away. In the laying of hands, now, that persons may receive the Holy Ghost, do we look, that they should speak with tongues? Or when we laid hands on these infants, did each one of you look to see whether they would speak with tongues, and, when he saw that they did not speak with tongues, was any of you so wrong-minded as to say, these have not received the Holy Ghost . . . If then the witness of the presence of the Holy Ghost be not now given through these miracles, by what is it given, by what does one get to know that he has received the Holy Ghost? Let him question his own heart. If he love his brother, the Spirit of God dwelleth in him.[112]

Augustine later retracted this seemingly cessationist view, saying,

> what I said is not to be so interpreted that no miracles are believed to be performed in the name of Christ in the present time. For when I wrote that book, I myself had recently learned that a blind man had been restored to sight . . . and I knew about some

---

110. Cf. Colver, "Baptism in the Holy Spirit," 22.
111. Cf. Ruthven, *On the Cessation of the Charismata*, 30.
112. Augustine, *Epistle of St. John*, homily 6.10 (pp. 497–98).

others, so numerous even in these times, that we cannot know about all of them nor enumerate those we know.[113]

It is yet to be determined herein if Calvin was a cessationist, but it is variously interpreted that he adopted and popularized the earlier cessationism of Augustine without acknowledging his later retractions.[114] Vinson Synan, for example, asserts that Calvin made cessationist statements in reaction to the Catholic charge that Reformers did not have authenticating miracles in their movement like those the founders of the Catholic Church had in the NT. In response to the Catholic's charge, Calvin said the miraculous gifts were only intended for the beginning of Christianity and had long since ceased to operate in the church.[115] With this response, Calvin not only discounted the miracles claimed by the clerics of the Catholic mystical tradition of his day, but he seemingly implied that the functioning of the *charismata* ended with the early church and would not be needed anymore.

9.4.2 Calvin's cessationism

To clearly understand Calvin's views regarding cessationism, though, it is important to consider his writings on the subject before agreeing or disagreeing with his interpreters. Admittedly, even after a painstaking study of his comments relative to the cessation of the *charismata*, Calvin's views appear to be ambiguous. This assessment can be understood after considering his remarks on the *charismata* as well as the offices from which they are exercised.

In terms of the *charismata*, Calvin says "that gift of healing, like the rest of the miracles [such as tongues and prophecy], which the Lord willed to be brought forth for a time, has vanished away to make the new preaching of the Gospel marvelous forever . . . it now has nothing to do with us."[116] So, the *charismata* were temporary gifts used as tools to manifest the presence of God as a witness toward confirming and establishing the church. Having been established, the church no longer needs *charismata* or miraculous gifts to witness about, or to hear from, God.[117] But, the church should continuously preach about the *charismata* used in NT time.

Calvin's writings about the offices that exercise the *charismata*, however, convey a slightly different, if not puzzling, understanding. For Calvin,

---

113. Augustine, *Retractions* 1.13.7. Cited in Elbert, *Calvin and the Spiritual Gifts*, 253.
114. Engammare, "Calvin," 648; cf. Colver, "Baptism in the Holy Spirit," 22.
115. Synan, "Speaking in Tongues," 324.
116. Calvin, *Institutes*, 2.4.19.18.
117. Cf. Calvin, *Institutes*, 2.4.3.8.

"the offices of pastor and teacher have not ceased in the church of this day," but relative to the offices of apostles, prophets, and evangelists, the Lord "now and again revives them as the need of the times demands," but such an action is extraordinary, for "in duly constituted churches it has no place."[118] Such a revival has even happened in Calvin's time, through Martin Luther, whom he considers an apostle.[119] Additionally, in regard to prophets, Calvin notes, "this class either does not exist today or is less commonly seen."[120] If Calvin correlates offices to functioning in the *charismata*, this latter statement suggests that he is not altogether a cessationist, for while he is not personally aware of charismatic activity, he does not claim that they have ceased in the officers of the church.

9.4.3 Calvin's interpreters on cessationism

Influenced by Calvin's work, however, contemporary scholars have argued for cessationism in at least five different ways. First, there is an exegetical claim that 1 Corinthians 13:8–10 teaches cessationism, based on an interpretation of "the end goal" in those verses to be Scripture.[121] The text reads, "love never fails, but as for prophecies, they will be discontinued, as for tongues, they will cease, as for knowledge, it will be discontinued. For we know in part, and we prophesy in part, but whenever the end goal [*tò téleion*] comes, that which is in part will be discontinued." The interpretation of these verses as proof for cessationism, however, is not without its detractors,[122] including the fact that I have already argued that the end goal Paul is referring to is the *Parousia* of Jesus Christ.

Second, theological dispensationalist asserts that the *charismata* were for biblical times and not the present dispensation.[123] This is despite the biblical evidence that seems to suggest that if the church needs to be edified, regardless of the dispensation, the *charismata* will be needed (Eph 4:12–13), for the spiritual gift, or office of the *diakonia*, becomes evident through charismatic activity.

Third, historically, it is claimed that the miraculous gifts ceased after the apostolic period. But there are at least two reasons to explain why the

118. Calvin, *Institutes*, 2.4.3.4.
119. Cf. Calvin, *Defensio adversus Pighium* (CR 6.250).
120. Calvin, *Institutes*, 2.4.3.4.
121. Cf. Unger, *New Testament Teaching on Tongues*, 96.
122. Cf. Mallone, *Those Controversial Gifts*, 17–19; Talbert, "Paul's Understanding of the Holy Spirit," 103.
123. Cf. Ryrie, *Dispensationalism Today*.

charismata may have appeared to cease in the post-apostolic era. One of these explanations is that as the post-apostolic church became more structured, power and the *charismata* were assumed to be prerogatives of the bishop and "exceptional Christians," such as those to be martyred. Thus, the laity increasingly did not participate in the *charismata*.[124]

Another reason, as Paul Tillich observes, is that subsequent to the Second Ecumenical Council at Constantinople (381 C.E.), when the divinity of the Spirit became "established," the Spirit was no longer "experienced" by most of the people as immanent or applicable to their daily lives. Instead, the Spirit became, to them, the transcendent God, and was replaced by the Virgin Mary in piety. The German theologian and existentialist philosopher wrote, "in the moment in which he was deified in the same sense that Christ was considered divine, the Spirit was replaced in actual piety by the Holy Virgin. The Virgin who gave birth to God acquired divinity herself to a certain extent, at least for popular piety."[125] Being replaced in "actual piety" includes the exercise of spiritual gifts, which was a part of popular piety up to that point.[126]

Fourth, some cessationists want correct theology—as found in the Bible—without the power the Bible speaks of. For them, subsequent to the apostolic era, there is no longer any need for the miraculous, since the gospel has adequately been dispersed. These cessationists have chosen to simply focus on the doctrine that has been established by the apostles, in order to fight against or control those they consider to be heretics because of their belief in and continuous practicing of the *charismata*.[127]

But scholars such as Stanley Burgess have documented the continuance of the *charismata* throughout church history.[128] Whenever the *charismata* appear to cease, it is usually because it is forced into groups that are considered marginal, fringe, or heretic by the institutionalized church. Montanism is an example of this in the ancient church, and classical Pentecostalism is an example in the contemporary church.

The final way in which contemporary scholars, influenced by Calvin's work, have argued for cessationism is an experiential assertion that those who claim to be functioning in the *charismata* today are inauthentic

---

124. McDonnell and Montague, *Christian Initiation*, 41.

125. Tillich, *History of Christian Thought*, 78.

126. McDonnell, *Christian Initiation*, argues that BHS occurs at water baptism and is Christian initiation and impartation of charismatic gifts. This view does not belong to private piety, but to public official liturgy, and was normative throughout the first eight centuries of the church.

127. Tillich, *History of Christian Thought*, 41.

128. Burgess, *Holy Spirit*.

practitioners of a "satanic counterfeit," because they do not evidence love and are emotionally unstable.[129] But even though there are some who may abuse the functioning of the *charismata*, such inauthentic spirituality is no reason to suggest that the *charismata* should cease functioning in the church. Related to this is the issue of gender criteria for authentic spirituality.

9.5 Are There Gender Criteria Relative to Authentic Spirituality in the Worship Service?

Are there gender criteria relative to the functioning of the *charismata* in the worship service? This is an issue raised in the contemporary context concerning the *mulier taceat* (let the women be silent) of 1 Corinthians 14:34–36. The apostle Paul says, "Let the women be silent in the churches. For it is not permitted for them to speak, but [to] be subject, just as even the law says. And if they wish to learn something, let them ask their own husbands at home, for it is shameful for a woman to speak in church. Or did the word of God come out from you, or come upon you only?"

Is Paul saying that women should not communicate in the worship service? If Paul allows for women to communicate in the worship service, to what extent does he do so? These questions are very important when one considers, as Arnold Bittlinger points out, that communication in the worship service should be a conversation between God and his people.[130] For, if women are not allowed to speak in the worship service, it begs further questions: Can women understand when God communicates to his people? Or, can women receive revelations from God? Are women allowed to communicate with God, whether through psalms or some form of spiritual gifts? And even more important, are women to be considered among the people of God?

9.5.1 Calvin's interpretation of the *mulier taceat*

For Calvin, with this command Paul is merely seeking to advance what is proper and edifying in a duly regulated assembly.[131] In such a gathering, because "it is the dictate of common sense, that female government is improper and unseemly . . . authority to teach (and to preach/prophesy) is not suitable to the station that a woman occupies, because, if she teaches, she

---

129. MacArthur, *Charismatics*, 174–80.
130. Bittlinger, "Charismatic Worship Service," 223.
131. Calvin, *Commentary*, 468–69.

presides over all the men while it becomes her to be under subjection."[132] This, however, does not mean that women were not allowed to speak in the worship service, "for a necessity may occur of such a nature as to require that a woman should speak in public."[133] Such exercise of the *charismata* by a woman should not occur "where there is a church in a regularly constituted state," where prophets and other men who are able to teach are available.[134] Thus, Calvin does not interpret the *mulier taceat* as a command that women cannot speak in the worship service. To Calvin, Paul is saying that the Corinthian women should not be the regular authoritative communicators in the worship service. This, however, does not speak to whether Calvin would support women communicating in the church of his day, but if he assumes that the charismatic activity (1 Cor 11:5) exercised by the Corinthian women ceased in his day, then he would probably also assert that women were no longer to speak in his contemporary worship service.

9.5.2 Contemporary interpretations of the *mulier taceat*

Surprisingly, contemporary scholarship agrees in the interpretation of Paul and Calvin, that is, at least in terms of the issue of propriety and edification as criteria for communicating in the worship service. But that is where the consensus ends. Among contemporary scholars, there are various interpretations of what kind of "order" is intended by Paul. In his article entitled "Learning in the Assemblies: 1 Corinthians 14:34–35," Craig Keener identifies various interpretations of the *mulier taceat*: 1) only males are allowed to authoritatively teach, preach, and judge in public worship service; 2) there was a need to avoid conduct that was offensive to the Graeco-Roman community; 3) at issue was questioning by those who were insufficiently learned; 4) at issue was tongues speech.[135]

The Lutheran Church of Australia's (LCA) Commission on Theology and Inter-Church Relations has also dealt extensively with how to interpret the *mulier taceat*. The commission concludes that since Paul allowed women to prophesy and pray in public worship (1 Cor 11:5), the *mulier taceat* was "designed to serve Paul's fundamental pastoral and evangelical concern that worship be conducted with order and decorum, so that nothing prevents the word of God being clearly taught at church and the

---

132. Calvin, *Commentary*, 468.
133. Calvin, *Commentary*, 468.
134. Calvin, *Commentary*, 468–69.
135. Keener, "Learning in the Assemblies."

Gospel freely proclaimed in the community."[136] The charge to silence, therefore, applies only to authoritative teaching, preaching, and evaluation of prophecies in that setting.

This is synonymous with Calvin's stance on the subject. From such a perspective, the women prophesying in 1 Corinthians 11:5 were functioning in the acceptable role of simply being channels announcing what the Lord revealed. In the *mulier taceat*, Paul is talking about women being silent in terms of functioning charismatically in the higher offices of male teachers and preachers who evaluate prophecies. A woman may prophesy (not a public ministry role), "a woman may teach other women, she may teach children, she may take part in the private instruction of a man like Apollos, but when a congregation assembles for public worship, women have no authority to serve as the preachers and teachers,"[137] and they are not to be involved in the subsequent evaluation of the prophecy.[138]

Not only does the perspective of this commission subordinate women to men, but it also disparages the act of prophecy to simply channeling the words of God. While being a channel of God's word is not to be taken lightly, prophets were not limited to that function. For Paul, prophets were involved in teaching (1 Cor 14:19, 31), as well as reproving and holding individuals to account (cf. 14:24). Further, there does not seem to be any support for the one who prophesies not being involved in the orderly evaluation of prophecies.

Another reason why some interpreters of the charge to silence assert it is an indication that only males were allowed to authoritatively teach, preach, and evaluate prophecies is that the one who is genuinely spiritual should recognize it as a command from the Lord that is valid until the *Parousia* (1 Cor 14:37). Proponents of this view make clear that Paul does not affirm an abusively patriarchal male dominance, since instead of being about males having power over women, the verse is about responsible authority and its proper use of serving others.[139] That Paul never sanctions oppressive behavior is suggested by the Corinthian context (1 Cor 11:2–16). In 11:3 Paul says, "but I want you to understand that Christ is the head of every man, and the husband is the head of his wife, and God is the head of Christ." Women are to be "subject" to their own husbands, as men are to be subordinate to Christ—a relationship that does not negate male and female equality and unity in Christ (Gal 3:28).

136. Lutheran Church of Australia, "Permit," 66.
137. Lutheran Church of Australia, "Prohibit," 65.
138. Lutheran Church of Australia, "Permit," 73.
139. Lutheran Church of Australia, "Prohibit," 53–54.

Thus, husbands are to exercise authority in a self-sacrificial manner. The middle form of the verb *ŭpotassésthōsan* ("let them [women] be subject") in 1 Corinthian 14:34 also makes it clear that Paul is appealing for voluntary submission, on the part of the wives, to God's order for church and its worship service. This relationship of wives to their husbands is analogous to when the members of the church are subject to their pastors, promoting "the peace and harmony that result when every part of Christ's body functions properly and the body grows and build itself up in love (cf. 1 Cor 13; 14:33, 40)."[140]

A second interpretation of the *mulier taceat* suggests Paul was emphasizing a need to avoid conduct that was offensive to the Graeco-Roman community. In this ancient Mediterranean context, social space was divided along lines of public (males) and private (females). Engaging in casual conversation with men would subject a woman to charges of immorality. And it was socially unacceptable for women to speak when men were present. One exception to this latter ethos, however, is for inspired utterances such as prophecy or tongues.[141] In light of this context, it is understandable how Paul can allow women to pray or prophesy in the public worship service (1 Cor 11:5), and also charge them to be silent in the same setting (14:34) when they are not prophesying. Paul's charge to silence, then, apparently involved conduct that was offensive in the Graeco-Roman context. And what is at stake in the *mulier taceat* is not gender, but propriety, orderliness, and learning in society.[142]

Third, some commentators argue that the *mulier taceat* concerns a need for orderliness in the worship service, considering questioning by those who are insufficiently learned. For example, while the asking of questions was common for first-century Graeco-Roman public discourse, Keener notes that such was not the case if the questioner was insufficiently learned, as was the case for most women.[143] Likewise, the Lutheran Church of Australia asserts that some poorly instructed women were asking a series of questions that was affecting the order and decorum of the worship service in Corinth.[144]

But the idea that the *mulier taceat* concerns unlearned women who were interrupting worship with their questioning seems to imply that if the women were learned, they too would have authority to speak or ask

140. Lutheran Church of Australia, "Prohibit," 57.
141. Keener, "Learning in the Assemblies," 166.
142. Keener, "Learning in the Assemblies," 171.
143. Keener, "Learning in the Assemblies," 168; cf. Plutarch, *Lectures* 18, *Moralia* 48b.
144. Lutheran Church of Australia, "Permit," 66, 75.

questions in the worship service. If this is true, perhaps the outspoken women in 1 Corinthians 11:5 were speaking with authority and were not just channels of divine revelation. Additionally, would it also not be the same scenario for men who were unlearned? That is, since it is frowned upon for the unlearned to ask questions, unlearned men would also have to be silent. One could conclude that only learned individuals could communicate authoritatively in the worship service. In other words, only those who were equipped, whether charismatically or through formal training, could exercise their voice in public worship.

Finally, for some the *mulier taceat* concerns a need for order in the worship service due to an abuse of tongues. Indeed, based on the context of 1 Corinthians 12–14, it is more likely that the *mulier taceat* refers to tongues speakers, since they are mentioned throughout the entire pericope. It is noteworthy that tongues speakers were also commanded by Paul to be silent in the worship service if their speech would remain unintelligible and disrupt the order of the public gathering (1 Cor 14:30). To be sure, the Corinthians were boastful and competitive, and they esteemed tongues as a sign of being spiritually mature—a status symbol. Thus, they spoke simultaneously and unintelligibly with little concern about being understood by others. In fact, it stands to reason that Paul issued the *mulier taceat* because the women were creating the same type of disorder in the community gatherings that was caused by uninterpreted tongues.

Because 1 Corinthians 14 is an explanation of why one should pursue spiritual gifts and love, and even more that one may prophesy (14:1), or as we now know—because of Paul particularly contrasting the gift of tongues with prophecy—an exhortation to edifying conduct, the second interpretation of the *mulier taceat*—that Paul was emphasizing a need to avoid conduct that was offensive to the Graeco-Roman community and to communicate in a way that is decent and in order—seems to be the most reasonable. The second interpretation of the *mulier taceat*—that Paul was emphasizing a need to avoid conduct that was offensive to the Graeco-Roman community and a need to communicate in a way that is decent and in order—seems to be the most reasonable. Savage and Heinrich Schlier agree with this notion when they say that Paul is offering a corrective to divisive speech marked by arrogance and pride.[145] Indeed, such offensive or disorderly conduct is inclusive of uninterpreted tongues and unlearned questions, but must also include certain "prophetic" speech. If Paul is encouraging controlled speech and manifestations of the gifts of the Spirit, in general, that are edifying for

---

145. Cf. Schlier, *Zeit der Kirche*, 223–24; and Savage, *Power Through Weakness*, 74–78.

the church, then, the other three interpretations of the *mulier taceat*, though they employ 11:5 to justify their claim, do not thoroughly address Paul's principle of orderliness or edification in the worship service.

Proponents of the other three views on the *mulier taceat* do not seem to adequately consider that 1 Corinthians 11:5 allows women to both pray and prophesy. And this praying, based on the context of discussing prophecy and tongues, is a reference to the private exercise of uninterpreted tongues unto God, as well as prophecy that is done in an orderly manner. This is because disorderly communication, such as public tongues that are either uninterpreted or not done in turn, must be avoided in the worship service (1 Cor 14:27-28), just as disorderly prophetic speech that is not done in turn must be avoided in the worship service (vv. 29-32).

There are various implications of this observation. First, it could be argued that Paul is not implying that the offices of teaching, preaching, and judging are off limits to all women, but only saying that those women who are communicating in a disorderly manner in the worship service—whether through uninterpreted tongues, disorderly prophecy, or inappropriate questioning—should be silent. A second implication is related to the first, and considers that utterances like prophecy, tongues, and "learned" questioning were acceptable in the worship service, but they must be exercised in an orderly way, or else be silenced. Finally, while in the *mulier taceat* Paul is specifically addressing a situation involving women, generally speaking, since asking unlearned questions would be considered disruptive of the worship service, and it is not just women who are often unlearned; one can deduce that anyone asking unlearned questions would be considered disruptive of order in the worship service and should be silent.

9.6 Conclusion

Having considered the thoughts of the apostle Paul, Calvin, and their interpreters relative to the functioning of tongues, the questions regarding the notion of the cessation of the *charismata*, and gender criteria relative to authentic spirituality in the worship service, the following conclusions can be made.

First, like prophecy, tongues have an edifying role in the church. That is, on the one hand, uninterpreted tongues are edifying to individual members as they mysteriously speak to God. Such speech can serve to give thanks, fellowship with, and develop a relationship with God, and therefore has doxological purposes. In this regard, tongues can be a form of inspired prayer, or even a psalm in which one mysteriously presents their supplications to God, or sing his praises. This kind of tongues is mysterious because only God can understand it. It serves as a way of communicating to God without being comprehended or intercepted by evil spirits. Perhaps it is because of the possibility of the latter scenario that the author of Ephesians encourages the Ephesian church to "pray in the Spirit" in order to persevere against the devises of the devil (Eph 6:18).

On the other hand, in the context of the gathering of members of the church, uninterpreted tongues should not be practiced unless there is an interpreter. Such tongues cannot edify others because it is unintelligible. Uninterpreted tongues, therefore, should only be communicated to God, in private. When interpreted, however, the gift of tongues, like prophecy, can be edifying to those who hear and understand it.

Moreover, tongues can be an initial evidence of being baptized with the Spirit, but should not be considered the initial evidence. This is because tongues, like other *charismata*, evidence divine presence. But the presence of God should not be limited to *charismata*, in general, or tongues, in particular. Instead of the doctrine of initial evidence, a more holistic view of baptism with the Spirit should be embraced. Such a view allows for the manifestation of the Spirit in every area of life, and, in addition to gifts of the Spirit, the fruit of the Spirit, and the edification of the church, for example, should be criteria for being baptized with the Spirit. In brief, speaking in tongues should not be forbidden in the church, but such a practice should be done decently and in order that the church and the rest of the world can be impacted for the glory of God.

Second, in light of the facts that 1) Augustine was not a cessationist; 2) it can be argued that Calvin was also not a cessationist; 3) church history documents the continuance of the *charismata*—including in the contemporary Pentecostal and charismatic movements; and 4) the Bible does not teach cessationism, but a charismatic manifestation of the Spirit in a loving and edifying way, it is appropriate to also suggest that the *charismata* did not cease with the NT church, and the contemporary church should continue to exercise the *charismata* until the *Parousia* of Jesus Christ.

Finally, with respect to whether Paul prescribed a gender criterion relative to the exercise of the *charismata* in the worship service, it is conclusive that only those who are gifted—whether through the triune God or from being formally trained—and are communicating in a loving and orderly or edifying way should be allowed to communicate in the worship service. And this makes sense, since being gifted as a criterion for communicating in the worship service bridged the gap between, on the one hand, a culture that recognized the authority that came from being gifted, but otherwise rejected, not only the message, but the right for some to communicate if they did not conform to culturally acceptable socially stratified profiles.

On the other hand, the Christian ethos, based in the example of Christ, and as articulated by the apostle Paul, while it also values communication by those who are gifted, does not conform to the cultural limiting of speech based on socially accepted stratification protocols. Instead, the Christian ethos maintains that all are potential dialogue partners with God, and can be considered the people of God. Such acceptance of people is ontological, for it is based on human beings being made in the image of God.

In this way of thinking, giftedness as a criterion for communicating in the worship service, then, allows for all people, regardless of their race, gender, or socioeconomic status (12:13), to communicate in the worship service. This allows both for the optimal communication of God's message to all, and all to praise God, since the worship service will not be limited only to the dialogue that takes place between certain people and God. This infers not only the value of the message brought by the people of God, but also holds those same people accountable to the discernment of the community, and is a basis for further growth of community members as they also allow the message to convict them.

This giftedness, on the other hand, also suggests that only those communicating in an edifying and orderly manner should be allowed to communicate in the worship service, for it implies that one is in control of their spirit, allowing for the Spirit of God to work through them; and love, which is characteristic of Christ, should be evident. This means that those communicating in the worship service, instead of communicating a self-exalting message, are functioning in service of Christ.

In brief, what is at stake in the *mulier taceat* is not gender, but propriety, orderliness, and learning in society.[146] "It is not the superiority of men over women that is central to Paul's argument, but a precisely attuned interconnection of abolition and conservation of the distinction between men and women."[147] For Paul, communication in the worship service manages the tension of being in a culture but not being of the culture. Thus, social roles involving one's gender are abolished, allowing both males and female to communicate in the worship service—under the authority of the triune God.

However, the "anthropological distinction between men and women is not abolished by faith and baptism, but remains fully valid."[148] To be sure,

---

146. Keener, "Learning in the Assemblies," 171.
147. Van der Watt, *Identity, Ethics, and Ethos*, 210.
148. Van der Watt, *Identity, Ethics, and Ethos*, 211.

there are no gender criteria relative to the functioning of the *charismata* in the worship service. The people of God, whether male or female, can all receive revelations from God and can be sovereignly authorized to communicate them to his people. There is no law limiting authoritative communication in the worship service to males. And, it is not in essence shameful for a woman to speak in church.

Part IV
Conclusion

Chapter 10

Authentic Spirituality in Pluralistic Contexts

This work has addressed the problem of discerning authentic spirituality in any context, but especially relevant to pluralistic environments of competing truth claims. This problem was dealt with from an ethical perspective in consideration of evidence from the ancient contexts of the OT and NT, as well as scholars throughout church history up to the contemporary context. The notion of how to live and communicate what is authentically spiritual was specifically considered by constructing a general perspective for what is authentically spiritual. Additionally, hermeneutical considerations associated with the communication of divine truths—especially in the context of the worship service—were considered.

The former issue necessitated the seeking of answers to at least three major concerns. First, there was a need to present a more balanced, ontological, and biblical criterion for discerning authentic spirituality, and fill a void in existing scholarship, which almost universally overlooks the role of the Trinity, in general, and the Spirit, in particular. Second, considering the context of a world in turmoil, and seemingly innumerable spiritual concerns, this study has sought ways in which the church could continue the mission of Christ in revealing how to be saved, both for present needs and for eternity. Finally, this study has sought out a manner of living that can bridge religious impasses between believers and a post-Christendom and pluralistic context where individuals offended by the person of Jesus Christ also consider themselves to be authentically spiritual.

In regards to the latter concern, unlike much of theological communication, which is based on either a modernist dichotomizing epistemology—which creates "objective" and "subjective" categories, and asserts, for example, that concepts such as faith and reason, spirit and matter, are antithetical—or a subjectivizing postmodernist epistemology that seems to disregard the value of traditional authoritative sources such as the Bible, this study has sought to consider all relevant sources of truth in determining criteria for authentic spirituality. That is why natural and supernatural modes of communication were dealt with, including sources from the East, West, and the Global South, as well as those that are contemporary and traditional in nature.

Emergent from this study is a clear and constructive perspective regarding the discernment of authentic spirituality, in terms of both living and communicating what is characteristic of God. Essentially, there is no one criterion. But the evidence gathered suggest that there is a combination of factors that, when taken together, do serve as criteria for authenticating spirituality.

Concerning how to live as authentically spiritual, such behavior must be inseparably linked with evidence of spiritual manifestations, love, and godly edification (1 Cor 14:1). These traits are characteristic of the triune God, who is Spirit (John 4:24), love (1 John 4:8, 16), and is peaceable and orderly (1 Cor 14:33).[1] In light of this truth, in a pluralistic and post-Christendom context, where individuals often consider themselves to be spiritual yet are offended by the person of Jesus Christ, a criteriology that includes the spiritual manifestations (and is not exclusive of Jesus), instead of being reductionistically christological, may be a way forward in bridging religious impasses.

But authentic spirituality is only possible in those who have received a revelation of Jesus Christ—and this occurs through the Spirit. This was true in the NT, for example, in the life of the apostle Paul (Gal 1:12, 15–16; 2:2), but it was also true regarding the OT people of God. When the OT people of God considered the combination of Spirit-led ecstasy and the traditionally accepted word of God to be criteria for what is authentically spiritual, they proleptically appropriated the revelation of Jesus Christ (cf. Rom 16:25–26).

In the contemporary context, and ever since the historic revelation of Jesus recorded in the Bible, the people of God live their lives in light of the same traditionally accepted revelation. This Jesus reveals the Father (Luke 10:22) and is inseparably linked to the word of God (John 1:1; 1 John 5:7), and the Spirit, who continually witnesses of him (John 14:26; 15:26). To be sure, "in him [Jesus] dwells all the fullness of the Godhead bodily" (Col 2:10), and it is through Jesus that one has access to the Father, by the Spirit (Eph 2:18).

It is by the Spirit that the revelation of Jesus Christ is received, or confession of Jesus as Lord is made (1 Cor 12:3). Upon receiving this revelation, the Holy Spirit indwells the believer (Rom 8:9) and sovereignly distributes

---

1. Being of order is similar to being edifying—God is edifying. When things are done in an orderly way, people can be spiritually strengthened.

charismata, which are to be exercised for the common good. These gifts of the Spirit, by themselves, because of their subjectivity, are not criteria for what is authentically spiritual. Perhaps this is why they have been neglected in scholarship on this subject.[2] Despite the subjectivity of spiritual manifestations, however, they are always manifested in authentic revelatory experiences. In fact, without the Spirit of God, one would not be able to live as authentically spiritual (cf. Phil 2:13; 1 Cor 12:7), for it is the Spirit of God who empowers ethical behavior that is revelatory of the triune God (Rom 8:9–14). Consequently, the role of the Spirit is integral in both the discernment of and participation in all that is revelatory of God.

When the Spirit is truly manifested, or more precisely, when one is being authentically spiritual, love, which is a supernatural grace of God or fruit of the Spirit (Gal 5:22), must also be evident (1 Cor 12:31—13:3). This love is personified in Christ, who gave his life for all (John 15:13). Because of this, by the power of the Holy Spirit, love is to be the principle of Christian ethics, by which the one who is truly spiritual should regulate all their actions.[3] And, if there is a christological criterion for authentic spirituality, love should rightly be considered as such. Because of the subjectivity concerned with what is true love, however, actions that are authentically spiritual must not only evidence manifestations of the Spirit and the love of Christ, but they must also be edifying for the people of God (1 Cor 14:1).

Activities that are revelatory of God are spiritually strengthening (1 Cor 12:7; 14:3). For example, *charismata* can be self-edifying when tongues are exercised in private to God (14:2, 4), but when exercised publicly they are comprehensible and edifying to the church (14:5). In such edifying acts, however, one should also be able to discern that the word of God is affirmed, the action is conducted properly and according to order (14:40), and it remains open to the intervention of the triune God. Such edification is exemplified in Jesus Christ. The very fact that Jesus personifies love and is the Savior of the world is evidence that Christ is edifying. His selfless life, teachings, death, resurrection, and ascension to intercede for others (Rom 8:34) attest the same.

In short, the one who is truly spiritual has received a revelation of Jesus Christ, and is empowered to live a charismatic, loving, and edifying kind of life. This witness should be discernible to the world as authentic spirituality that is representative of the triune God. When discerned, such Christlikeness can also serve as a check and balance between overtly rationalistic and

---

2. Cf. Dunn, *Jesus and the Spirit*, 293–97; Thiselton, *First Corinthians*, 916; Fee, *First Corinthians*, 574–82.

3. Calvin, *Commentary*, 418.

abusively subjectivizing communication, for the one who is truly spiritual employs both their mind and spirit toward understanding and communicating to the world all that is representative of the character of God revealed in Christ.

In fact, those who are authentically spiritual are commissioned to "go into the entire world and proclaim the good news [the gospel of Jesus Christ] to all" (Mark 16:15). That was Christ's mission and it is to be the mission of his church. It is the responsibility of the body of Christ to pattern their every action after the example of their Lord by lovingly exercising their spiritual gifts for the good of all. The church is to serve as an effective witness by discerning the authenticity of spiritual claims in the world, so that believers and unbelievers alike might grow in their knowledge of God, and all might come to confess Jesus as Lord, to the glory of God.

To be a most effective witness, it should be discernible that one's proclamation or communication is done in a way that is sensitively Trinitarian, contextual, and considerate of traditions. This is true in any context. But it is especially relevant for effective communication about the things of God in a pluralistic context.

Trinitarian communication that emphasizes the *perichoretic* reality of who God is, that is, one *ousia* ("essence") but three *hypostases* ("persons"), may also serve to more effectively bridge religious impasses. This is because it highlights the principle of unity (one *ousia* of the Godhead)—despite very real diversity (*hypostases* of the Godhead)—which is at the heart of the Christian ethos. Despite being united in Christ, Christians possess a diversity of gifts from the same empowering Spirit who indwells them, to the intent that the common good is served.

This Christian ethic, though it may appear to be exclusive, or intolerant of those of other faiths, because of the Christian belief in Jesus as the Lord, is actually inclusive, socially tolerant, and conducive to growth, because it considers that believers are all given gifts, which are needed for their edification, as well as that of the people of God. For all are equally loved by God. In other words, social stratification—whether based on economic status, ethnicity, or gender—that is belittling of individuals is replaced with the notion that all who are gifted by God qualify to function in the *charismata*, in particular, and generally be representative of authentic spirituality.

Sensitively Trinitarian communication can also help to bridge religious impasses by being robustly christocentric in that it focuses on, and evidences, the love personified in Christ. Instead of "subjective" talk about who God is, this kind of communication concerns a more "objective" revelation of God via the person of the historical Jesus (John 14:9), who died on the cross for the sins of all people (John 3:16). And rather than emphasizing differences between people—as is often done in religious talk—Jesus' emphasis on the importance of all people being united—even as the triune God is (John 17:22)—should be discernible.

Communication that is authentically revelatory of God is also done in a contextual manner that is edifying and comprehensible to all. Such exchange of ideas does not put obstacles in the way of the gospel of Christ, but "become all things to all people, that I [one] might by all means save some" (1 Cor 9:22). In this way, believers and unbelievers alike can discern, understand, and benefit from the revelation of God. This infers at least two understandings.

In the first place, like Jesus, the one who is authentically spiritual should communicate not only through their spoken words, but also through their actions. For Jesus' words and actions are one and the same (John 1:1). They are always consistent with each other, and convey the reality of who God is. For Christians to attain this ideal, they should willingly glean from, dialogue with, and be accountable to feedback from all who are impacted by the Spirit, regardless of their life circumstances.

The other inference one can make regarding contextual communication is that it is considerate of existential and ontological realities that reveal the things of God. Rather than simply expressing only what appears to be either rational or supernatural, contextual communication expresses the phenomenological truth of Christ regardless of its source and how it is obtained.

This means, for example, that authentic revelatory claims are considerate of traditions—even as Jesus and Paul continuously appealed to the established authority of their Hebrew tradition.[4] The truly spiritual person, then, unlike much of the contemporary postmodern context, continuously communicates in consideration of accepted traditional understandings such as that of the Bible and confessional creeds. They, therefore, take advantage of a check against anthropocentric understandings that are contrary to the revelation of God. Being considerate of traditions also serves to affirm the value of relationships that transfer wisdom from generation to generation, as classical truths are gleaned and applied to one's context as the Spirit directs.

From this biblical, Trinitarian, contextual, and traditional perspective, it can be surmised that to live and communicate what is authentically spiritual, one needs to have had a revelation of Jesus Christ. This could have happened either directly or indirectly through Scripture, or some other means

4. The traditional hermeneutic of Paul has already been established in this study. Jesus' reliance on this same tradition is evident in Gospel passages such as Matt 21:42; 22:29; Luke 4:21; 24:27, 32; John 5:39; 7:38.

the Lord sovereignly employs in communicating with his people, and it will be evident by some spiritual manifestation. Having received a revelation of Jesus Christ, the individual is then empowered by the Holy Spirit to live and communicate what is authentically spiritual. This includes the ability to exercise Christlike love and be edifying in all things.

Believers are more likely to be discerning of such authentic revelation because of the indwelling Holy Spirit, who confers to them the ability to employ both rational and supernatural means of discernment. Unbelievers, on the other hand, though they are also able to discern the things of God, do so based only on rational criteria.

The church is therefore to be considered the sphere in which authentically spiritual living takes place. And the worship service is a means toward this end, because its purpose is to usher in the presence of God, for dialogue to take place, to the intent of transforming individuals into the image of Christ through the Spirit. Since all *charismata* evidence divine presence, in the worship service, the exercise of all gifts of the Spirit should therefore be encouraged in all who would lovingly and orderly function in them.

From this perspective, all who have received a revelation of Jesus Christ have the responsibility of patterning their every action after the example of their Lord. They are to lovingly exercise their spiritual gifts so that all may be edified. Concomitantly, the one who is authentically spiritual should communicate in ways that are sensitively Trinitarian, contextual, and considerate of traditions, to the intent that all may grow in the knowledge of the Lord Jesus Christ. That is the measure of authentic spirituality—for any context!

Bibliography

Ackerman, David. "Fighting Fire with Fire: Community Formation in 1 Cor 12-14." *Evangelical Review of Theology* 29 (2005) 347-62.
Agersnap, Soren. *Baptism and the New Life: A Study of Romans 6:1-14*. Arhus: Arhus University Press, 1990.
Albright, William. *Archaeology and the Religion of Israel*. Baltimore: John Hopkins Press, 1942.
Alkier, Stefan. *Wunder und Wirklichkeit in den Briefen des Apostels Paulus: Ein Beitrag zu einem Wunderverständnis jenseits von Entmythologisierung und Rehistorisierung*. Tubingen: Siebeck, 2001.
Anderson, Gerald. *The Theology of the Christian Mission*. New York: McGraw-Hill, 1961.
Apuleius. *Metamorphoses*. Translated by J. Arthur Hanson. Loeb Classical Library. Cambridge, MA: Harvard University Press, 1989.
Aquinas, Thomas. *Summa Theologiae Vol. 45 (2a2ae 171-178): Prophecy and Other Charisms*. Translated by Roland Potter. New York: Cambridge University Press, 2006.
Aristides, Aelius. *Orations*. Edited by E. H. Warmington. Loeb Classical Library. Cambridge, MA: Harvard University Press, 1973.
Armerding, Carl. "Prophecy in the Old Testament." In *Handbook of Biblical Prophecy*, edited by Carl Armerding and W. Ward Gasque. Grand Rapids: Baker Book House, 1977.
Augustine. *The Epistle of St. John*. Homily 6.10. In vol. 7 of *The Nicene and Post-Nicene Fathers*, series 1, edited by Philip Schaff. 1886-89. Reprint, Peabody, MA: Hendrickson, 1994.
———. *Retractions*. In *On Free Choice of the Will*, translated by Anna S. Benjamin and L. H. Hackstaff. New York: Penguin Putnam, 1964.
Aune, David. *Prophecy in Early Christianity and the Ancient Mediterranean*. Grand Rapids: Eerdmans, 1983.
———. "Religion, Graeco-Roman." In *Dictionary of New Testament Background*, edited by Craig Evans and Stanley Porter, 917-26. Downers Grove, IL: InterVarsity, 2000.
Baker, J. "Prophecy, Prophets." In *New Bible Dictionary*, edited by I. Howard Marshall, A. R. Millard, J. I. Packer, and D. J. Wiseman, 964-75. 3rd ed. Downers Grove, IL: InterVarsity, 1996.
Barrett, C. K. *A Commentary on the First Epistle to the Corinthians*. London: Black, 1971.

---. "Paul's Opponents in II Corinthians." *New Testament Studies* 17 (1971) 245–56.
Barrett, David, editor. *World Christian Encyclopedia: A Comparative Study of Churches and Religions in the Modern World, AD 1900–2000*. Oxford: Oxford University Press, 1982.
Barth, Christoph. *God with Us: A Theological Introduction to the Old Testament*. Grand Rapids: Eerdmans, 1991.
Barton, Steven. "Paul's Sense of Place: An Anthropological Approach to Community Formation in Corinth." *New Testament Studies* 32 (1986) 225–46.
---. "Social Values and Structures." In *Dictionary of New Testament Background*, edited by Craig Evans and Stanley Porter, 1127–34. Downers Grove, IL: InterVarsity, 2000.
Bauer, Walter. *A Greek English Lexicon of the New Testament and Other Early Christian Literature*. Edited by Frederick William Danker. 3rd ed. Chicago: University of Chicago Press, 2000.
Baumgarten, Jorg *Paulus und die Apokalyptik*. Neunkirchen-Vluyn: Neukirchener, 1975.
Beker, J. Christian. *Paul the Apostle: The Triumph of God in Life and Thought*. Philadelphia: Fortress, 1980.
Best, Ernest. "Interpretation of Tongues." *Scottish Journal of Theology* 28 (1975) 45–62.
Betz, Hans, and Margaret Mitchell. "Corinthians, First Epistle to the." In vol. 1 of *Anchor Bible Dictionary*, edited by David Freedman, 1139–48 New York: Doubleday, 1992.
Beyer, Herman. 1965. "διακονέω." In vol. 2 of *Theological Dictionary of the New Testament*, edited by G. Kittel and G. Friedrich, translated by G. Bromiley, 81–87. Grand Rapids: Eerdmans, 1964–76.
Bezuidenhout, Marthinus. *Pauliniese kriteria ten opsigte van die Beoefening van die charismata: 'n eksegetiese studie van 1 Kor. 12–14*. Pretoria: University of Pretoria Press, 1980.
---. "The Trinitarian Nature of the Pauline Criteria Concerning the practice of the Charismata." In *The Reality of the Holy Spirit in the Church*, edited by Petrus Gräbe and W. Hatting, 93–104. Pretoria: J. L. van Schlaik, 1997.
Bittlinger, Arnold. "Charismatic Worship Service in the New Testament and Today." *Studia Liturgica* 9 (1973) 215–29.
---. *Gifts and Graces: A Commentary on 1 Corinthians 12–14*. Grand Rapids: Eerdmans, 1968.
---. "The Significance of Charismatic Experiences for the Mission of the Church." *International Review of Mission* 75 (1986) 117–22.
Blenkinsopp, Joseph. *A History of Prophecy in Israel*. Philadelphia: Westminster, 1983.
Boff, Leonardo. *Trinity and Society*. Translated by Paul Burns. New York: Orbis, 1988.
Bray, Gerald, editor. *1–2 Corinthians*. Ancient Christian Commentary on Scripture 7. Downers Grove, IL: InterVarsity, 1999.
Brooner, Oscar. *Isthmia: The Temple of Poseidon*. Vol. 1. Princeton, NJ: American School of Classical Studies at Athens, 1971.
Bruce, F. F. *1 & 2 Corinthians*. New Century Bible. London: Oliphants, 1971.
Bultmann, Rudolf. *Theology of the New Testament*. Vol. 1. New York: Scribner, 1951.
Burgess, Stanley. *The Holy Spirit: Ancient Christian Traditions*. Peabody, MA: Hendrickson, 1984.
Callan, Terence. *Dying and Rising with Christ: The Theology of Paul the Apostle*. Mahwah, NJ: Paulist, 2006.

Calvin, John. *Commentary on the Epistle of Paul the Apostle to the Corinthians.* Translated by John Pringle. Grand Rapids: Eerdmans, 1948.

———. *The Institutes of Christian Religion.* Vols. 20 and 21. Edited by John McNeill, translated by Ford Lewis Battles. Philadelphia: Westminster, 1960.

Carrington, Philip. *The Primitive Christian Catechism.* Cambridge: Cambridge University Press, 1940.

Carson, Donald. *Showing the Spirit: A Theological Exposition of 1 Corinthians 12–14.* Grand Rapids: Baker, 1987.

Cartledge, Mark. "Charismatic Prophecy and New Testament Prophecy." *Themelios* 17 (1991) 17–19.

Chantraine, Heinrich. *Freigelassene und sklaven im Dienst des romischen kaiser: Studien zu ihrer Nomenklatur, Forschungen zur antiken Sklavere,* 1. Wiesbaden: Steiner, 1967.

Cicero. *De Officiis.* Translated by Walter Miller. Loeb Classical Library. Cambridge, MA: Harvard University Press, 1990.

Colver, Randy. "The Baptism in the Holy Spirit, the *Charismata*, and Cessationism." 2006. http://www.netministry.com/clientfiles/62181/mw_colverbaptismintheholyspirit.pdf.

Collins, John. "The Mediatorial Aspect of Paul's Role as *Diakonos*." *Australian Biblical Review* 40 (1992) 34–44.

Collins, Raymond. *First Corinthians.* Sacra pagina. Minnesota: Liturgical, 1999.

Conzelmann, Hans. *1 Corinthians.* Hermeneia. Philadelphia: Fortress, 1975.

———. "Χαρισμα." In vol. 9 of *Theological Dictionary of the New Testament*, edited by G. Kittel and G. Friedrich, translated by G. Bromiley, 402–14. Grand Rapids: Eerdmans, 1964–76.

———. "Korinth und die Mädchen der Aphrodite. Zur Religionsgeschichte der Stadt Korinth." *NAG* 8 (1968) 247–61.

Crenshaw, James. *Prophetic Conflict: Its Effect upon Israelite Religion.* Berlin: De Gruyter, 1971.

Cunningham, Richard. "Theologizing in a Global Context: Changing Contours." *Review and Expositor* 94 (1997) 351–62.

Dabney, Lyle. "Starting with the Spirit: Why the Last Should now be First." In *Starting with the Spirit*, edited by Gordon Preece and Stephen Pickard. Adelaide: ATF, 2001.

Dahl, Nils. *Studies in Paul: Theology for the Early Christian Mission.* Minneapolis: Augsburg, 1977.

Dautzenberg, Gerhard. *Urchristliche Prophetie: Ihre Erforschung, ihre Voraussetzungen im Judentum und ihre Struktur.* Kohlhammer, 1975.

Dayton, Donald. *Theological Roots of Pentecostalism.* Peabody, MA: Hendrickson, 1987.

Dihle, Albrecht. "Demut." *Reallexikon für Antike und Christentum* 3 (1957) 735–78.

Dio Chrysostom. *Orations.* Translated by J. W. Cohoon. Loeb Classical Library. Cambridge, MA: Harvard University Press, 1971.

Dodd, C. H. *Gospel and Law.* Cambridge: Cambridge University Press, 1951.

Duff, A. M. *Freedmen in the Early Roman Empire.* Cambridge: Heffer, 1958.

Dunn, James. *Baptism in the Holy Spirit.* London: SCM, 1970.

———. *The Christ and the Spirit.* Vol. 2, *Pneumatology.* Grand Rapids: Eerdmans, 1998.

———. *Jesus and the Spirit: A Study of the Religious and Charismatic Experience of Jesus and the First Christians as Reflected in the New Testament.* London: SCM, 1975.

———. "Prophetic I-Sayings and the Jesus Tradition: The Importance of Testing Prophetic Utterances within Early Christianity." *New Testament Studies* 24 (1978) 175–98.

———. *Theology of Paul the Apostle*. Grand Rapids: Eerdmans, 1998.

Eck, Diana. "Globalization & Religious Pluralism." Gifford Lectures, University of Edinburgh, May 15, 2009. http://www.youtube.com/watch?v=MowDxV4vOqU.

———. *A New Religious America: How a Christian Country Has Now Become the World's Most Religiously Diverse Nation*. San Francisco: HarperCollins, 2001.

Elbert, Paul. "Calvin and the Spiritual Gifts." *Journal of the Evangelical Theological Society* 22 (1979) 235–56.

Elias, Jacob. *Remember the Future: The Pastoral Theology of Paul the Apostle*. Scottdale, PA: Herald, 2006.

Engammare, Max. "Calvin: A Prophet without a Prophecy." *Church History* 67 (1998) 643–61.

Epictetus. *Diatribae*. Translated by W. A. Oldfather. Loeb Classical Library. Cambridge, MA: Harvard University Press, 1985.

Eriksson, Anders. *Traditions as Rhetorical Proof: Pauline Argumentation in 1 Corinthians*. Stockholm: Almqvist & Wiskell, 1998.

Ewert, David. "Glossolalia in the Church Today." In *Encounter with the Holy Spirit*, edited by Geo Bunk, 174–88. Scottdale, PA: Herald, 1972.

Fee, Gordon. *The First Epistle to the Corinthians*. New International Commentary on the New Testament. Grand Rapids: Eerdmans, 1987.

———. *God's Empowering Presence: The Holy Spirit in the Letters of Paul*. Peabody, MA: Hendrickson, 1994.

———. *Gospel and Spirit: Issues in New Testament Hermeneutics*. Peabody, MA: Hendrickson, 1991.

———. *Paul, The Spirit, and the People of God*. Peabody, MA: Hendrickson, 1996.

———. *Pauline Christology*. Peabody, MA: Hendrickson, 2007.

———. "Tongues—Least of the Gifts? Some Exegetical Observations on 1 Corinthians 12–14." *Pneuma* 2 (1980) 3–14.

———. "Toward a Pauline Theology of Glossolalia." In *Pentecostalism in Context: Essays in Honor of William W. Menzies*, edited by Wonsuk Ma and Robert P. Menzies, 24–37. Sheffield: Sheffield Academic, 1997.

Finley, Moses, and Henk Pleket. *The Olympic Games: The First Thousand Years*. London: Chatto and Windus, 1976.

Fitzmyer, Joseph. *According to Paul: Studies in the Theology of the Apostle*. New York: Paulist, 1992.

———. *First Corinthians*. Anchor Yale Bible 32. New Haven, CT: Yale University Press, 2008.

Forbes, Christopher. *Prophecy and Inspired Speech in Early Christianity and Its Hellenistic Environment*. Tubingen: Mohr, 1995.

Fry-Brown, Teresa. *Delivering the Sermon: Voice, Body, and Animation in Proclamation*. Minneapolis: Fortress, 2008.

Furnish, Victor Paul. *Theology and Ethics in Paul*. Nashville: Abingdon, 1968.

Gadamer, Hans-Georg. *Truth and Method*. Translated by Joel Weinsheimer and Donald Marshall. 2nd ed. New York: Continuum, 2004.

Gangel, Kenneth. *Unwrap Your Spiritual Gifts*. Wheaton, IL: Victor, 1983.

———. *You and Your Spiritual Gifts*. Chicago: Moody, 1975.

Gardiner, Edward. *Greek Athletic Sports and Festivals.* London: MacMillan, 1910.
Garland, David. *1 Corinthians.* Baker Exegetical Commentary on the New Testament. Grand Rapids: Baker, 2003.
Garnsey, Peter. *Social Status and Legal Privilege in the Roman Empire.* Oxford: Oxford University Press, 1970.
Giesebrecht, Friedrich. *Die Berufsbegabung der altestamentlichen Propheten.* Göttingen: Vandenhoeck & Ruprecht, 1897.
Gillespie, Thomas. *The First Theologians: A Study in Early Christian Prophecy.* Grand Rapids: Eerdmans, 1994.
Godet, Frédéric. *Commentary on St Paul's First Epistle to the Corinthians.* Vol. 2. Edinburgh: T. & T. Clark, 1886.
Goff, James, Jr. *Fields White unto Harvest.* Fayetteville: University of Arkansas Press, 1988.
Gordon, R. L. "Mithraism and Roman Society: Social Factors in the Explanation of Religious Change in the Roman Empire." *Religion* 2 (1972) 92–121.
Goudge, H. *The First Epistle to the Corinthians.* Westminster Commentaries. London: Methuen, 1915.
Gräbe, Peter. "A Perspective from Regent University's Ph.D. Program in Renewal Studies: Theology in the Light of the Renewing Work of the Holy Spirit." *Pneuma* 27 (1995) 124–29.
Grether, Oskar. *Name und Wort Gottes im Alten Testament.* Glessen: Topelmann, 1934.
Grosheide, Frederik. *Commentary on the First Epistle to the Corinthians.* Grand Rapids: Eerdmans, 1953.
Grudem, Wayne. *The Gift of Prophecy in the New Testament and Today.* Eastbourne: Kingsway, 1988.
Gunkel, Hermann. "The Secret Experiences of the Prophets." *Expositor,* 9th series, 1 (1924) 356–66, 427–35.
Haldar, Alfred. *Associations of Cult Prophets among the Ancient Semite.* Upsala: Almqvist & Wiskell, 1945.
Harink, Douglas. *Paul among the Postliberals: Pauline Theology beyond Christendom and Modernity.* Grand Rapids: Brazos, 2003.
Hauerwas, Stanley. *Sanctify Them in the Truth: Holiness Exemplified.* Nashville: Abingdon, 1998.
Hays, Richard. "Ecclesiology and Ethics in 1 Corinthians." *Ex Auditu* 10 (1994) 31–43.
———. *The Moral Vision of the New Testament: Community, Cross, New Creation; A Contemporary Introduction to New Testament Ethics.* San Francisco: Harper, 1996.
Helyer, Larry. *The Witness of Jesus, Paul and John: An Exploration in Biblical Theology.* Downers Grove, IL: InterVarsity, 2008.
Hempel, J. "Vom irrenden Glauben." *Zeitschrift für systematische Theologie* 7 (1930) 631–60.
Hilber, John. "Diversity of OT Prophetic Phenomena and NT Prophecy." *Westminster Theological Journal* 56 (1994) 243–58.
Hildebrandt, Wilf. *An Old Testament Theology of the Holy Spirit.* Peabody, MA: Hendrickson, 1996.
Hill, David. "Christian Prophets as Teachers or Instructors in the Church." In *Prophetic Vocation in the New Testament and Today,* edited by Johannes Panagopoulos. Leiden: Brill, 1977.
———. *New Testament Prophecy.* Atlanta: John Knox, 1979.

Himmighofer, Traudel. *Die Zürcher Bibel*. Mainz: Philipp von Zabern, 1995.
Hollenweger, Walter. "Gifts of the Spirit: Natural and Supernatural." In *The New International Dictionary of Pentecostal Charismatic Movements*, edited by Stanley Burgess and Eduard van Der Maas, 667–68. Grand Rapids: Zondervan, 2002.
Holscher, Gustav. *Die Propheten*. Leipzig: J. Hinrichs, 1914.
Horn, Friedrich. Das *Angeld des Geistes: Studien zur paulinischen Pneumatologie*. Gottingen: Vandenhoeck & Ruprecht, 1992.
Huey, F. B. *Yesterday's Prophets for Today's World*. Nashville: Broadman, 1980.
Hüffmeier, Wilhelm, editor. *The Church of Jesus Christ: The Contribution of the Reformation towards Ecumenical Dialogue on Church Unity* (*Die Kirche Jesu Christi: Der reformatorische Beitrag zum okumenischen Dialog über die kirchliche Einheit*). 4th Assembly of the churches participating in the Leuenberg Agreement, May 3–10, 1994, Vienna. Text in English and German. Frankfurt: Lembeck, 1996.
Hutton, Rodney. *Charisma and Authority in Israelite Society*. Minneapolis: Fortress, 1994.
Hynson, Leon. "Speaking the Word; Prophecy and Glossolalia; 1 Corinthians 14:1–33." *Evangelical Journal* 24 (2006) 34–37.
Jenkins, Philip. "A New Religious America." *First Things* 125 (2002) 25–28.
Jensen, Alexander. *Theological Hermeneutics*. London: SCM, 2007.
Johansson, Nils. "1 Cor xiii and 1 Cor xiv." *New Testament Studies* 10 (1963–64) 383–92.
Jung, Franz. ΣΩTHP: *Studien zur Rezeption eines hellenistischen Ehrentitels im Neuen Testament*. Munster: Aschendorff, 2002.
Juvenal. *Satires*. Translated by G. G. Ramsay. Loeb Classical Library. Cambridge, MA: Harvard University Press, 1993.
Käsemann, Ernst. "The Motif of the Body of Christ." In *Perspectives on Paul*. Philadelphia: Fortress, 1971.
———. "On the Subject of Primitive Christian Apocalyptic." In *New Testament Questions of Today*. Philadelphia: Fortress, 1969.
Keck, Leander. "The Accountable Self." In *Theology and Ethics in Paul and His Interpreters: Essays in Honor of Victor Paul Furnish*, edited by Eugene Lovering Jr. and Jerry Summney, 1–13 Nashville: Abingdon, 1996.
Keener, Craig. *1–2 Corinthians*. New Cambridge Bible Commentary. New York: Cambridge University Press, 2005.
———. "Learning in the Assemblies: 1 Corinthians 14:34–35." In *Discovering Biblical Equality: Complimentarity without Heirarchy*, edited by Ronald W. Pierce and Rebecca Merrill Groothuis, 161–71. Downers Grove, IL: InterVarsity, 2004.
Keown, Gerald. "The Prophet as Encourager." *Perspectives in Religious Studies* 35 (2008) 155–61.
Kistemaker, Simon. *First Corinthians*. Grand Rapids: Baker, 1993.
Kleinknecht, Hermann. "πνεῦμα, πνεῦμα τικός." In vol. 6 of *Theological Dictionary of the New Testament*, edited by G. Kittel and G. Friedrich, translated by G. Bromiley, 332–58. Grand Rapids: Eerdmans, 1964–76.
Kuhl, Curt. *The Prophets of Israel*. Translated by Rudolph Ehlrich and J. P. Smith. Richmond: John Knox, 1960.
Lactantius. *De Mortibus Persecutorum*. Bibl Patr. Ecc. Lat. XI. Philadelphia: University of Pennsylvania Press, 1984.

Lasor, William Sanford, David Allan Hubbard, and Frederic Wm. Bush. *Old Testament Survey: The Message Form and Background of the Old Testament*. Grand Rapids: Eerdmans, 1996.

Latte, Kurt. *Die Religion der Römer*. Tubingen: Mohr-Siebeck, 1927.

Leith, John. "Calvin's Doctrine of the Proclamation of the Word and Its Significance for Today in the Light of Recent Research." *Review and Expositor* 86 (1989) 29–44.

Lewis, I. M. *Ecstatic Religion: An Anthropological Study of Spirit Possession and Shamanism*. Baltimore: Penguin, 1971.

Lindblom, Johannes. *Prophecy in Ancient Israel*. Oxford: Basil Blackwell, 1962.

Lindemann, Andreas. *Der Erste Korintherbrief*. Tubingen: Mohr-Siebeck, 2000.

———. "Pauline Mission and Religious Pluralism." In *Theology and Ethics in Paul and His Interpreters: Essays in Honor of Victor Paul Furnish*, edited by Eugene Lovering Jr. and Jerry Summney, 275–88. Nashville: Abingdon, 1996.

Livy. Translated by Evan Sage. Loeb Classical Library. Cambridge, MA: Harvard University Press, 1985.

Lohse, Eduard. "Changes of Thought in Pauline Theology? Some Reflections on Paul's Ethical Teaching in the Context of his Theology." In *Theology and Ethics in Paul and His Interpreters: Essays in Honor of Victor Paul Furnish*, edited by Eugene Lovering Jr. and Jerry Summney, 146–60. Nashville: Abingdon, 1996.

Lucian. *Anacharsis*. Translated by A. Harmon. Loeb Classical Library. Cambridge, MA: Harvard University Press, 1992.

Lutheran Church of Australia Commission on Theology and Inter-Church Relations. "1 Corinthians 14:33b–38 and 1 Timothy 2:11–14 Permit the Ordination of Women." *Lutheran Theological Journal* 39 (2005) 66–83.

———. "1 Corinthians 14:33b–38 and 1 Timothy 2:11–14 Prohibit the Ordination of Women." *Lutheran Theological Journal* 39 (2005) 51–65.

MacArthur, John. *The Charismatics*. Grand Rapids: Zondervan, 1978.

Macchia, Frank. *Baptized in the Spirit: A Global Pentecostal Theology*. Grand Rapids: Zondervan, 2006.

MacGorman, J. W. "Glossolalic Error and Its Correction: 1 Corinthians 12–14." *Review & Expositor* 80 (1983) 389–400.

MacMullen, Ramsay. *Paganism in the Roman Empire*. New Haven, CT: Yale University Press, 1981.

———. *Roman Social Relations, 50 B.C. to A.D. 284*. New Haven, CT: Yale University Press, 1974.

Malherbe, Abraham. *Early Christianity and Classical Culture: Studies in Honor of Abraham J. Malherbe*. Atlanta: SBL, 2003.

———. *Social Aspects of Early Christianity*. Baton Rouge: Louisiana State University Press, 1977.

Mallone, George. *Those Controversial Gifts: Prophecy, Dreams, Visions, Tongues, Interpretation, Healing*. Downers Grove, IL: InterVarsity, 1983.

Mare, W. Harold. " 1 Corinthians." *The Expositor's Bible Commentary*, vol. 10, ed. Frank Gaegelem. Grand Rapids: Zondervan, 1976.

Martial. *Epigrams*. Translated by D. R. Shackleton Bailey. Loeb Classical Library. Cambridge, MA: Harvard University Press, 1993.

McDonald, Lee Martin, and Stanley Porter. *Early Christianity and Its Sacred Literature*. Peabody, MA: Hendrickson, 2000.

McDonnell, Killian, and George Montague. *Christian Initiation and Baptism in the Holy Spirit: Evidence from the First Eight Centuries.* Collegeville, MN: Liturgical, 1991.

McNamara, Martin. "Discernment Criteria in Israel: True and False Prophets." In *Discernment of the Spirit and of Spirits*, 3–13 New York: Seabury, 1979.

McRay, J. R. "Corinth." In *Dictionary of New Testament Background*, edited by Craig Evans and Stanley Porter, 227–31. Downers Grove, IL: InterVarsity, 2000.

Menzies, William, and Robert Menzies. *Spirit and Power: Foundations of Pentecostal Experience.* Grand Rapids: Zondervan, 2000.

Meeks, Wayne. *The First Urban Christians: The Social World of the Apostle Paul.* New Haven, CT: Yale University Press, 1983.

Meyer, Heinrich. *Critical and Exegetical Handbook to the Epistles to the Corinthians.* Vol. 1. Edinburgh: T. & T. Clark, 1892.

Mitchell, Margaret. *Paul and the Rhetoric of Reconciliation: An Exegetical Investigation of the Language and Composition of 1 Corinthians.* Louisville: Westminster/John Knox, 1991.

Mofatt, James. *The First Epistle of Paul to the Corinthians.* London: Hodder and Stoughton, 1938.

Moretti, Luigi. *Inscrizioni Agonistiche Greche.* Rome: Angelo Signorelli, 1953.

Moule, C. F. D. "Obligation in the Ethics of Paul." In *Christian History and Interpretation: Essays in Honor of John Knox*, edited by W. R. Farmer, C. F. D. Moule, and R. R. Niebuhr, 389–406. Cambridge: Cambridge University Press, 1967.

Mowinckel, Sigmund. "'The Spirit' and the 'Word' in the Pre-Exilic Reforming Prophets." *Journal of Biblical Literature* 53 (1934) 199–227.

Munck, Johannes. *Paul and the Salvation of Mankind.* London: SCM, 1959.

Neuhaus, Richard. "One Nation under Many Gods." *First Things*, 2001, 71–79.

Nilsson, Martin. *The Dionysiac Mysteries of the Hellenistic and Roman Age.* New York: Arno, 1975.

———. "Problems of the History of Greek Religion in the Hellenistic and Roman Age." *Harvard Theological Review* 36 (1943) 251–75.

Nock, Arthur. *Essays on Religion and the Ancient World.* Vol. 1. Edited by Zeph Stewart. Oxford: Clarendon, 1972.

O'Connor, J. Murphy. *St. Paul's Corinth: Texts and Archaeology.* Wilmington, DE: Liturgical, 2002.

Omar, A. Rashied. "Islam Beyond Tolerance: The Qur'anics Concept of Ta'aruf." *Brethren Life and Thought* 53 (2008) 15–20.

Oswald, Eva. *Falsche Prophetie im Alten Testament.* Tubingen: Mohr, 1962.

Packer, J. I. *Keep in Step with the Spirit.* Old Tappan, NJ: InterVarsity, 1984.

Painter, John. "Paul and the Πνευματικοι at Corinth." In *Paul and Paulinism: Essays in Honor of C. K. Barrett*, edited by M. D. Hooker and S. G. Wilson. London: SPCK, 1982.

Palamas, Gregory. *The Triads.* Edited by John Meyendorff, translated by Nicholas Gendle. New York: Paulist, 1983.

Pearson, B. W. R. "Associations." In *Dictionary of New Testament Background*, edited by Craig Evans and Stanley Porter, 136–38. Downers Grove, IL: InterVarsity, 2000.

Pell, George Cardinal. "Intolerant Tolerance." *First Things* 195 (2009) 9–10.

Peters, Francis. *The Harvest of Hellenism: A History of the Near East from Alexander the Great to the Triumph of Christianity.* New York: Simon and Schuster, 1970.

Petronius. *Satyricon*. Translated by Michael Heseltine. Loeb Classical Library. Cambridge, MA: Harvard University Press, 1969.
Pinnock, Clark. "The Work of the Holy Spirit in Hermeneutics." *Journal of Pentecostal Theology* 2 (1993) 3–23.
Pitkin, Barbara. "Prophecy and History in Calvin's Lectures on Daniel (1561)." In *Geschichte der Daniel-Auslegung in Judentum, Christentum und Islam: Studien zur Kommentierung des Danielbuches in Literatur und Kunst*, edited by Katharina Bracht and David Du Toit, 323–47. New York: De Gruyter, 2007.
Plutarch. *Moralia*. Translated by Harold North Fowler. Loeb Classical Library. Cambridge, MA: Harvard University Press, 1991.
Powell, Benjamin. "Greek Inscriptions from Corinth." *American Journal of Archaeology* 7 (1903) 26–71.
Quell, Gottfried. *Wahre und falsche Propheten: Versuch einer Interpretation*. Gütersloh: Bertelsmann, 1952.
Quintilian. *Institutio Oratorio*. Translated by H. E. Butler. Loeb Classical Library. Cambridge, MA: Harvard University Press, 1980.
Reekman, Tony. "Juvenal's Views on Social Change." *Ancient Society* 2 (1971) 117–61.
Reisling, Jannes. "Prophecy, the Spirit and the Church." In *Prophetic Vocation in the New Testament and Today*, edited by Johannes Panagopoulos. Leiden: Brill, 1977.
Ridderbos, Herman. *Paul: An Outline of His Theology*. Translated by John Richard De Witt. London: SPCK, 1977.
Ridderbos, J. "The Nature of Prophecy." *Evangelical Quarterly* 12 (1940) 112–22.
Robeck, Cecil, Jr. "Prophecy, Prophesying." In *Dictionary of Paul and His Letters*, edited by Gerald Hawthorne and Ralph Martin, 755–62. Downers Grove, IL: InterVarsity, 1993.
Robert, Louis. "Le grand nom de Dieu." *Hellenica* 10 (1955) 100.
Robertson, A. T., and Alfred Plummer. *A Critical and Exegetical Commentary on the First Epistle of St. Paul to the Corinthians*. International Critical Commentary. Edinburgh: T. & T. Clark, 1914.
Robinson, Theodore. "Daría." *Expository Times* 46 (1934–35) 41–44.
———. "Die prophetischen Bücher im Lichte neuer Entdeckungen." *Zeitschrift für die Alttestamentliche Wissenschaft*, n.f., 4 (1927) 3–9.
Rosner, Brian. *Paul, Scripture, and Ethics: A Study of 1 Corinthians 5–7*. Leiden: Brill, 1994.
Rousselle, Aline. "Body Politics in Ancient Rome." In *A History of Women in the West, 1: From Ancient Goddesses to Christian Saints*, edited by G. Duby and M. Perot, 296–337. Cambridge, MA: Harvard University Press, 1992.
Rowe, Arthur. "1 Corinthians 12–14: The Use of a Text for Christian Worship." *Evangelical Quarterly* 77 (2005) 119–28.
Rowley, H. H. "The Nature of Prophecy in Light of Recent Study." *Harvard Theological Review* 38 (1945) 1–38.
Ruthven, Jon. *On the Cessation of the Charismata: The Protestant Polemic on Postbiblical Miracles*. Sheffield: Sheffield Academic, 1997.
Ryrie, Charles. *Dispensationalism Today*. Chicago: Moody, 1965.
Samarin, William. "Sacred and Profane." *Crux* 9 (1972) 4–11.
Sanders, James. "Canonical Hermeneutics: True and False Prophecy." In *From Sacred Story to Sacred Text*, 89–105. Philadelphia: Fortress, 1987.

Savage, Timothy. *Power Through Weakness: Paul's Understanding of the Christian Ministry in 2 Corinthians*. New York: Cambridge University Press, 1996.
Sawyer, John. *Prophecy and the Prophets of the Old Testament*. Oxford: Oxford University Press, 1987.
Schatzmann, Siegfried. *A Pauline Theology of the Charismata*. Peabody, MA: Hendrickson, 1987.
Schlier, Heinrich. *Die Zeit der Kirche: Exegetische Aufsätze und Vorträge*. Freiburg: Herder, 1972.
Schnelle, Udo. *Apostle Paul: His Life and Theology*. Translated by M. Eugene Boring. Grand Rapids: Baker, 2003.
Schrage, Wolfgang. *The Ethics of the New Testament*. Translated by David Green. Philadelphia: Fortress, 1988.
―――. *Der erste Brief an die Korinther*. Evangelisch-katholischer Kommentar zum Neun Testament 7/3. Düsseldorf: Benziger, 1999.
Schweizer, Eduard. "The Service of Worship: An Exposition of 1 Corinthians 14." *Interpretation* 13 (1959) 400–408.
Scranton, Robert. *Corinth: Monuments of the Lower Agora and North of the Archaic Temple*. Vol. 1. Princeton, NJ: ASCSA, 1951.
Seneca. *Epistulae morales*. Translated by Richard Gammere. Loeb Classical Library. Cambridge, MA: Harvard University Press, 1920.
Seneca. *Moral Essays (Dialogues)*. Translated by J. W. Basore. 3 vols. Loeb Classical Library. Cambridge: Harvard University Press, 1928.
Sevenster, Gerhard. *Paul and Seneca*. Novum Testamentum Supplements 4. Leiden: Brill, 1961.
Smith, Dennis. "The Egyptian Cults at Corinth." *Harvard Theological Review* 70 (1977) 201–31.
Solivan, Samuel. *The Spirit, Pathos, and Liberation: Toward an Hispanic Pentecostal Theology*. Sheffield: Sheffield Academic, 1998.
Spicq, Ceslaus. *Agape in the New Testament*. St. Louis: Herder, 1965.
Stauffer, Richard. "Les Discours à la première personne dans les sermons de Calvin." *Revue d'histoire et de philosophie religieuses* 45 (1965) 46–78.
Strabo. *Geographica*. Translated by Horace Jones. Loeb Classical Library. Cambridge, MA: Harvard University Press, 1988.
Stronstad, Roger. *The Charismatic Theology of St. Luke*. Peabody, MA: Hendrickson, 1984.
Synan, Vinson. "Speaking in Tongues." *One in Christ* 19 (1983) 323–31.
―――. *The Century of the Holy Spirit: 100 Years of Pentecostal and Charismatic Renewal*. Nashville: T. Nelson, 2001.
Tacitus I. Translated by M. Hutton and W. Peterson. Revised by R. M. Ogilvie, E. H. Warmington, and Michael Winterbottom. Loeb Classical Library. Cambridge, MA: Harvard University Press, 1914.
Talbert, Charles. "Paul's Understanding of the Holy Spirit: The Evidence of 1 Corinthians 12–14." *Perspectives in Religious Studies* 11 (1984) 95–108.
Tertullian. *Against Marcion*. Translated by Peter Holmes. Edinburgh: T. & T. Clark, 1870.
Theissen, Gerd. *Psychological Aspects of Pauline Theology*. Edinburgh: T. & T. Clark, 1987.

———. *The Social Setting of Pauline Christianity: Essays on Corinth*. Philadelphia: Fortress, 1982.

Theophrastus. *Characters*. Edited and translated by Jeffrey Rusten, I. C. Cunningham, and A. D. Knox. Loeb Classical Library. Cambridge, MA: Harvard University Press, 1993.

Thiselton, Anthony. *The First Epistle to the Corinthians*. New International Greek Testament Commentary. Grand Rapids: Eerdmans, 2000.

———. *The Living Paul: An Introduction to the Apostle's Life and Thought*. Downers Grove, IL: InterVarsity, 2009.

Thorsen, Don. *The Wesleyan Quadrilateral: Scripture, Tradition, Reason & Experience as a Model of Evangelical Theology*. Lexington, KY: Emeth, 2005.

Tillich, Paul. *A History of Christian Thought: From Its Judaic and Hellenistic Origins to Existentialism*. Edited by Carl E. Braaten. New York: Simon & Schuster, 1967.

Torrey, R. A. *The Person and Work of the Holy Spirit*. New York: Revell, 1910.

Troupe, Carol. "One Body, Many Parts: A Reading of 1 Corinthians 12:12–27." *Black Theology* 6 (2008) 32–45.

Turner, Max. "Spiritual Gifts Then and Now." *Vox Evangelica* 15 (1985) 7–64.

———. "Tongues: An Experience for All in the Pauline Churches?" *Asian Journal of Pentecostal Studies* 1 (1998) 231–53.

Twelftree, Graham. *People of the Spirit: Exploring Luke's View of the Church*. Grand Rapids: Baker, 2009.

Unger, Merril. *New Testament Teaching on Tongues*. Grand Rapids: Kregel, 1971.

Van der Watt, Jan. Editor. *Identity, Ethics, and Ethos in the New Testament*. New York: De Gruyter, 2006.

Van Winkle, D. "1 Kings XIII: True and False Prophecy." *Vetus Testamentum* 39 (1989) 31–43.

Vielhauer, Philipp. *Oikodome: Das Bild vom Bau in der christlicken Literatur vom Neuen Testament bis Clemens Alexandrinus*. Heidelberg: Lebenslauf, 1940.

Ward, James. *The Prophets*. Nashville: Abingdon, 1982.

Ward, Wayne. "The Significance of Tongues for the Church." In *Speaking in Tongues: Let's Talk about It*, edited by Watson Mills, 143–51. Waco, TX: Word, 1973.

Watson, D. F. "Roman Social Classes." In *Dictionary of New Testament Background*, edited by Craig Evans and Stanley Porter, 999–1004. Downers Grove, IL: InterVarsity, 2000.

Weaver, P. R. C. *Familia Caesaris: A Social Study of the Emperor's Freedmen and Slaves*. Cambridge: Cambridge University Press, 1972.

Wesley, John. "The More Excellent Way." Edited by Edward Purkey with corrections by Ryan Danker and George Lyons. Based on the text from *The Sermons of John Wesley*, edited by Thomas Jackson (1872). Wesley Center for Applied Theology at Northwest Nazarene University, 1999. http://wesley.nnu.edu/john-wesley/the-sermons-of-john-wesley-1872-edition/sermon-89-the-more-excellent-way/.

———. *A Plain Account of Christian Perfection*. New York: Methodist Book Concern, 1925. Translated by J. Arthur Hanson. Loeb Classical Library. Cambridge, MA: Harvard University Press, 1989.

Wilckens, Ulrich. "Σοφία." *Theologische Wörterbuch zum Neun Testament* 7 (1964) 497–529.

Williams, J. Rodman. "Baptism in the Holy Spirit." In *The New International Dictionary of Pentecostal and Charismatic Movements*, edited by Stanley Burgess and Eduard van der Maas, 389–406. Grand Rapids: Zondervan, 2002.

Wilson, Robert. "Early Israelite Prophecy." In *Interpreting the Prophets*, edited by James Mays and Paul Achtemeier. Philadelphia: Fortress, 1987.

Wimber, John, and Kevin Springer. *Power Evangelism*. San Francisco: Harper, 1992.

Wiseman, James. "Corinth and Rome I: 228 B.C.–A.D. 267." *Aufstieg und Niedergang der romischen Welt* 2 (1979) 497.

———. *The Land of Ancient Corinthians: Studies in Mediterranean Archaeology*. Goteborg: Paul Astroms, 1978.

Witherington, Ben. *Conflict and Community in Corinth: A Socio-Rhetorical Commentary on 1 and 2 Corinthians*. Grand Rapids: Eerdmans, 1995.

———. *Women in the Earliest Churches*. Cambridge: Cambridge University Press, 1988.

Wolter, Michael. "Pauline Ethics according to 1 Corinthians." In *Identity, Ethics, and Ethos in the New Testament*, edited by Jan Van der Watt, 199–217. New York: De Gruyter, 2006.

Yarbrough, O. Larry. *Not Like the Gentiles: Marriage Rules in the Letters of Paul*. Society of Biblical Literature Dissertation Series 80. Atlanta: Scholars, 1985.

Yong, Amos. "Between the Local and the Global: Autobiographical Reflections on the Emergence of the Global Theological Mind." In *Shaping a Global Theological Mind*, edited by Darren C. Marks. Aldershot: Ashgate, 2008.

———. *The Spirit Poured Out on All Flesh: Pentecostalism and the Possibility of Global Theology*. Grand Rapids: Baker Academic, 2005.

Yong, Amos, and Peter Heltzel, editors. *Theology in Global Context: Essays in Honor of Robert Cummings Neville*. New York: T. & T. Clark, 2004.

Name Index

Ackerman, David, 107, 134, 147, 177
Agersnap, Soren, 177
Albright, William, 18, 177
Alkier, Stefan, 177
Anderson, Gerald, 177
Apuleius, 32, 177
Aquinas, Thomas, 68-70
Aristides, Aelius, 34, 177
Armerding, Carl, 177
Augustine, 156, 157, 166, 177
Aune, David, 3, 51, 95, 96, 134, 177

Baker, J., 3, 7,13, 18, 23, 177
Barrett, C. K., 38, 98, 99, 177, 184
Barrett, David, 114, 115, 178
Barth, Christoph, 178
Barton, Steven, 30, 100, 178
Bauer, Walter, 4, 178
Baumgarten, Jorg, 178
Beker, J., 85, 130, 178
Best, Ernest, 107, 146, 150, 151, 155, 178
Betz, Hans, 52, 178
Beyer, Herman, 59, 178
Bezuidenhout, Marthinus, xvi, 1, 42-43, 53-57, 61-64, 70-73, 76, 81, 87-89, 105, 178
Bittlinger, Arnold, 123, 125, 133, 147, 160, 178
Blenkinsopp, Jos, 5, 178
Boff, Leonardo, xiv, 50, 178
Bray, Gerald, 43, 178
Brooner, Oscar, 34, 178
Bruce, F. F., 99, 178

Bultmann, Rudolf, 178
Burgess, Stanley, 159, 172, 178, 188

Callan, Terence, 123, 129, 178
Calvin, John, 86, 117, 134-39, 141-42, 144, 147-51, 156-62, 165-66, 173, 179-80, 183, 185-86
Carrington, Philip, 179
Carson, Donald, 66, 179
Cartledge, Mark, 138, 179
Chantraine, Heinrich, 179
Cicero, 130, 179
Colver, Randy, 134, 156, 157, 179
Collins, John, 179, 59
Collins, Raymond, 179, 100
Conzelmann, Hans, 35, 43, 45, 48, 51, 65, 75, 98, 179
Crenshaw, James, 8, 13-20, 22, 25, 179
Crinagorus, 33
Cunningham, Richard, 179

Dahl, Nils, 38, 179
Dautzenberg, Gerhard, 141, 143, 179
Dayton, Donald, 53, 179
Dihle, Albrecht, 179
Dio Chrysostom, 179
Dodd, C. H, 179
Duff, A. M, 30, 179
Dunn, James, 4, 42-43, 52, 53, 58, 64, 65, 76, 106, 116, 152, 153, 173, 179

Eck, Diana, 109-115, 180
Elbert, Paul, 137, 157, 180

Elias, Jacob, 130, 180
Engammare, Max, 157, 180
Epictetus, 180
Eriksson, Anders, 47, 48, 100, 180
Ewert, David, 107, 180

Fee, Gordon, 31, 33, 42, 47, 51, 53, 60,
    63, 64, 66, 75, 78, 80, 90, 94,
    97–100, 107, 118–19, 129–31,
    151, 153, 155, 173, 180
Finley, Moses, 180
Fitzmyer, Jos, 43–44, 47, 49, 51–52, 123,
    180
Forbes, Christopher, 154, 180
Fry-Brown, Teresa, 144, 180
Furnish, Victor Paul, 180–3

Gadamer, Hans-Georg, xv, 27, 96,
    101–2, 180
Gangel, Kenneth, 141, 143, 180
Gardiner, Edward, 181
Garland, David, 48, 55, 96–97, 181
Garnsey, Peter, 181
Gehazi, 4
Giesebrecht, Friedrich, 7, 11, 181
Gillespie, Thomas, 91, 140–42, 181
Godet, Frédéric, 66, 181
Goff Jr., James, 152, 181
Gordley, Matthew, ix
Gordon, R. L., 181
Goudge, H., 66, 181
Gräbe, Peter, ix, 178, 181
Grether, Oskar, 10, 181
Grosheide, Frederik, 76, 181
Grudem, Wayne, 137–38, 181
Gunkel, Hermann, 5, 8, 181

Haldar, Alfred, 6, 181
Hananiah, 4, 15, 17, 18
Harink, Douglas, 124–25, 143, 181
Hauerwas, Stanley, 181
Hays, Richard, 123, 127–31, 181
Helyer, Larry, 31, 181
Hempel, J., 14, 181
Hilber, John, 3, 23–24, 26, 181
Hildebrandt, Wilf, 3–4, 109, 181
Hill, David, 140–43, 47, 181
Himmighofer, Traudel, 136, 182

Hollenweger, Walter, 68–70, 182
Holscher, Gustav, 5–9, 182
Horn, Friedrich, 182
Huey, F., 182
Hutton, Rodney, 32, 182
Hynson, Leon, 145, 155, 182

Jenkins, Philip, 113, 182
Jensen, Alexander, 182
Johansson, Nils, 80, 182
Jung, Franz, 182
Juvenal, 182, 185

Käsemann, Ernst, 71, 182
Keck, Leander, 130, 182
Keener, Craig, 43, 56–57, 97, 101, 161,
    163, 167, 182
Keown, Gerald, 23, 182
Kistemaker, Simon, 99, 182
Kleinknecht, Hermann, 46, 48, 55, 182
Kuhl, Curt, 182

Lactantius, 182
Latte, Kurt, 31, 183
Leith, John, 142, 183
Lewis, I. M., 10, 183
Lindblom, Johannes, 5, 8, 10, 12, 183
Lindemann, Andreas, 43, 46, 51, 98,
    112, 183
Livy, 34, 183
Lohse, Eduard, 183
Lovering, Jr., Eugene, 182–83
Lucian, 183
Lutheran Church of Australia, 137, 142,
    161–63

MacArthur, John., 160, 183
Macchia, Frank, 153–54, 183
MacGorman, J. W., 123, 127, 145–46,
    183
MacMullen, Ramsay, 30–31, 183
Malherbe, Abraham, 183
Mallone, George, 138, 148, 152, 155,
    158, 183
Mare, W. Harold, 154, 183
McDonald, Lee Martin, 183
McDonnell, Killian, 152, 159, 184

NAME INDEX

McNamara, Martin, 4, 6, 12, 17–23, 25, 184
McRay, J. R., 34, 184
Menzies, William and Robert, 53, 180, 184
Meeks, Wayne, 30, 38, 51, 184
Meyer, Heinrich, 66, 184
Miriam, 4, 16
Mitchell, Margaret, 52, 91, 178, 184
Mofatt, James, 37, 184
Montague, George, 159, 184
Moretti, Luigi, 34, 184
Moule, C. F. D, 184
Mowinckel, Sigmund, 6–13, 19, 20, 22, 25–26, 184
Munck, Johannes, 37, 184

Neuhaus, Richard, 113, 115, 184
Niebuhr, R. R., 184
Nilsson, Martin, 31, 184
Nock, Arthur, 184

O'Connor, J. Murphy, 184
Omar, A. Rashied, 112, 184
Oswald, Eva, 18, 22, 184

Packer, J. I., 137, 141, 177, 184
Painter, John, 37, 184
Palamas, Gregory, 58, 184
Paul, The Apostle, xiii–xiv, 3, 26–27, 31, 32, 43, 79, 112, 130, 137, 141, 160, 165, 167, 172, 184, 186
Pearson, B. W. R., 184
Pell, George Cardinal, 118, 184
Peters, Francis, 30, 184
Petronius, 185
Pinnock, Clark, 143, 185
Pleket, Henk, 180
Plummer, Alfred, 66, 185
Plutarch, 163, 185
Porter, Stanley, 177–78, 183–84, 187
Powell, Benjamin, 185

Quell, Gottfried, 12–13, 18–19, 22, 185
Quintilian, 185

Reekman, Tony, 185
Reisling, Jannes, 143, 185

Ridderbos, Herman, 185
Ridderbos, J., 5, 13, 185
Robeck, Cecil Jr., 185
Robert, Louis, 185
Robertson, A. T., 66, 185
Robinson, Theodore, 8, 44–46, 185
Rosner, Brian, 185
Rousselle, Aline, 39, 185
Rowe, Arthur, 107, 134, 185
Rowley, H. H., 12, 185
Ruthven, Jon, 156, 185
Ryrie, Charles, 158, 185

Samarin, William, 148, 185
Sanders, James, 21–22, 25, 185
Saul, 4
Savage, Timothy, 29–31, 34, 37, 41, 164, 186
Sawyer, John, 5, 186
Schatzmann, Siegfried, 42, 48–49, 52, 57, 64–67, 76, 186
Schlier, Heinrich, 37, 51, 164, 186
Schnelle, Udo, 31–32, 130, 141, 186
Schrage, Wolfgang, 76, 186
Schweizer, Eduard, 107, 139–40, 186
Scranton, Robert, 186
Seneca, 30, 99, 123, 186
Sevenster, Gerhard, 99, 186
Smith, Dennis, 33, 186
Solivan, Samuel, 186
Spicq, Ceslaus, 80, 186
Springer, Kevin, 126, 188
Stauffer, Richard, 186
Story, Lyle, ix
Strabo, 33, 186
Stronstad, Roger, 153, 186
Summney, Jerry, 182–83
Synan, Vinson, 134, 145, 151–52, 157

Tacitus, 186
Talbert, Charles, 142, 145, 158
Tertullian, 43, 186
Theissen, Gerd, 186
Theophrastus, 187
Thiselton, Anthony, 35, 42, 45, 48–51, 53, 56–57, 59, 63–66, 75–76, 80, 91, 95–96, 100, 102, 116, 118, 129, 173, 187

Thorsen, Don, 143, 187
Tillich, Paul, 159, 187
Torrey, R. A., 152, 187
Troupe, Carol, 123, 187
Turner, Max, 134–35, 138, 142, 150, 187
Twelftree, Graham, ix, 125, 187

Unger, Merril, 81, 158, 187

Van der Watt, Jan, ix, 89, 167, 187–88
Van Winkle, D., 24, 187
Vielhauer, Philipp, 91, 187

Ward, James, 187
Ward, Wayne, 134, 145–46, 187
Watson, D. F., 187
Weaver, P. R. C., 187
Wesley, John, 79, 143

Wilckens, Ulrich, 37, 187
Williams, J. Rodman, 188
Willis Abigail, v, ix
Willis Anna, v, ix
Willis Bonnie, v, ix
Willis John, v, ix
Willis Sarah, v, ix
Willis Stephen, v, ix
Wilson, Robert, 6, 8–9, 24, 188
Wimber, John, 126, 143, 188
Wiseman, James, 33, 188
Witherington, Ben, 99, 188
Wolter, Michael, 45, 188

Yarbrough, O. Larry, 188
Yong, Amos, ix, 85–86, 110–11, 188

Zedekiah, 4

Subject Index

accountability, 87–88, 128, 130
ancient context, 109, 115, 118n35,119
anthropocentric understandings, 175
Apostle Paul, xiii–xiv, 3, 26–27, 31, 32, 43, 79, 112, 130, 137, 141, 160, 165, 167, 172, 184, 186
appropriate communication, 133–35
Assemblies of God, 151, 153
authentic revelation, xi, xiii, 81, 90–91, 94, 176
authenticity, 12–13, 22, 25, 75, 83, 125, 174

baptism in the Spirit, 145, 152–53
Body of Christ, 43, 51, 54, 59–60, 62, 65, 70–72, 100, 123–24, 126, 140, 155, 174

capitalistic ethos, 115
cessationism, 156-59, 166
charismata, xii, 3, 32–37, 39–52, 54–55, 57–84, 86–91, 96, 100, 102, 105, 107n1, 121, 123, 125, 127–30, 134–35, 139,141, 144–45, 147–48, 152–61, 166, 173–74, 176
charismatic worship, 123, 133, 160
Christendom, xiii–xiv, 110, 113, 118, 171–72
Christian ethos, 46, 61, 99, 118, 167, 174
Christian exclusivism, 32, 34, 34n32, 39–40, 103, 117, 172, 174
Christian initiation, 152, 152n126
Christian maturity, 154
Christian perfection, 79
Christian pluralist, 11, 131

Christians, xi, 31–33, 37–38, 55, 61, 69–70, 73, 79, 85, 112, 114, 117, 127–28, 174, 175
Christlikeness, 131, 173
Christocentric, xiii–xiv, 42, 54, 173, 174
Christological criterion, 42, 53–54, 56, 87, 173
Church, xi, xiii, 30, 35–45, 49–51, 71, 73, 84–86, 91–94, 97–101, 104, 107–09, 114–19, 121–40, 142–47, 150, 152–68, 173–74, 176
confessional criterion, xvi, 53–56
contemporary context, 96, 108–172
contexts, 21–25
contextual theology, xvi, 82–88
contextuality, 111–12
Corinth, 30, 31, 33–36, 45, 84, 118, 134–35
Corinthian context, 33, 39, 45, 72, 91, 99, 162
criteriology, xii–xiii, 4, 172
criterion of common benefit, xvi, 61–70, 73
criterion of edification, 89–106
criterion of love, 75–88

direct revelation, 136–37, 139, 142, 147
discernment of spirits, 64, 66–67, 124
diversity, xiii, 33n22, 49, 56–57, 60, 61–62, 67, 71, 73, 84, 103, 110–18, 144, 174
divine message criteria, 14–17, 18n75
divine revelation, xi, 3, 56, 59, 78, 86, 139, 142, 164
division, iv, 36, 50

193

ecstasy, 6–13, 24–26, 172
ecumenical Council, 159
ecumenical pneumatology, 153
edification, 38–39, 59–60, 63–65, 84, 88, 89–132, 136, 151, 154–55
Enlightenment, 12, 116, 120
eschatology, 51, 141
ethics, 51, 129–33, 141, 173

faith, xi–xii, xv, 16–17, 20, 22, 24–25, 38–39, 41, 45, 51, 62, 64–65, 77, 83–84, 92, 101, 111–13, 116, 118, 124, 127–28, 139, 146, 167, 171, 174
foretelling, 136–36, 139, 141, 143
forthtelling, 136–37, 139, 143
Fruit of the Spirit, 78, 80, 88, 128, 154, 166, 173

gender criteria, 134–35, 145, 160–68
gift of tongues, xi, 63, 65, 90–91, 93, 102, 134–36, 144–55, 164, 166
gifted, 38, 84, 101, 126, 129, 136, 166–67, 174
gifts of healing, 60, 64–66, 129
gifts of the Spirit, xii, xiin2, 47, 51, 59n23, 60–62, 78, 81, 87, 93, 98, 100, 104, 106, 124, 128, 135, 146, 152, 155, 164, 166, 173, 176
globalization, xiii–xiv, 33,35, 85, 86, 109–111, 115, 172
glossolalia, 9, 51, 68, 76, 145–46, 148
grace of God, ix, 49, 57, 78–79, 130, 173
Graeco-Roman, 29–41, 46, 53, 73, 86, 99, 102–03, 115–18, 120, 123, 135, 161, 163–64
greater gifts, 155

Hermeneutics, 21–22, 25
Honestiores, 29
human foreign languages, 144–45, 147–50
Humiliores, 29

Idols, 38, 46, 5, 56, 100
image of God, 117, 167
inferior gift, 155

initial evidence, xi, 145, 151, 151n88, 152–55, 166
interpretation of scripture, 136, 141
interpretation of tongues, 44, 45n26, 60–62, 64–65, 67, 107n1, 133–35, 144, 146–48,
intolerance, 32, 103, 117–18

Jews, xi, 33, 36, 55, 85, 86, 114, 125

love, xiv, 38, 45, 51, 54, 63, 75–88, 90, 92, 101, 105–06, 111, 116–19, 126, 128–32, 135, 149, 153–54, 158, 160, 163–64, 172–74

manifestations of the Spirit, 34, 42, 45, 45n26, 47, 63, 69, 75, 77, 98, 105, 107n1, 128, 173
marginalization, 123
missionary purpose, 126
mulier taceat, 135, 160–68
Muslims, xi, 112, 114–15
mysteries in the Spirit, 91, 149

natural gifts, 68–69
New Testament, 3, 27–106
normativity, xi, 23, 73, 89, 146, 151–53, 159n126,
NT Apostles, 38, 138, 152, 158–59

Old Testament, 1–26, 142
ordinances, 39, 50
outer experiences, xv, 6–13, 25, 72–73

Pauline corpus, 3, 54, 54n5, 119
Pentecostal, 36, 91, 110, 150–53, 159, 166
perichoretic, xiv, 49–50, 53, 56, 56n10, 57, 59–60, 174
phenomenological pluralism, 110
phenomenology, 8, 10–13, 18, 23, 31–32, 47, 54, 64, 68–69, 106, 110, 145, 151, 175,
pluralism, 32, 36, 40, 102, 109–14, 117–18
post-Christendom, xiii–xiv, 110, 118n35, 172
postmodernism, xii, 116

SUBJECT INDEX

power evangelism, 126
preaching, 133, 138–43, 147, 157, 162, 165
prophecy, 3–26, 166, 44, 45n26, 62–64, 66–68, 76–77, 81, 83–84, 90–96, 98, 102–05, 107, 109, 120, 134–44, 147, 154, 157, 162–66
Prophet, 4–8
prophetic preaching, 140
protestant reformer, 86, 117
public tongues, 165
purpose of the church, 122, 124–27

Qur'an, xi, 111

rationalism, 30, 37, 116, 120
reductionism, 140, 172
Reformed, xiv, 131n34, 134–36, 144,
relativism, x1, 113, 116
resurrection, 40, 46, 51, 111, 125, 173
Revelation, xi–xiv, 3, 6–7, 10, 15–16, 22, 24–26, 35, 45, 56, 59, 61, 64, 73, 78, 81, 83–95, 101, 120–21, 127, 131–33, 136–43, 147, 164, 168, 172–76
revelation of Jesus Christ, xiv, 35, 45, 61, 64, 101, 120–21, 131, 172–73, 175–76

Sacramentalists, 152, 154
sacraments, 138, 152
sanctification, 123, 153–54
satanic counterfeit, 160
sexual immorality, 37–39, 46, 50, 119
social stratification, 32, 99, 103, 111, 174
soteria, 116, 31–32, 35
special revelation, 137
spiritual gifts, xii, xv, 42–52, 54–56, 59, 61–63, 68, 77–78, 81, 83, 85–86, 90, 102, 126–27, 159, 164, 176

spiritual things, xii, 35–36, 40–52, 55, 62, 64, 78, 85, 88, 90–94, 104–07, 119, 134
stratification, 32, 99, 103, 111, 167, 174
subsequence, 153
supernatural, 173, 175–76, xiii–xiv, 5, 30–32, 68–70, 78, 83–88, 102, 116, 120–21, 126, 135–37, 139, 142–43, 145–46, 148, 151
supernatural gifts, 69

Ta'aruf, 112
the American dream, 117
the word of Yahweh, 6–7, 10–13, 19–20, 24–25
theological dispensationalist, 158
tolerance, 32, 34, 39–40, 61, 103, 111–13, 117–18, 135
tongues, 44, 54, 61–69, 76–77, 81–84, 95–100, 102, 104–05, 107n1, 110, 133–36, 144–58, 161–67
tradition, xi–xii, xiv–xvi, 3–4, 6, 11–12, 20–22, 25–26, 38–39, 46, 95–96, 100–06, 113–16, 118, 126, 132, 139, 157, 171–72, 174–76
traditional theology, 95–103
trinitarian, xiv, 50, 53–74, 81, 86, 88–89, 106, 129–32, 174–76
trinitarian ethic, 131

unrighteousness, 37–38, 46, 50, 77–78, 80, 117, 123
upward mobility, 30–31, 35, 135
urbanization, 110

word of knowledge, 64, 77
word of wisdom, 64
works of power, 64–66

xenolalia, 145

Scripture Index

Old Testament

Genesis

12:1–3	16
17:1–22	16
28:10–17	16

Exodus

3:1—4:17	18n78
15:20	24n104
32:10–32	23
34:27–35	24n100

Numbers

12:1–15	24
12:6	16
14:11–20	24n103

Deuteronomy

13:1–3	16
18:15–22	23
18:15–19	23
18:21–22	14
34:10	23

1 Samuel

9:9	5
10:12	24n104
10:19–24	24n104

2 Samuel

7:4–17	23
23:2–4	95n16

1 Kings

22:5–8	15
22:14–17	16n96, 23
22:28	14n61

2 kings

3:17–20	24n104

Isaiah

7:3–4	15
7:11	24n104
7:17	16
11:1–5	95n16
28:7	17
28:11–12	96
30:8	14n61

Isaiah (continued)

38:5–6	23
38:7	24n104
38:22	24n104
42:5	23
44:3	23
45:14	97
48:16–20	95n16
59:21	95n16
61:1	95n16

Jeremiah

1:4–19	18n78
1:10	95n16
2:8	16
11:1–8	95n16
18:7–10	14
20:9	19
23:11	16n96
23:13	16
23:14	16n96
23:17	16n96
23:18	19n79
23:21–22	16n96, 19n79
23:25	16
23:31	16
23:32	16, 92
26:1–23	20
28	19, 21
28:9	14n61
28:10–11	12
29:10–15	95n16
38:21	9n36
42:4	23
42:7	16n96
43:1–3	18

Ezekiel

1–3	18n78
11:19	23
13:1–10	15n64
33:33	14n61
36:26–27	23
39:29	23

Hosea

1:2–3	16n96
1:2	18n78
12:13	23

Joel

2:28–29	100
2:28	16

Amos

2:10–11	23
2:11	40
3:7	5
3:8	19
7:1	9
7:14–15	18n78

Jonah

1:1	18n78

Micah

3:5–11	16n96
3:5	16
3:12	40

Zechariah

4:7	101

New Testament

Matthew

5:21–22	130
5:27–28	130
5:38–39	130
5:43–44	130
5:46–47	130
7:15–20	80
21:11	25
21:42	175
21:46	25
22:29	175n4

Mark

3:15	66
11:23	101
13:24–25	66
16:15	125, 174

Luke

2:10–11	111
2:28–32	111
4:21	175n4
5:17	66
10:22	117
24:27	175n4

John

1:1	172, 175
1:18	xiv, 131
3:16–18	112
3:16	80, 111, 125, 190
4:24	172
5:39	175n4
6:46	xiv
7:38	175n4
14:6	111
14:9	xiv
14:26	172

15:13	80, 129, 173
15:19	123
15:26	172
16:33	124

Acts

2:1–11	145
3:20–26	25
8:1	32, 38
10:34b–35	112
11:19	7
13:4–14	125n14
13:51	125n14
14:6	125n14
14:24–25	125n14
15:41—16:12	125n14
17:1	125n14
17:15	125n14
18	35
18:1–19	35
18:1–16	33
18:1	125n14
18:18–23	125n14
18:24	33n21, 36
19:21	125n14
20:2–6	125n14
20:13–17	125n14
21:1–8	126n14
21:17	126n14
36:26–27	7
39:29	7

Romans

1:3–4	54n5
1:11	44
1:16–18	31
1:16	31
2:11	149
3:9–23	24
5:5	78, 153
5:9	77
5:11–15	80
5:18	80, 123

Romans (continued)

6:1–14	177
6:11	123
8:9–14	124, 173
8:9	123
8:26–27	145
8:34	173
10:13	31
12:2	34n32, 40
12:5	62
12:6	62
12:7	62
12:8	62
13:1	116
14:12	130
15:4	122
15:16	36
16:25–26	61, 120, 172
16:25	120

1 Corinthians

1:1–9	36
1:1–2	36
1:2	122n1, 123, 124
1:4–7	36
1:5	64
1:7	129
1:9	36
1:10—4:21	36, 46, 50, 78n8
1:10	xiv
1:17	xiv, 94, 120n37
1:17—2:15	37, 64
1:18	64n36
1:19	95n16
1:22–24	116
1:23	xiv
1:24	64n36
1:26–29	30n6, 37
1:26–31	69
2:1–16	xiv
2:1	120n37
2:2–5	61, 131
2:4	64n36, 120n37
2:5	64n36
2:6	120n37
2:9	95n16
2:10	45, 56, 64
2:10–11	66
2:10–13	xiv, 35
2:13	46n29, 120n37
2:15	127
3:1–23	37
3:1	46n30, 50
3:4	36
3:10	xiv
3:21	69
4:6b–7	37
4:7	69
4:16–17	129
4:19–21	64n36
5:1	37, 39
5:1—6:20	37, 46, 50, 78n8
5:5	78
5:11	37
6:1–7	95n16
6:12–20	119
6:13–20	37
6:13	37
7:1–40	50
7:19	101
8:1–11:1	50
8:5–6	31
8:5	31, 34n31
8:6	32
8:6–7	64
8:1	50
9:9	95n16
9:19–27	111
9:21	101
9:22	85, 175
10:1–14	95n16
10:23	92
10:31	131
10:33	85
11:1	50
11:2–16	162
11:2–34	39, 50
11:3	162
11:5	99, 161, 162, 163, 164, 165
11:18–19	36, 37, 46, 50
11:18a	124

… SCRIPTURE INDEX …

12–14	xii, xvi, 1, 14n60, 27, 29, 35, 42n1, 43–56, 60, 69, 75, 76, 78, 95, 101, 103, 105–7, 116, 119, 120, 122, 128, 130, 133, 134, 155, 164	12:18–26	60, 71
		12:18	59, 60n25, 70, 71, 72, 123
		12:19–24	72
		12:19	84
		12:24	123
		12:25–26	72
		12:25	70, 128
12:1–31	vii, xvi, 53	12:27–30	60
12:1–3	xvi, 16, 34n32, 53, 54, 56n10, 85,	12:27	51
		12:28–30	61
12:1	xii, 40, 43, 51	12:28	70, 116
12:2	56, 85,	12:30	91, 150, 151
12:2–3	100, 101	12:31—33	173
12:3	42, 47, 50, 51, 53, 54, 56, 57, 80, 131, 172	12:31	47, 61, 62, 63, 73, 74, 76, 77, 78, 79, 85, 151, 155
12:4–11	xvi, 61, 62	13	54n5, 111
12:4–6	50, 56, 57, 61, 62, 63, 71, 72	13:1–13	75, 119, xvi
		13:1–3	16, 51n59, 77, 78, 82, 128, 154n103
12:4	xiin2, 3, 43, 45, 51, 52, 54, 57, 59, 63, 65, 68, 71, 146, 151,	13:1	15, 77, 83, 116, 145
		13:2	64n37, 77, 83, 101,
12:5	51, 59, 68n47–48, 71	13:3	51, 78
12:6	51, 54, 71, 58n18, 59, 60	13:4a	77
		13:4b–6a	78
12:7	34, 41n41, 51n59, 54, 63, 128, 131, 146, 173	13:4–7	77, 80, 128
		13:6b–7	78, 86
		13:8–10	58, 81, 151
12:7–11	45, 59, 63, 145	13:8–12	81, 82, 83
12:7–26	60	13:8	76, 81, 83, 158
12:8–10	62, 64, 154n103	13:10	81
12:9	32	14:1	34n29, 41n41, 45, 47, 48n43, 51n59, 60, 63, 78, 90, 105, 128, 130, 136, 143, 151, 154, 164, 172, 173
12:10	3, 148		
12:11	54, 63, 66, 67, 69, 82, 91, 125, 127, 148, 151		
12:12–30	xvi, 70		
12:12–17	59, 71, 72, 100	14:1–6	86, 154n103
12:12–27	187	14:1–40	xvi, 89
12:12–31	123	14:1–33	119, 182
12:12	59, 65, 70, 71, 123	14:2	51, 54n6, 65, 67, 90, 91, 99n37, 102, 104, 133, 146, 148, 149, 150, 151, 173
12:13	32, 36, 39, 56, 57, 70, 71, 83, 85, 100, 123, 131, 167		
12:14–26	54		

1 Corinthians (continued)

14:2–4	51, 66
14:3	83, 89n2, 91, 92, 95, 102, 104, 138, 140, 173
14:3–4	91, 92
14:4–5	124n7, 133n1, 63
14:4	65, 67, 91, 92, 94, 99n37, 146, 173
14:4a	91
14:4b	91
14:5–14	93
14:5–6	65, 99
14:5	67, 92, 93, 95, 148, 150, 151, 173
14:6–9	84
14:6	93, 111, 113, 120, 125n14, 133, 143
14:12	45, 92, 93, 94, 97, 124n7
14:13	67
14:14–15	146
14:15	84, 85, 93, 146
14:17	54n5, 92
14:18	36
14:19	124n7, 162
14:21	87, 93, 94, 96, 101, 101n46, 102
14:23	84, 93, 124, 135
14:23–25	86, 87, 96, 102
14:24–25	84, 92, 93, 125n14
14:24	84, 124, 162
14:25	86, 97, 124, 125, 93, 102, 104,
14:26–36	93, 102, 104,
14:26	84, 87, 92, 93, 98, 104, 124n7, 131, 133
14:27–28	67, 94, 146, 175
14:27	67, 98
14:28	63n32, 93, 94, 98, 124n7
14:29–33	94
14:29	67, 83, 87, 99, 124, 138
14:31	87
14:32	54, 67, 93, 94, 99, 138
14:33	137, 163, 172
14:33b–38	137n17
14:34–35	135, 161, 182
14:34–36	100, 160
14:34	94, 98, 99, 100, 163
14:36	84
14:37	45, 61, 84, 103, 104, 120, 162
14:40	54, 104, 124n7, 163, 173
15:1–4	95n16
15:45	95n16
15:54	95n16
15:56	95n16
15:1–58	40, 46, 51
15:22–25	81
15:50–55	81
15:58	40, 61
16:1–4	40, 51

2 Corinthians

1:12	120n37
5:14–15	79
5:21	79, 80
12:1–7	120
12:10	29

Galatians

1:1	120
1:12–16	xiv
1:12	61, 120, 131, 172
1:14	101
1:15–16	61, 120, 131, 172
2:2	xiv, 36, 61, 120, 172
2:8	36
3:26–28	131
3:27–28	127
3:28	32, 56, 162
5:13–14	78
5:16–21	78
5:16–23	79

5:22	78, 173
5:22–23	128
5:22–26	154
5:24–26	78

Ephesians

2:7	77
2:18	172
4:7–13	59
4:11	68n47, 68n48
4:12–13	158
6:18	166

Philippians

1:21	xiv, 131
2:9–11	54n5
2:13	173

Colossians

1:15–18	54n5
2:10	172

1 Thessalonians

2:11	92
4:13–18	137
5:9	31
5:20–21	67

1 Timothy

2:11–14	137n17, 183

2 Timothy

2:10	31, 120
3:1	32

Titus

3:4–6	80

Hebrews

1:3	87
5:9	31

1 Peter

1:5	31
1:13–16	123
4:10	3

2 Peter

2:10	116

1 John

4:8	77, 80, 149, 172
4:12	xiv, 131
4:16	77, 80, 149, 172
5:7	172
5:20	81

Revelation

1:9	80
21:2—22:5	137

www.ingramcontent.com/pod-product-compliance
Lightning Source LLC
Chambersburg PA
CBHW070323230426
43663CB00011B/2199